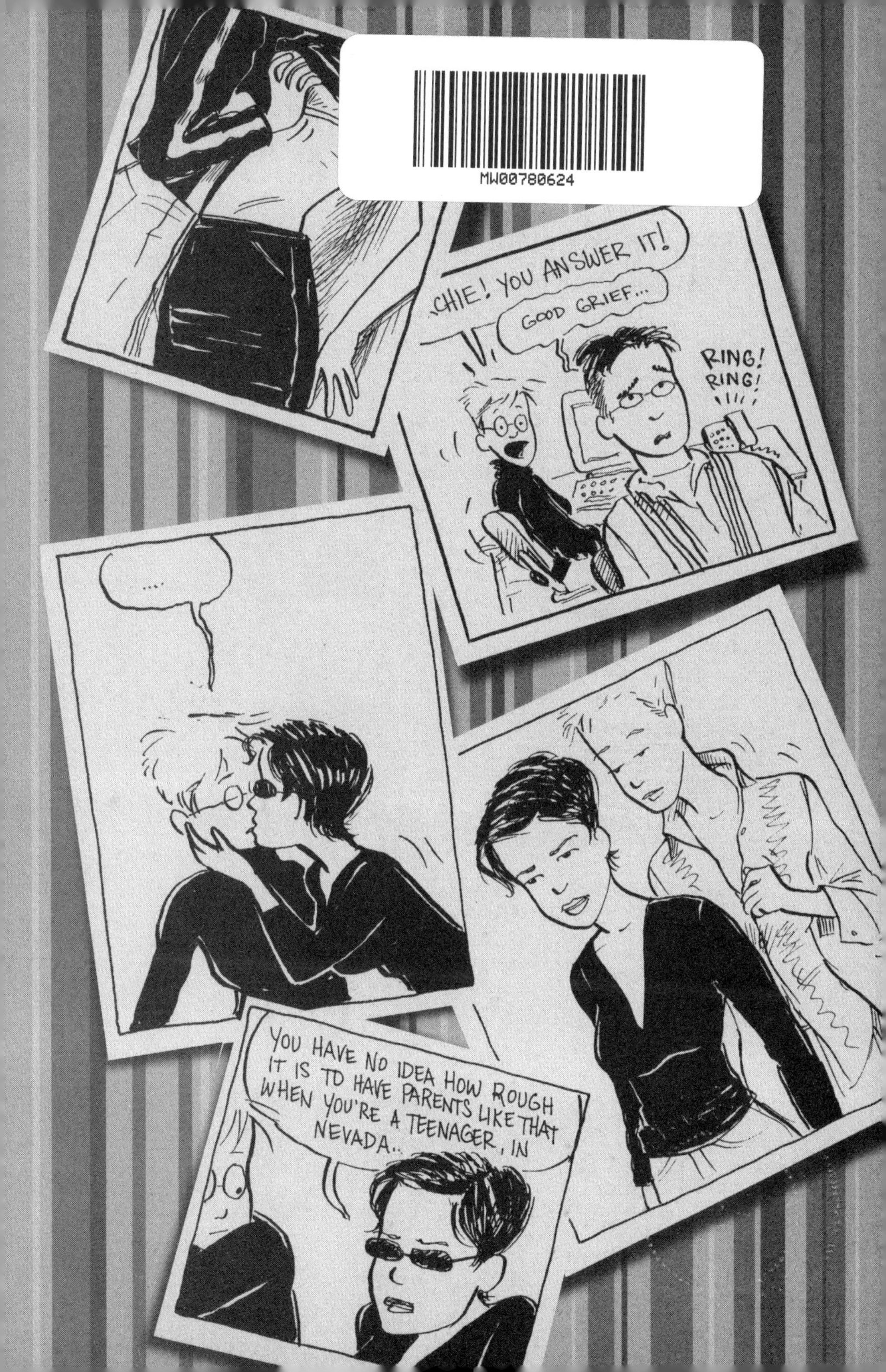

CHIE! YOU ANSWER IT!
GOOD GRIEF...
RING! RING!
....
YOU HAVE NO IDEA HOW ROUGH IT IS TO HAVE PARENTS LIKE THAT WHEN YOU'RE A TEENAGER, IN NEVADA...

Other Jane's World trade paperbacks:

VOL. 1, ISBN 0-9742450-0-3
VOL. 2, ISBN 0-9742450-1-1
VOL. 3, ISBN 0-9742450-7-0
VOL. 4, ISBN 0-9766707-3-9

JANE'S WORLD © PAIGE BRADDOCK 2006

Jane's World, Volume 5
ISBN 0-9766707-5-5

Jane's World
P.O. Box 88
Sebastopol, CA 95473

JanesWorld@mac.com

JaneComics.com

Co-Publisher
Adrienne Corso
AdrienneCorso@mac.com

Brian Miller
Hi-Fi colour design
www.hifidesign.com

Webmaster:
Michael Shermis
3WD World Wide Web Design
www.3WD.com

Printed in Canada

JANE'S WORLD VOL. 5

Story and art by Paige Braddock

Who's who in Jane's World...

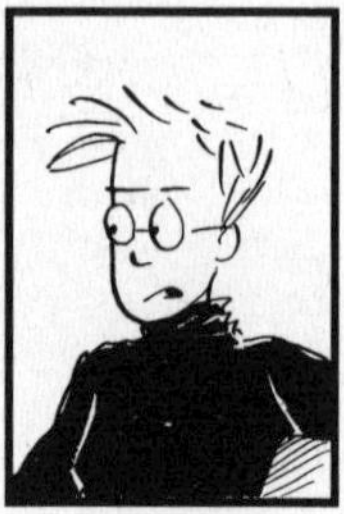

Jane
It's her comic!

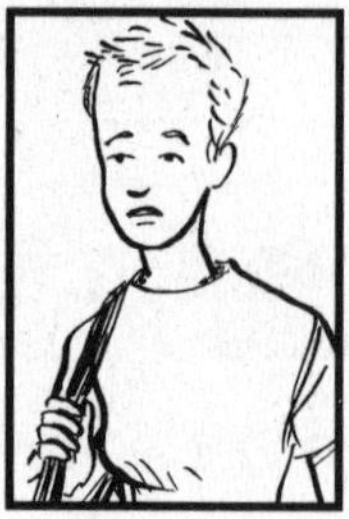

Jill
Trouble

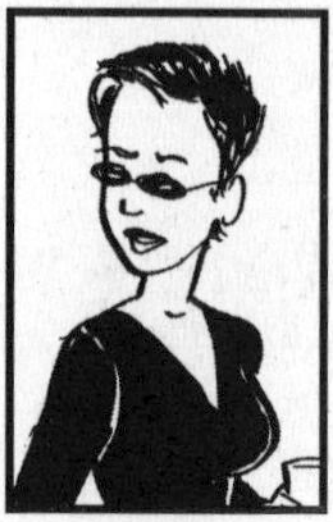

Chelle
Needs no introduction

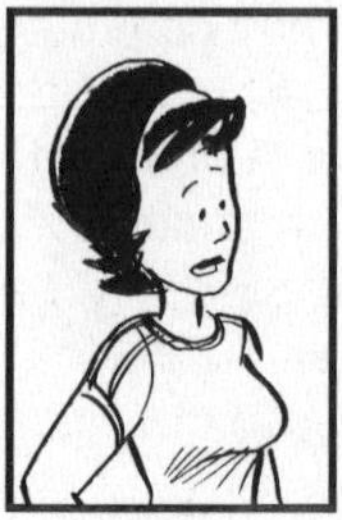

Talia
Jane's Ex GF

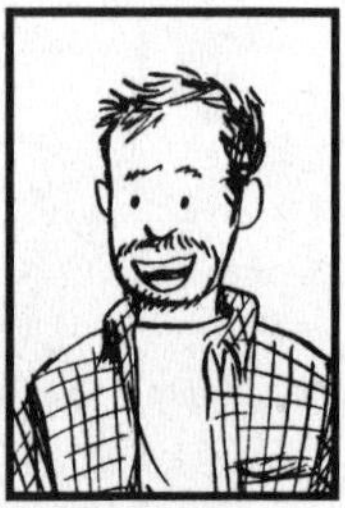

Ethan
Jane's roommate

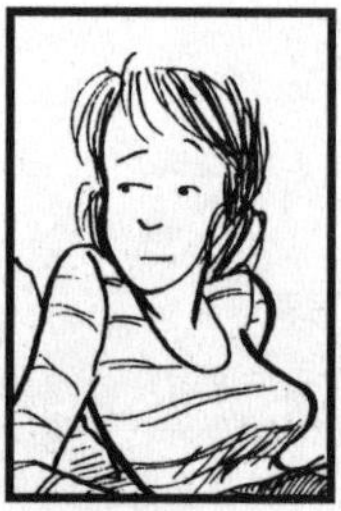

Dorothy
Jane's best friend

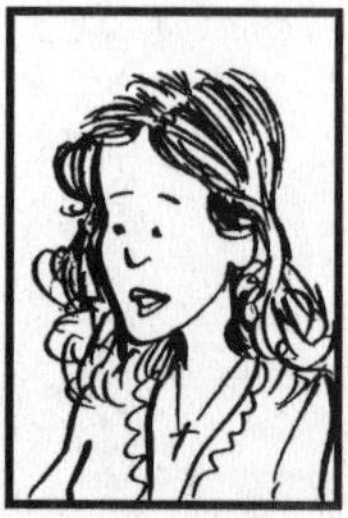

Skye
New girl in town

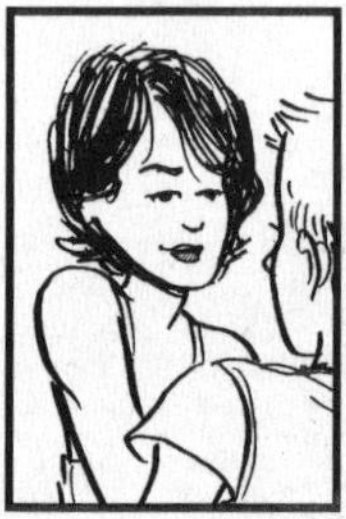

Virginia
Chelle's mother

Jane's World recap:

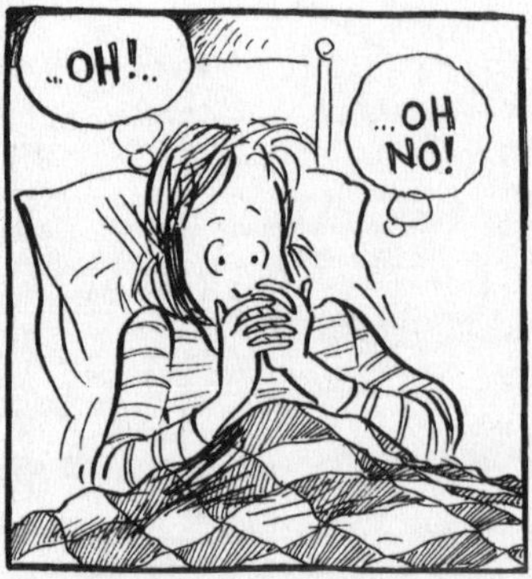
...OH!..
...OH NO!

Our last chapter started off with Dorothy waking up in a strange place. Okay, it wasn't that strange, it just wasn't her house. She'd had a little too much to drink at her grand re-opening party the night before and had ended up making a pass at Jane before falling asleep. She woke up the next morning and the events from the night before all came rushing back. Of course, being the model of maturity that she is (not), Dorothy snuck out of the house quickly before Jane woke up. Then Jane woke up not feeling so good about things only to have the rest of her day go downhill fast. She let Ethan find them a new rental unit, which ended up being a trailer... she got doused at lunch with four 16 oz. glasses of water... the newspaper where Jane works got bought out by some big corporation... the only real high point was getting to meet Skye. Unfortunately, Skye was the one who dumped the tray.

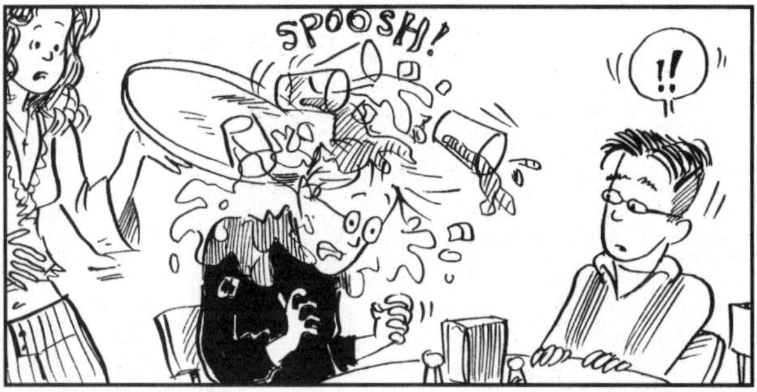
SPOOSH!
!!

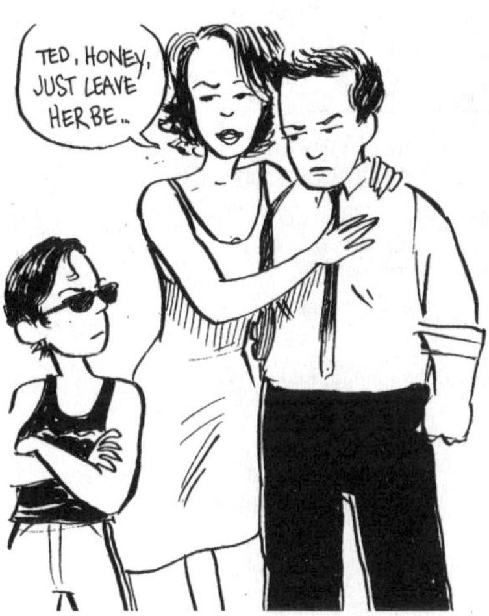
TED, HONEY, JUST LEAVE HER BE..

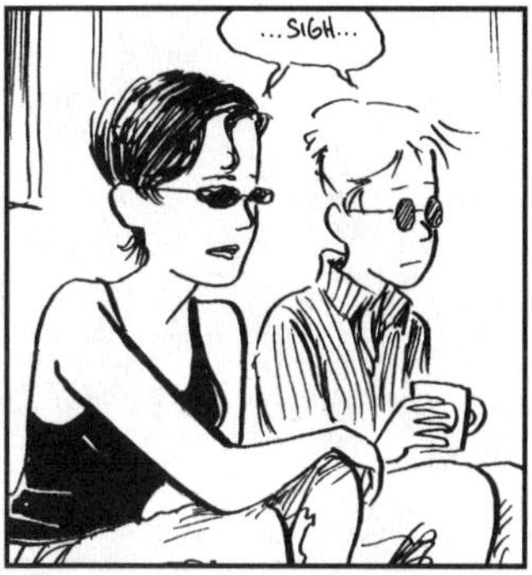
...SIGH...

Later, Chelle pays Jane a visit in the trailer park and we get a little flash-back sequence of not only Jane and Chelle's brief romantic encounter, but a flashback to teen Chelle as well. Chelle grew up in Nevada with a womanizing mother and a butch step mom, a woman named Ted.

Back in the present, Chelle and Jill have a fight. Chelle sends Jill packing. It's a long drive back to Nevada and Jill is so distracted by her thoughts that she doesn't realize she is being followed the last half hour of the trip...

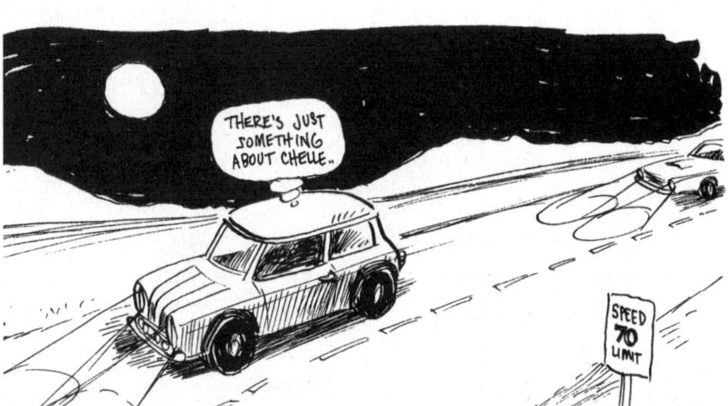
THERE'S JUST SOMETHING ABOUT CHELLE..
SPEED 70 LIMIT

Okay... here we go...

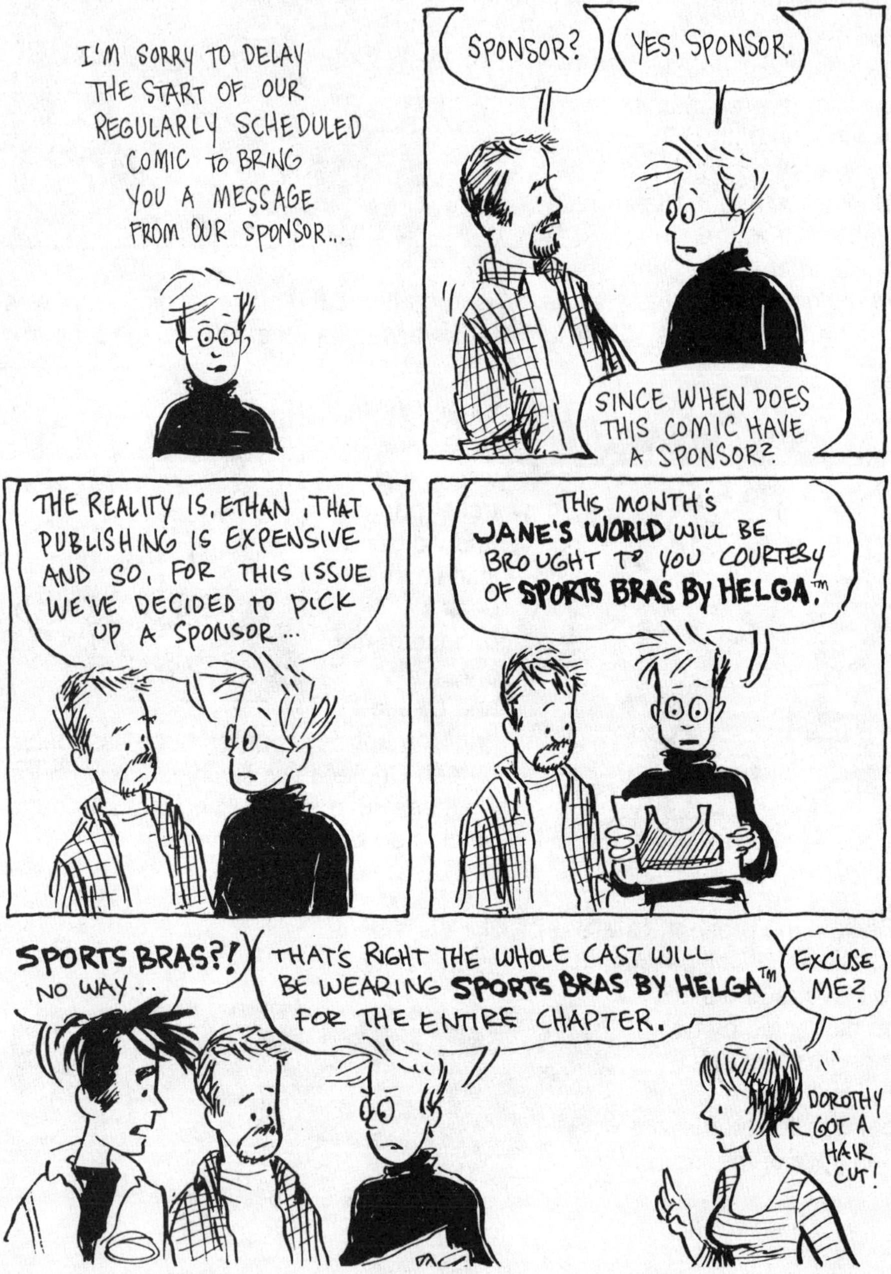
I'M SORRY TO DELAY THE START OF OUR REGULARLY SCHEDULED COMIC TO BRING YOU A MESSAGE FROM OUR SPONSOR...
SPONSOR?
YES, SPONSOR.
SINCE WHEN DOES THIS COMIC HAVE A SPONSOR?
THE REALITY IS, ETHAN, THAT PUBLISHING IS EXPENSIVE AND SO, FOR THIS ISSUE WE'VE DECIDED TO PICK UP A SPONSOR...
THIS MONTH'S JANE'S WORLD WILL BE BROUGHT TO YOU COURTESY OF SPORTS BRAS BY HELGA™.
SPORTS BRAS?! NO WAY...
THAT'S RIGHT THE WHOLE CAST WILL BE WEARING SPORTS BRAS BY HELGA™ FOR THE ENTIRE CHAPTER.
EXCUSE ME?
DOROTHY GOT A HAIR CUT!

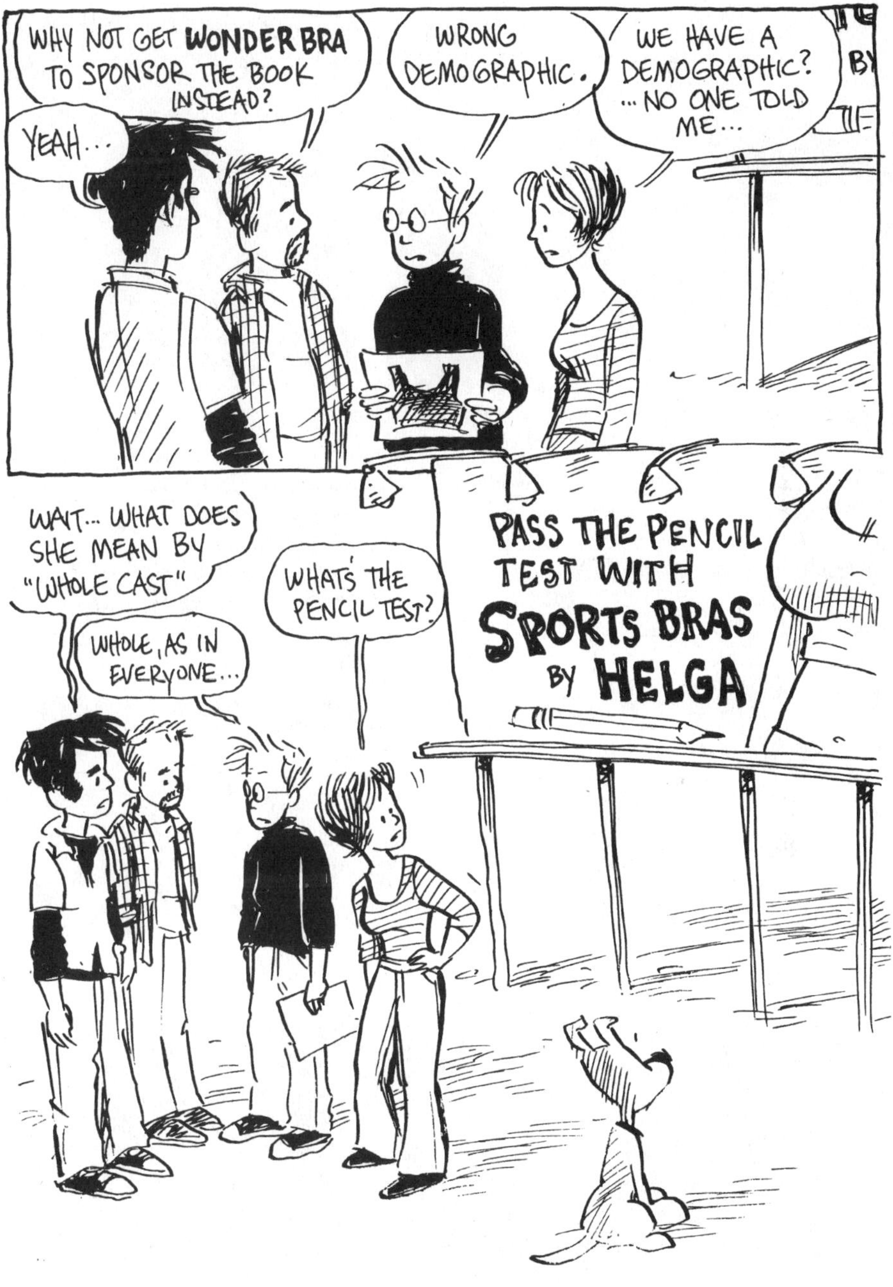
WHY NOT GET WONDERBRA TO SPONSOR THE BOOK INSTEAD?
YEAH...
WRONG DEMOGRAPHIC.
WE HAVE A DEMOGRAPHIC? ...NO ONE TOLD ME...
WAIT... WHAT DOES SHE MEAN BY "WHOLE CAST"
WHOLE, AS IN EVERYONE...
WHAT'S THE PENCIL TEST?
PASS THE PENCIL TEST WITH SPORTS BRAS BY HELGA

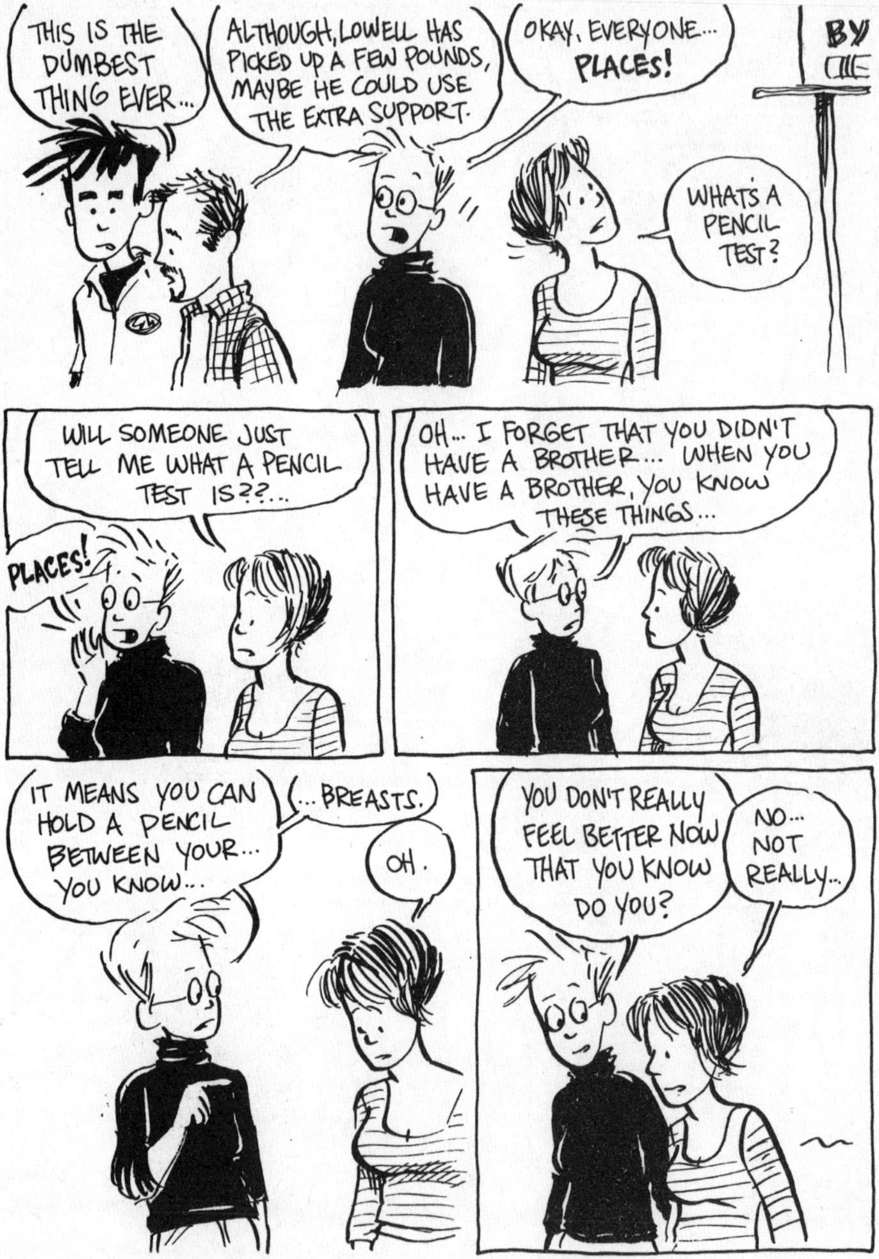
THIS IS THE DUMBEST THING EVER...
ALTHOUGH, LOWELL HAS PICKED UP A FEW POUNDS, MAYBE HE COULD USE THE EXTRA SUPPORT.
OKAY, EVERYONE... PLACES!
WHAT'S A PENCIL TEST?
WILL SOMEONE JUST TELL ME WHAT A PENCIL TEST IS??...
PLACES!
OH... I FORGET THAT YOU DIDN'T HAVE A BROTHER... WHEN YOU HAVE A BROTHER, YOU KNOW THESE THINGS...
IT MEANS YOU CAN HOLD A PENCIL BETWEEN YOUR... YOU KNOW...
... BREASTS.
OH.
YOU DON'T REALLY FEEL BETTER NOW THAT YOU KNOW DO YOU?
NO... NOT REALLY...

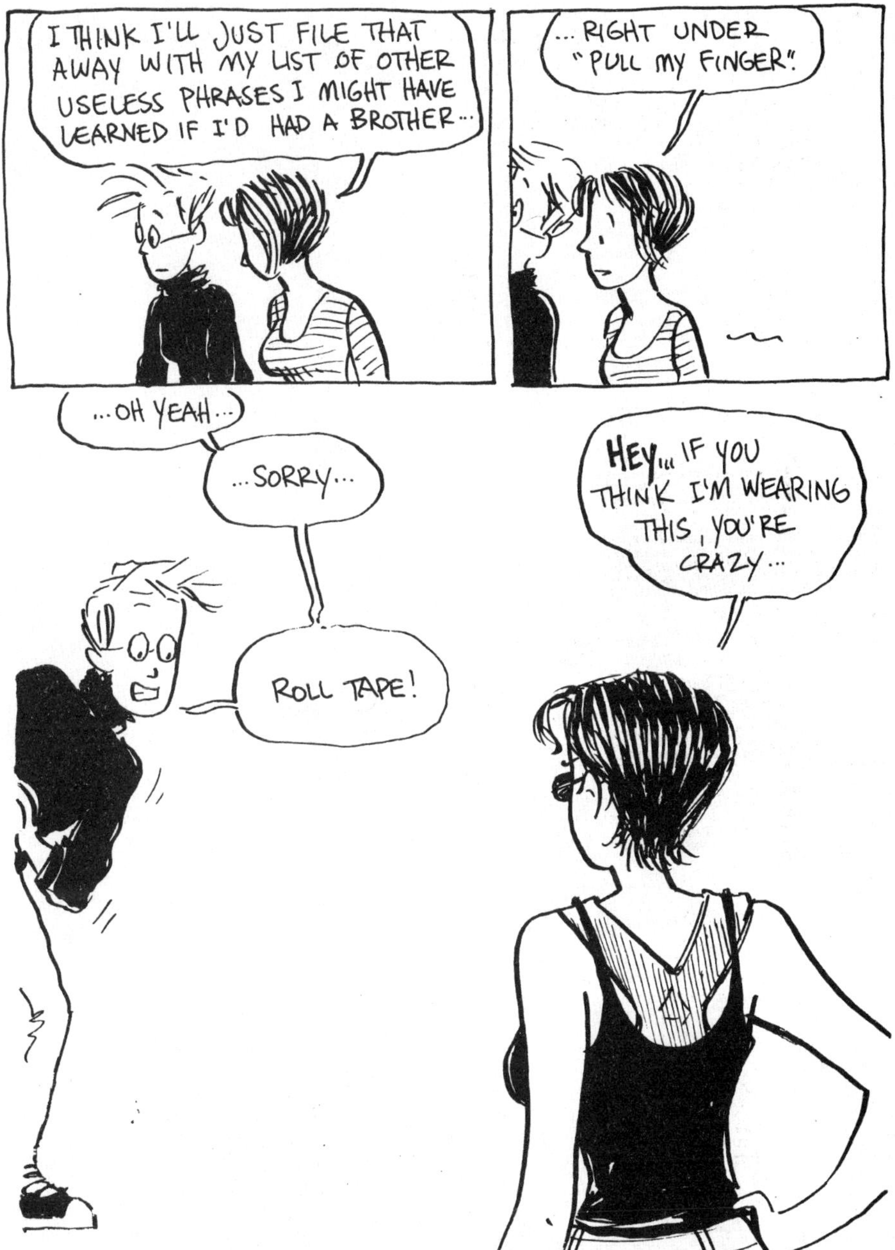
I THINK I'LL JUST FILE THAT AWAY WITH MY LIST OF OTHER USELESS PHRASES I MIGHT HAVE LEARNED IF I'D HAD A BROTHER...
... RIGHT UNDER "PULL MY FINGER".
...OH YEAH...
...SORRY...
ROLL TAPE!
HEY... IF YOU THINK I'M WEARING THIS, YOU'RE CRAZY...

Chapter One

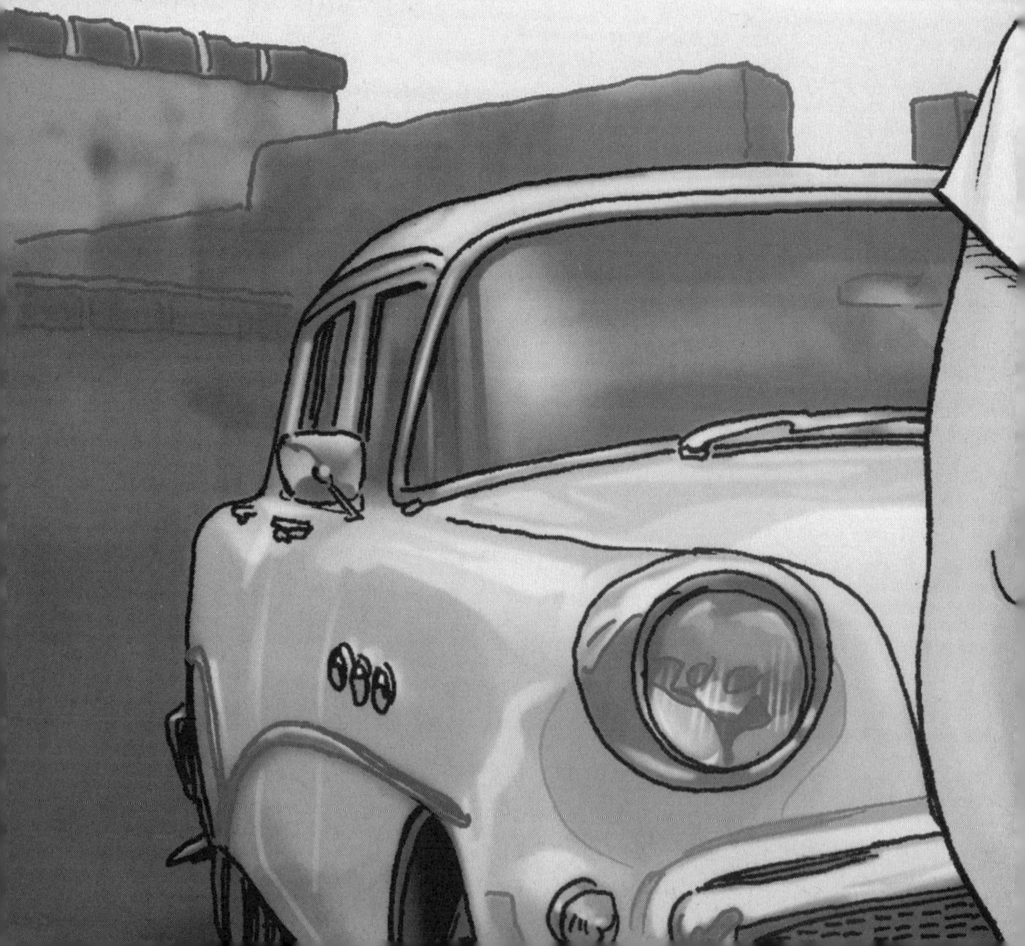

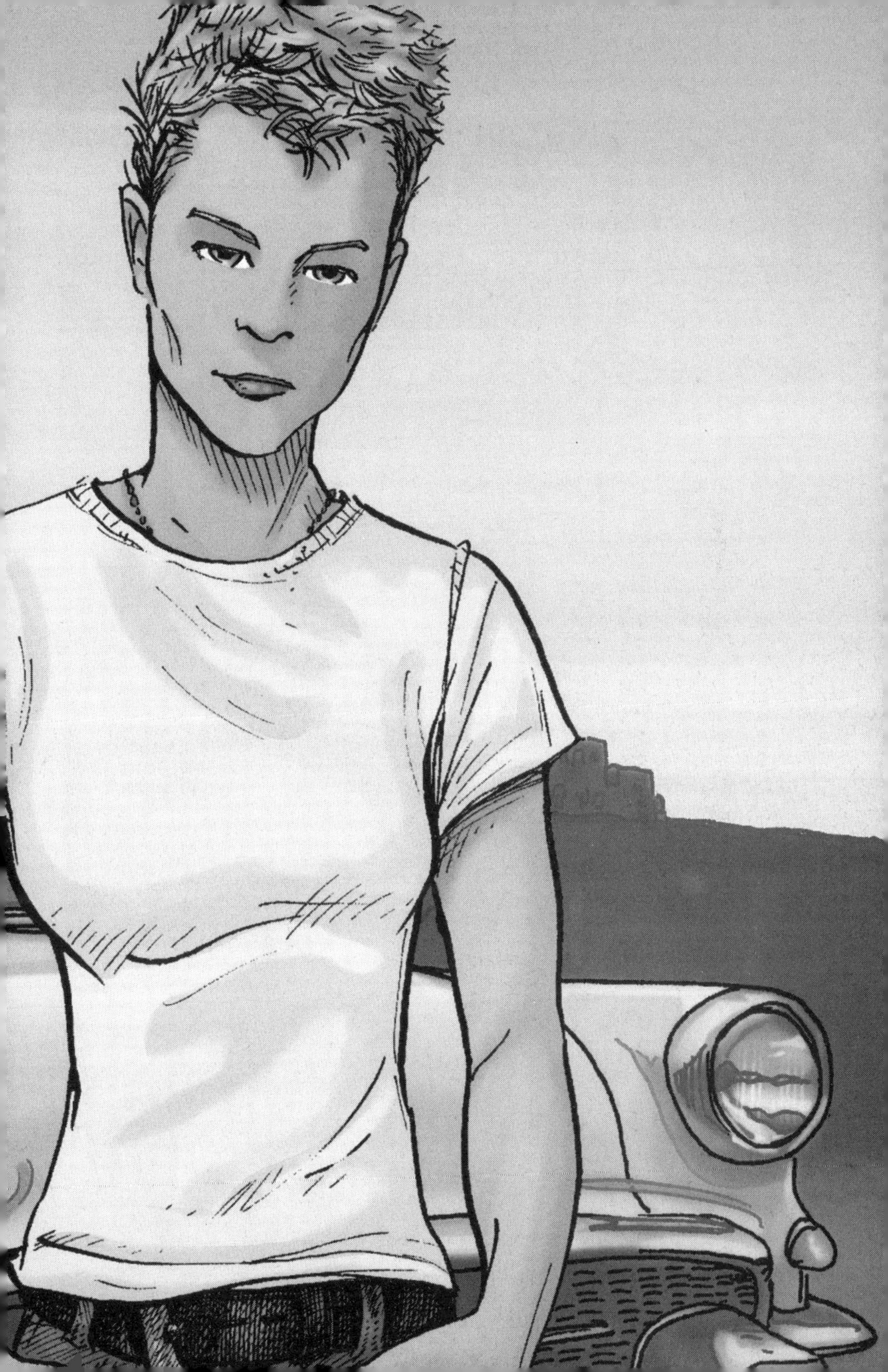

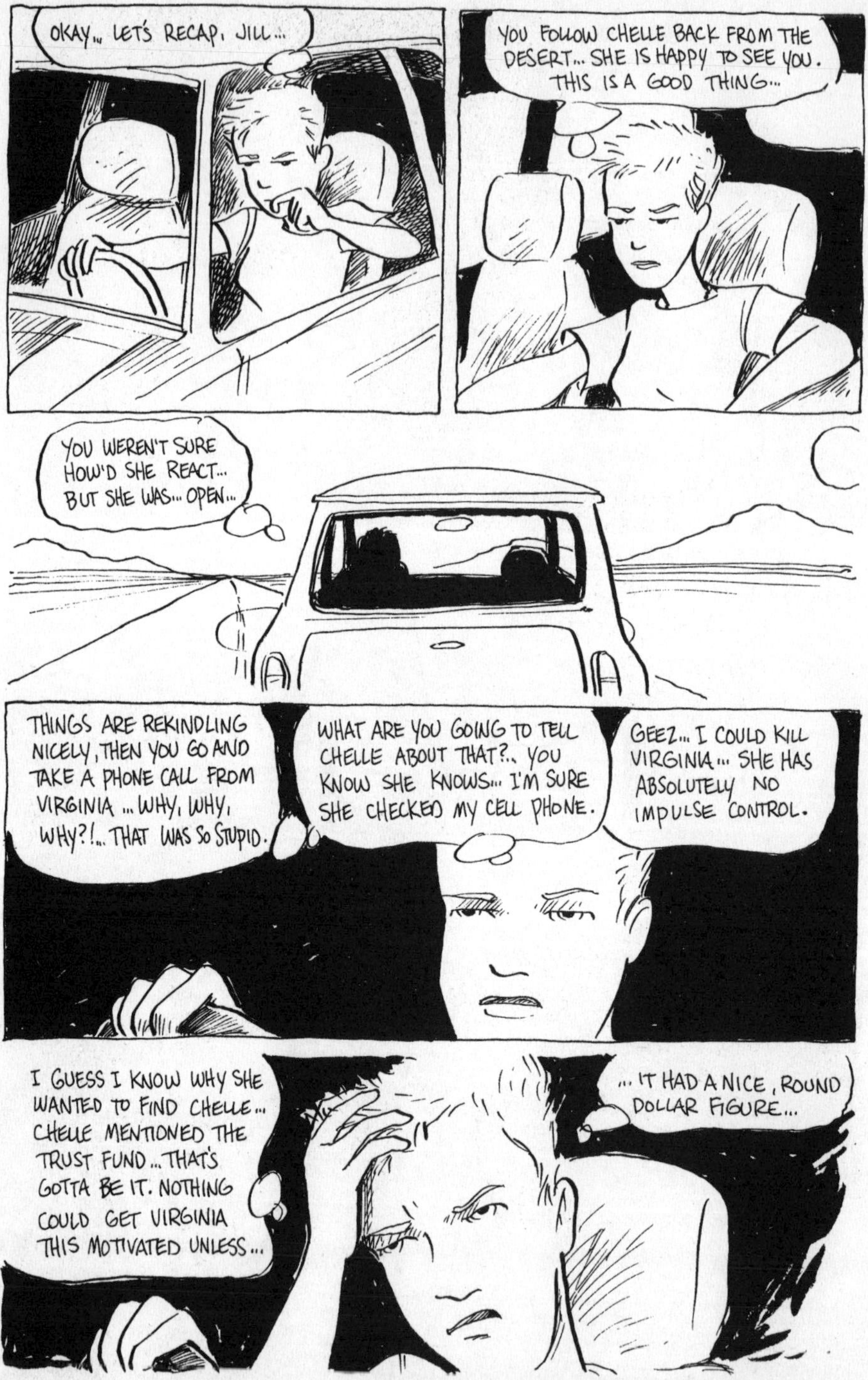
OKAY... LET'S RECAP, JILL...
YOU FOLLOW CHELLE BACK FROM THE DESERT... SHE IS HAPPY TO SEE YOU. THIS IS A GOOD THING...
YOU WEREN'T SURE HOW'D SHE REACT... BUT SHE WAS... OPEN...
THINGS ARE REKINDLING NICELY, THEN YOU GO AND TAKE A PHONE CALL FROM VIRGINIA ... WHY, WHY, WHY?!... THAT WAS SO STUPID.
WHAT ARE YOU GOING TO TELL CHELLE ABOUT THAT?.. YOU KNOW SHE KNOWS... I'M SURE SHE CHECKED MY CELL PHONE.
GEEZ... I COULD KILL VIRGINIA... SHE HAS ABSOLUTELY NO IMPULSE CONTROL.
I GUESS I KNOW WHY SHE WANTED TO FIND CHELLE... CHELLE MENTIONED THE TRUST FUND... THAT'S GOTTA BE IT. NOTHING COULD GET VIRGINIA THIS MOTIVATED UNLESS...
... IT HAD A NICE, ROUND DOLLAR FIGURE...

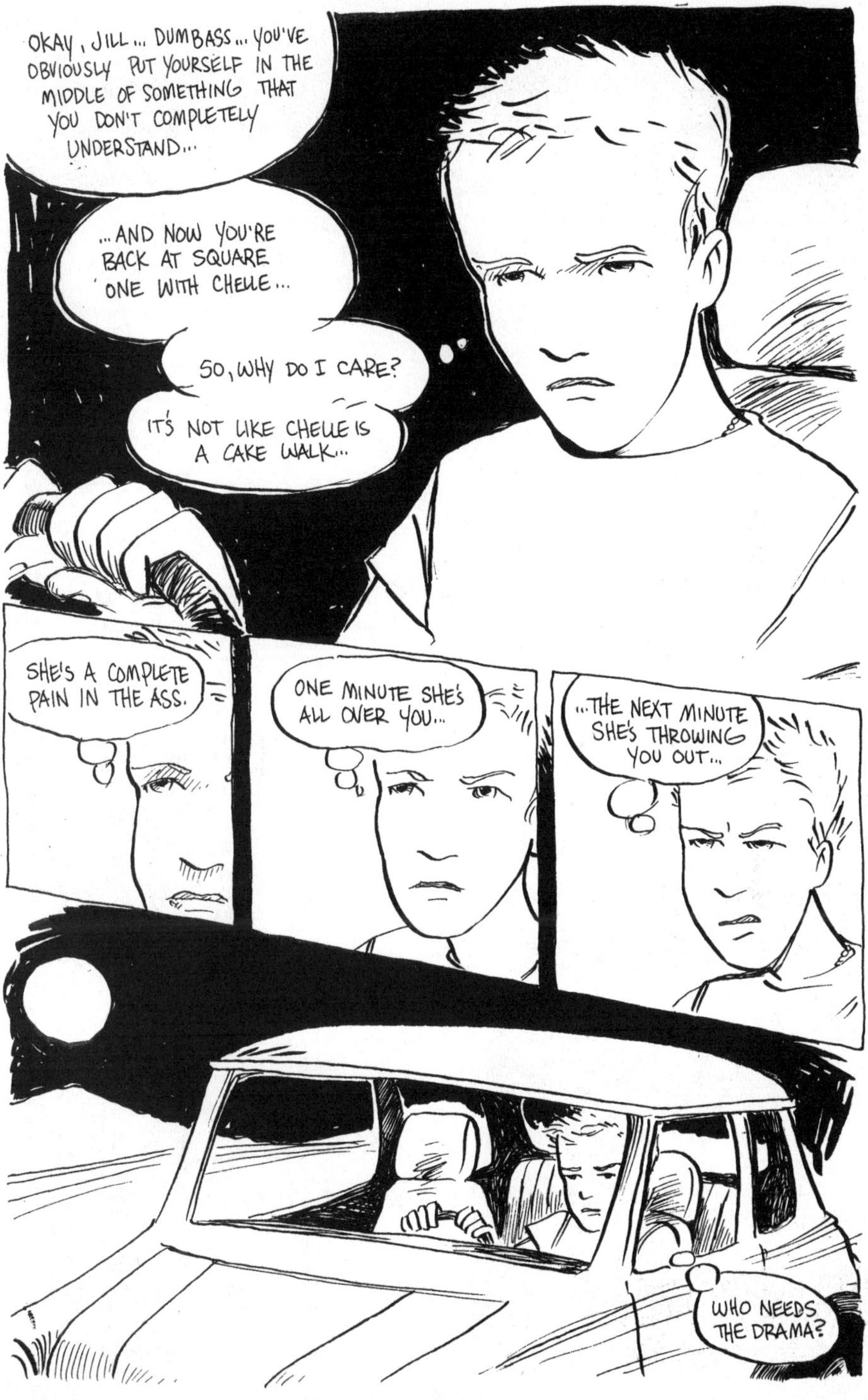
OKAY, JILL... DUMBASS... YOU'VE OBVIOUSLY PUT YOURSELF IN THE MIDDLE OF SOMETHING THAT YOU DON'T COMPLETELY UNDERSTAND...
...AND NOW YOU'RE BACK AT SQUARE ONE WITH CHELLE...
SO, WHY DO I CARE?
IT'S NOT LIKE CHELLE IS A CAKE WALK...
SHE'S A COMPLETE PAIN IN THE ASS.
ONE MINUTE SHE'S ALL OVER YOU...
...THE NEXT MINUTE SHE'S THROWING YOU OUT...
WHO NEEDS THE DRAMA?

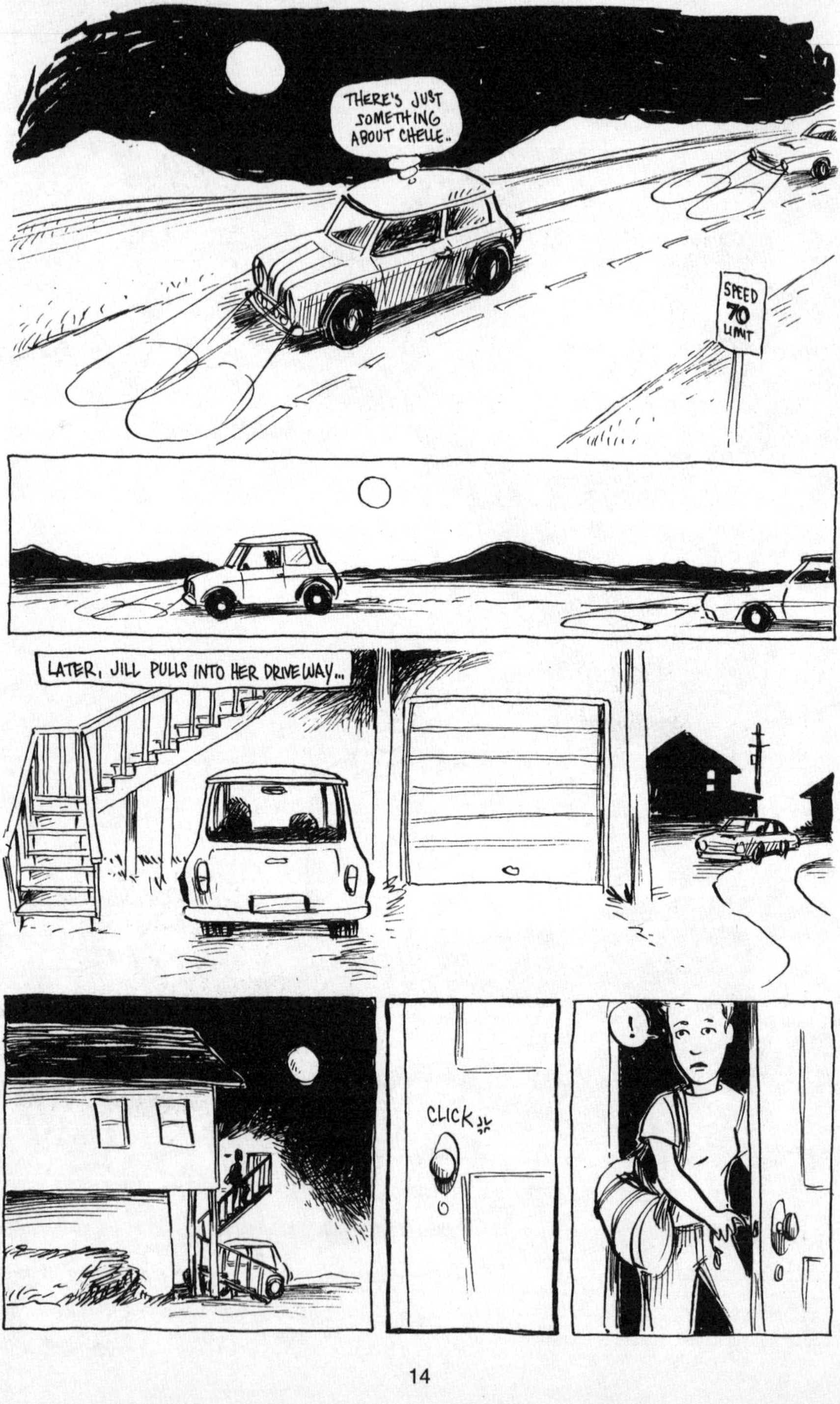
THERE'S JUST SOMETHING ABOUT CHELLE..
SPEED 70 LIMIT
LATER, JILL PULLS INTO HER DRIVEWAY...
CLICK
!

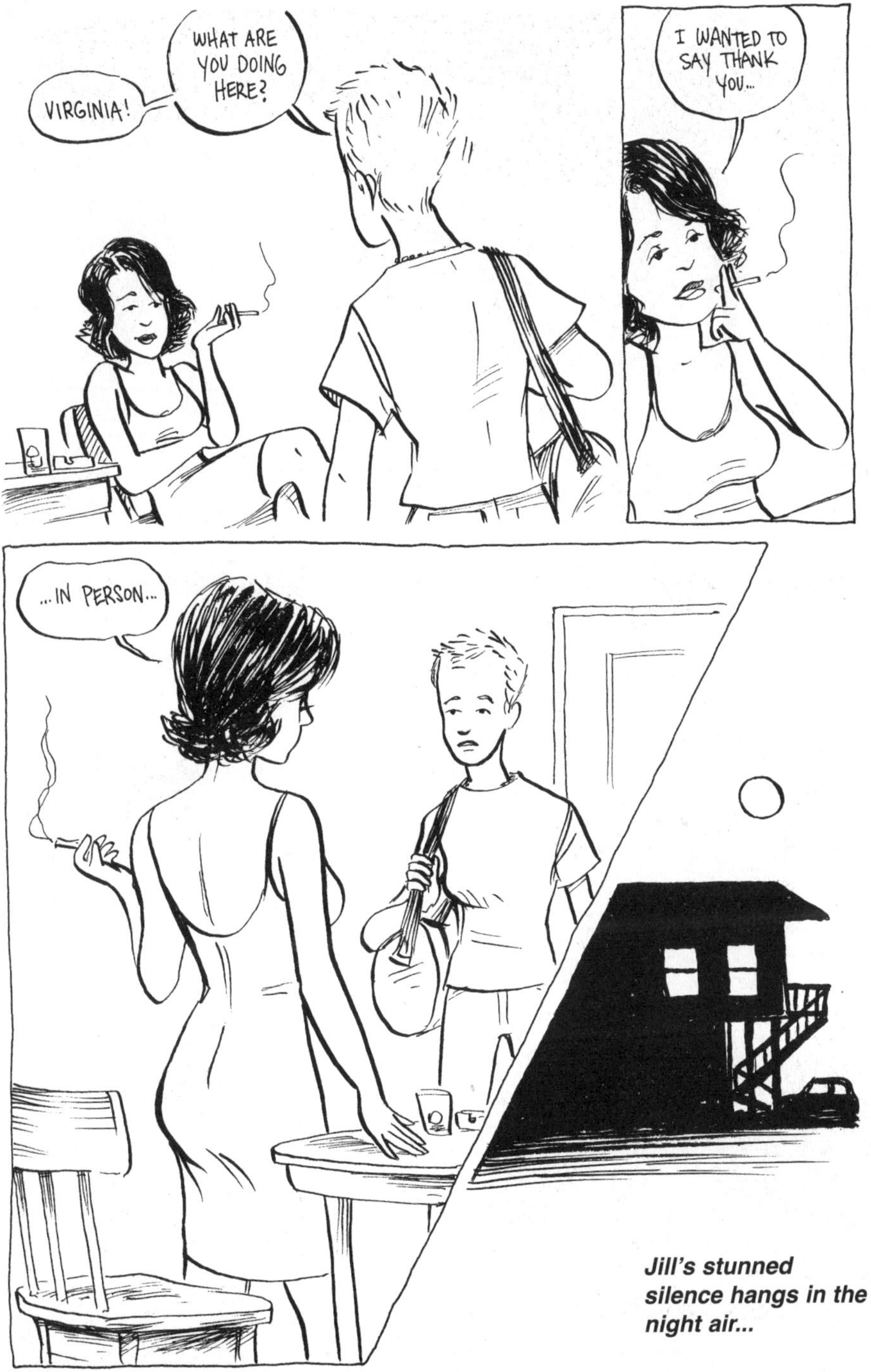
VIRGINIA!
WHAT ARE YOU DOING HERE?
I WANTED TO SAY THANK YOU...
...IN PERSON...
Jill's stunned silence hangs in the night air...

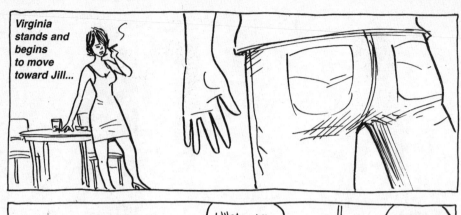

Virginia stands and begins to move toward Jill...

WHOA... JUST A MINUTE...

YOU KNOW I JUST SPENT THE WEEKEND WITH CHELLE?

SO THIS IS ALL JUST A LITTLE TOO...

CLOSE?...

...WEIRD.

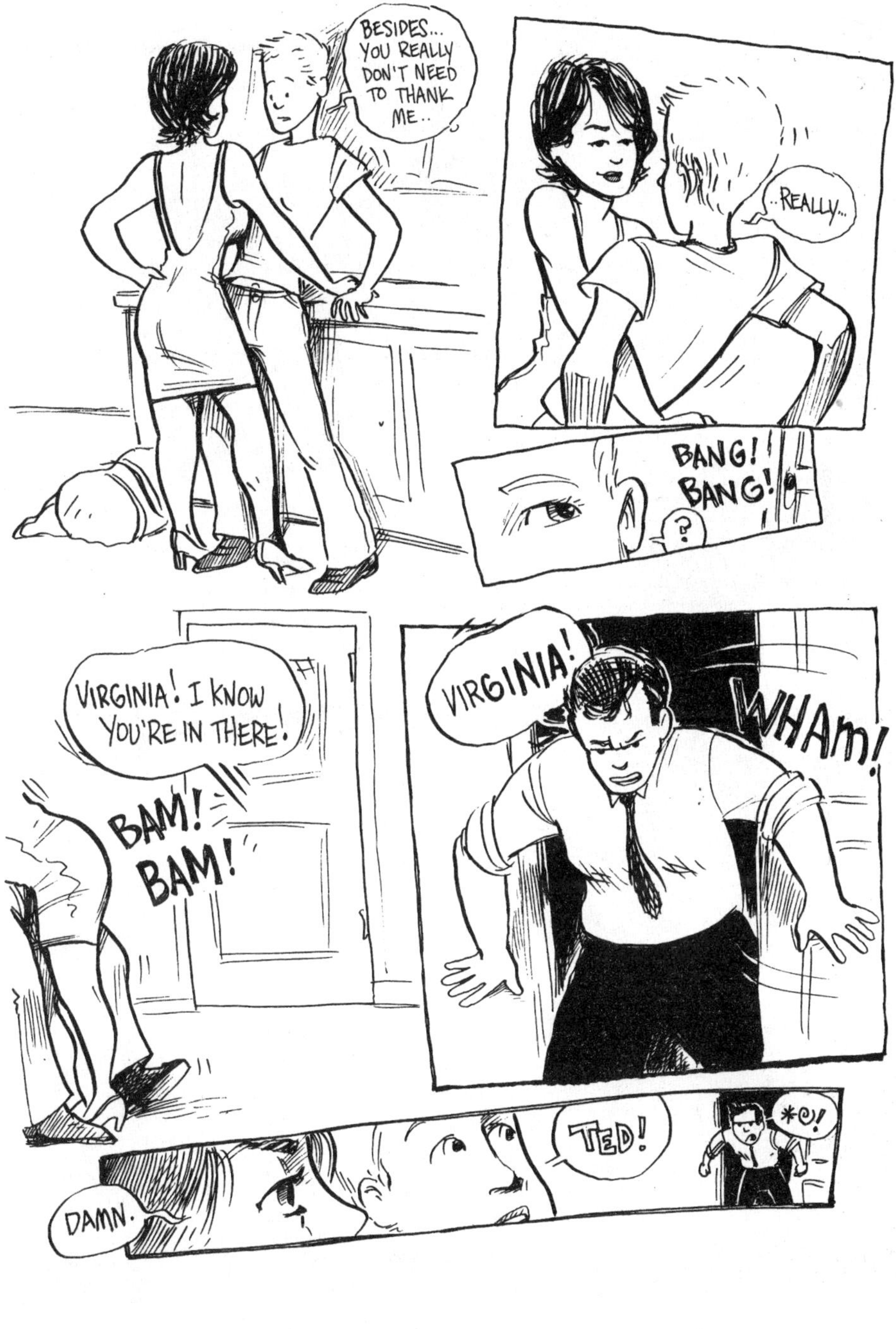

BESIDES... YOU REALLY DON'T NEED TO THANK ME..
..REALLY..
BANG! BANG!
?
VIRGINIA! I KNOW YOU'RE IN THERE!
BAM! BAM!
VIRGINIA!
WHAM!
TED!
*@!
DAMN.

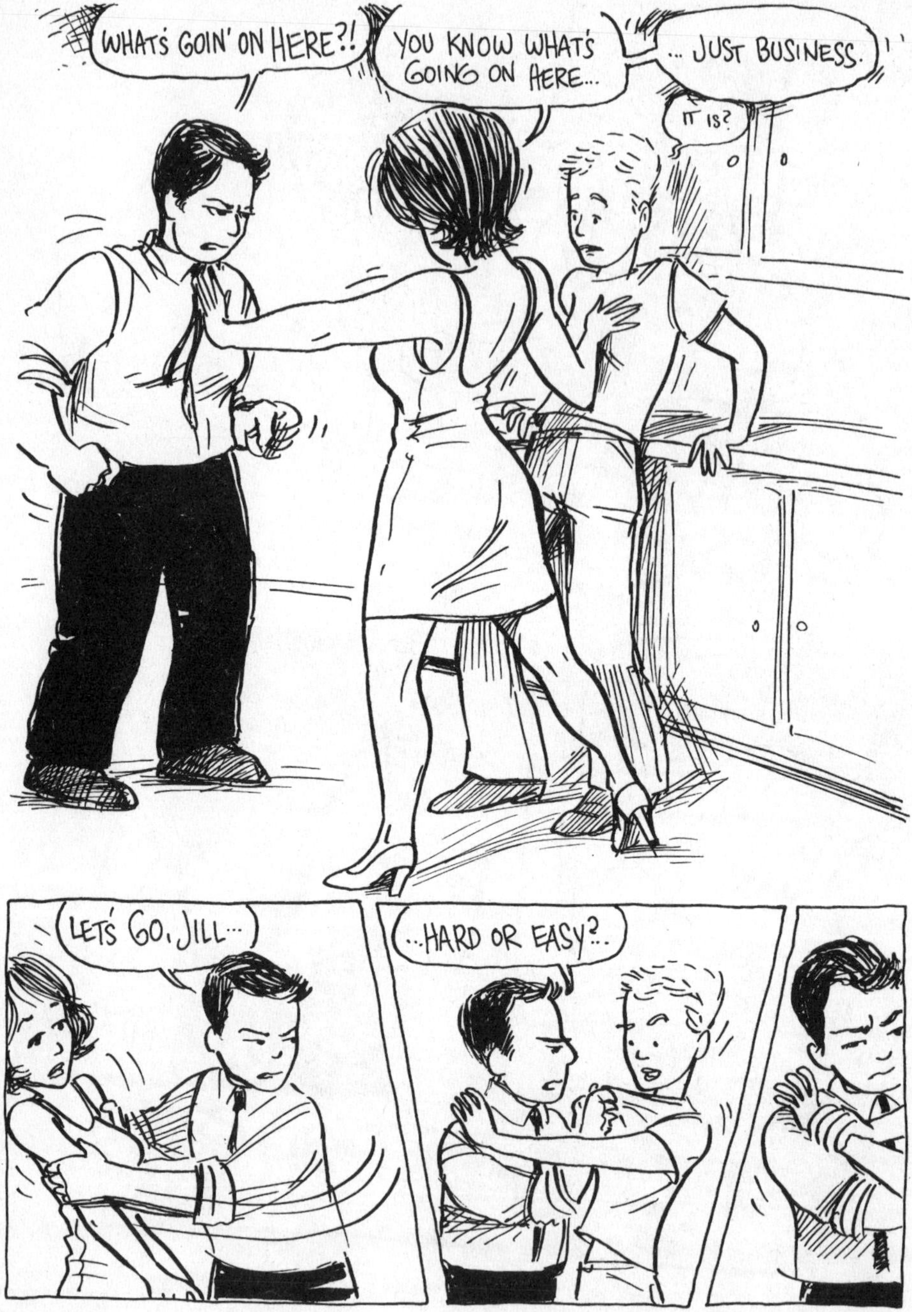
WHAT'S GOIN' ON HERE?!
YOU KNOW WHAT'S GOING ON HERE...
... JUST BUSINESS.
IT IS?
LET'S GO, JILL...
...HARD OR EASY?...

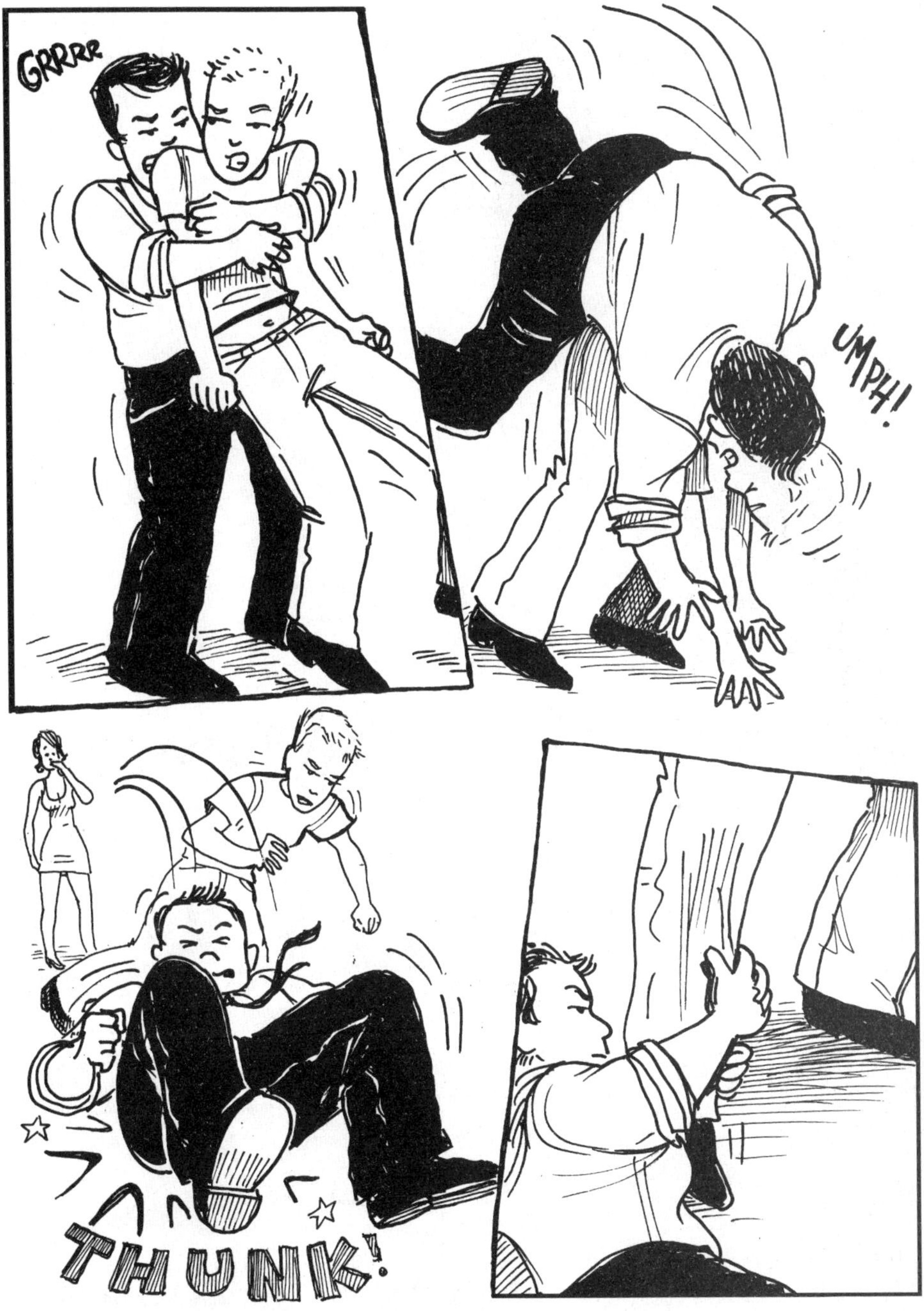
GRRRR
UMPH!
THUNK!

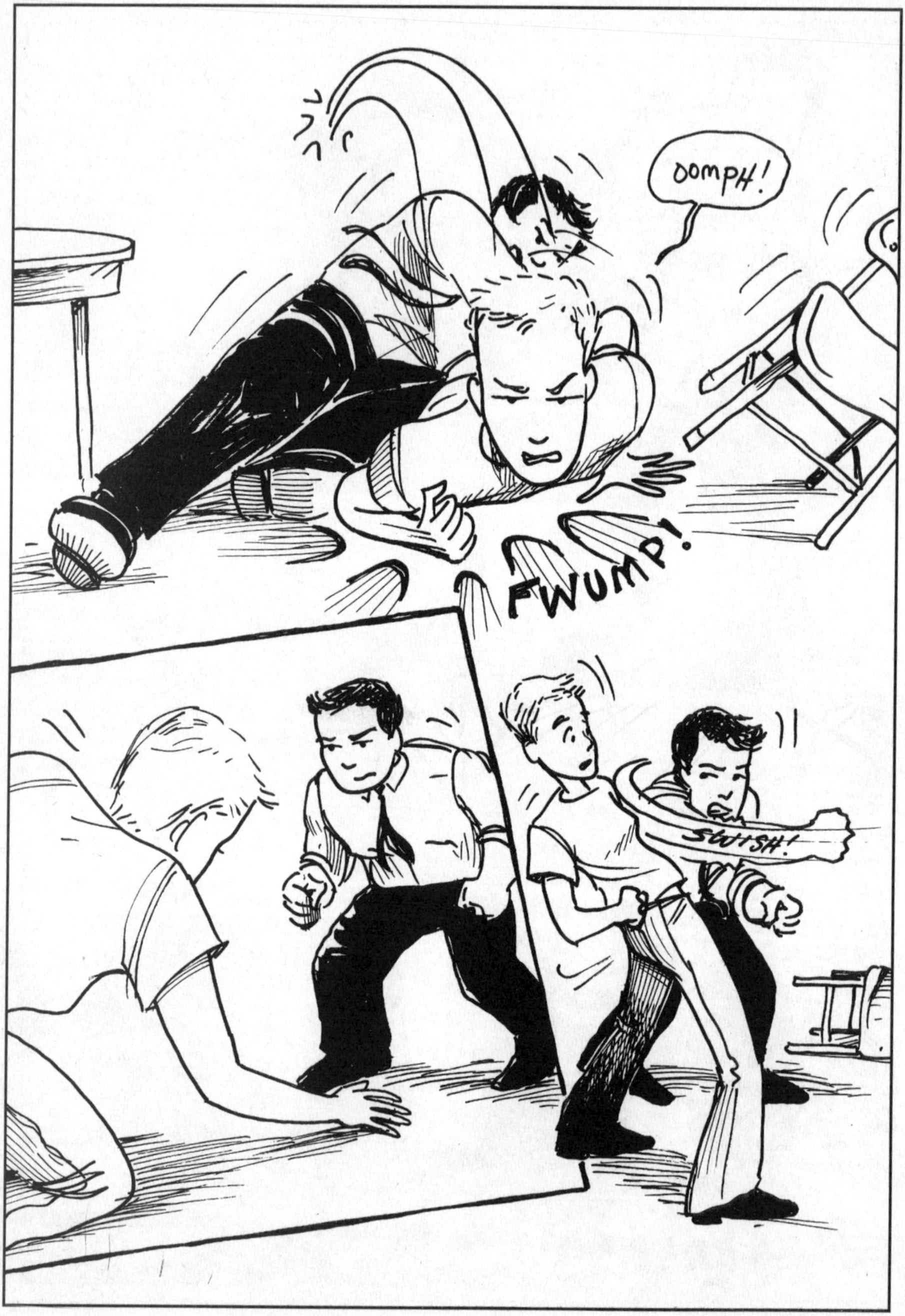
OOMPH!
FWUMP!
SWISH!

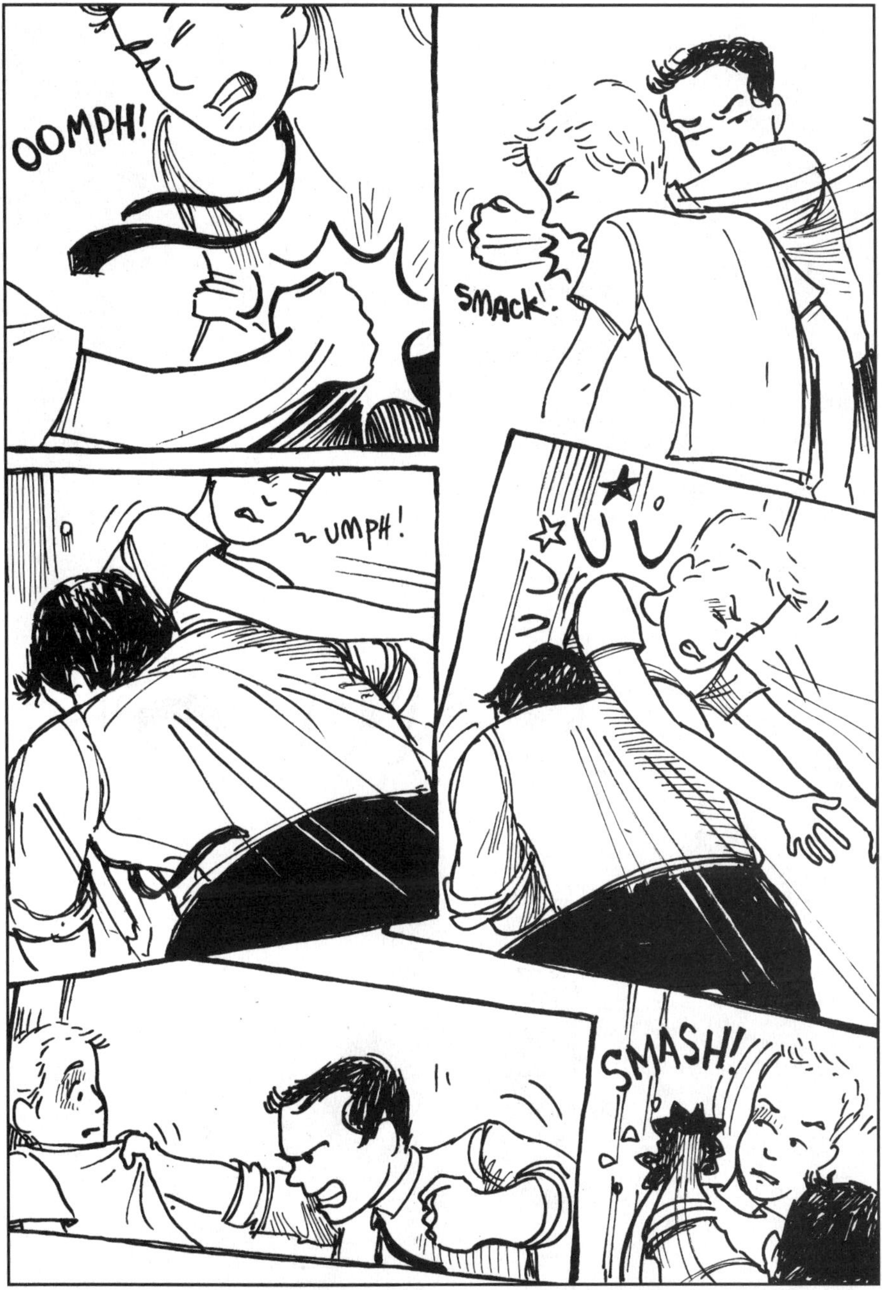
OOMPH!
SMACK!
~UMPH!
SMASH!

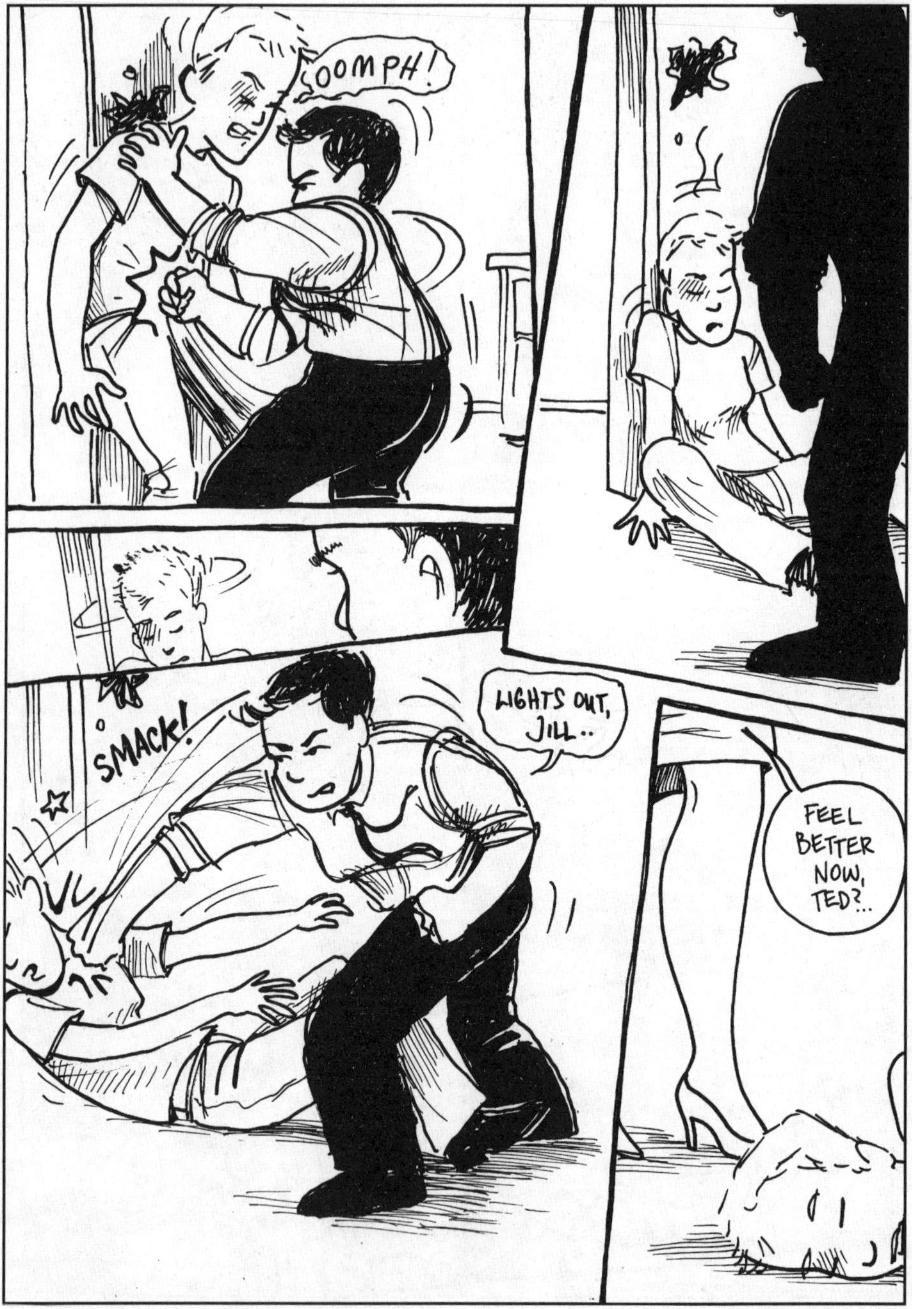
OOMPH!
SMACK!
LIGHTS OUT, JILL..
FEEL BETTER NOW, TED?...

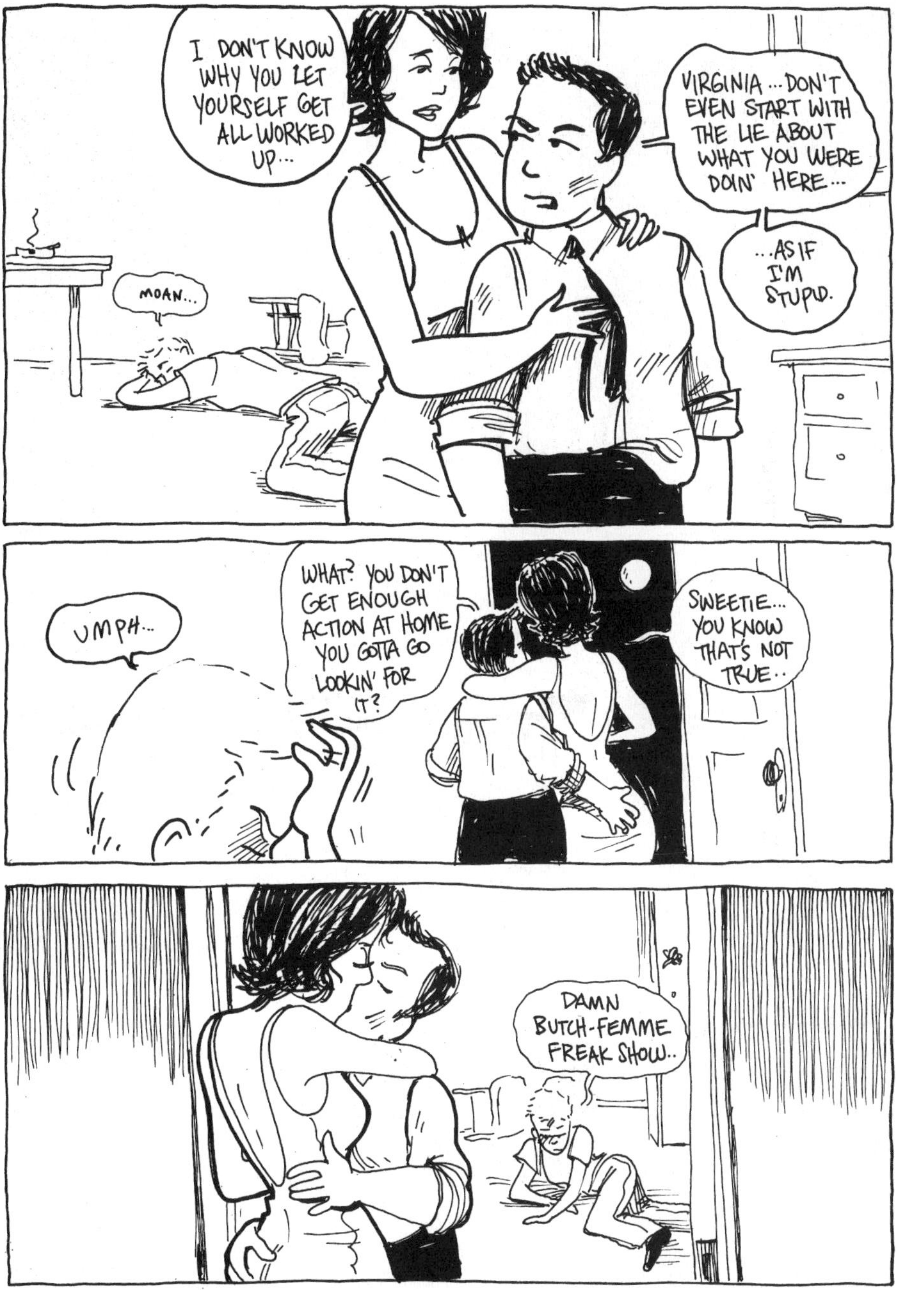
I DON'T KNOW WHY YOU LET YOURSELF GET ALL WORKED UP...
VIRGINIA ... DON'T EVEN START WITH THE LIE ABOUT WHAT YOU WERE DOIN' HERE...
...AS IF I'M STUPID.
MOAN...
UMPH...
WHAT? YOU DON'T GET ENOUGH ACTION AT HOME YOU GOTTA GO LOOKIN' FOR IT?
SWEETIE... YOU KNOW THAT'S NOT TRUE..
DAMN BUTCH-FEMME FREAK SHOW..

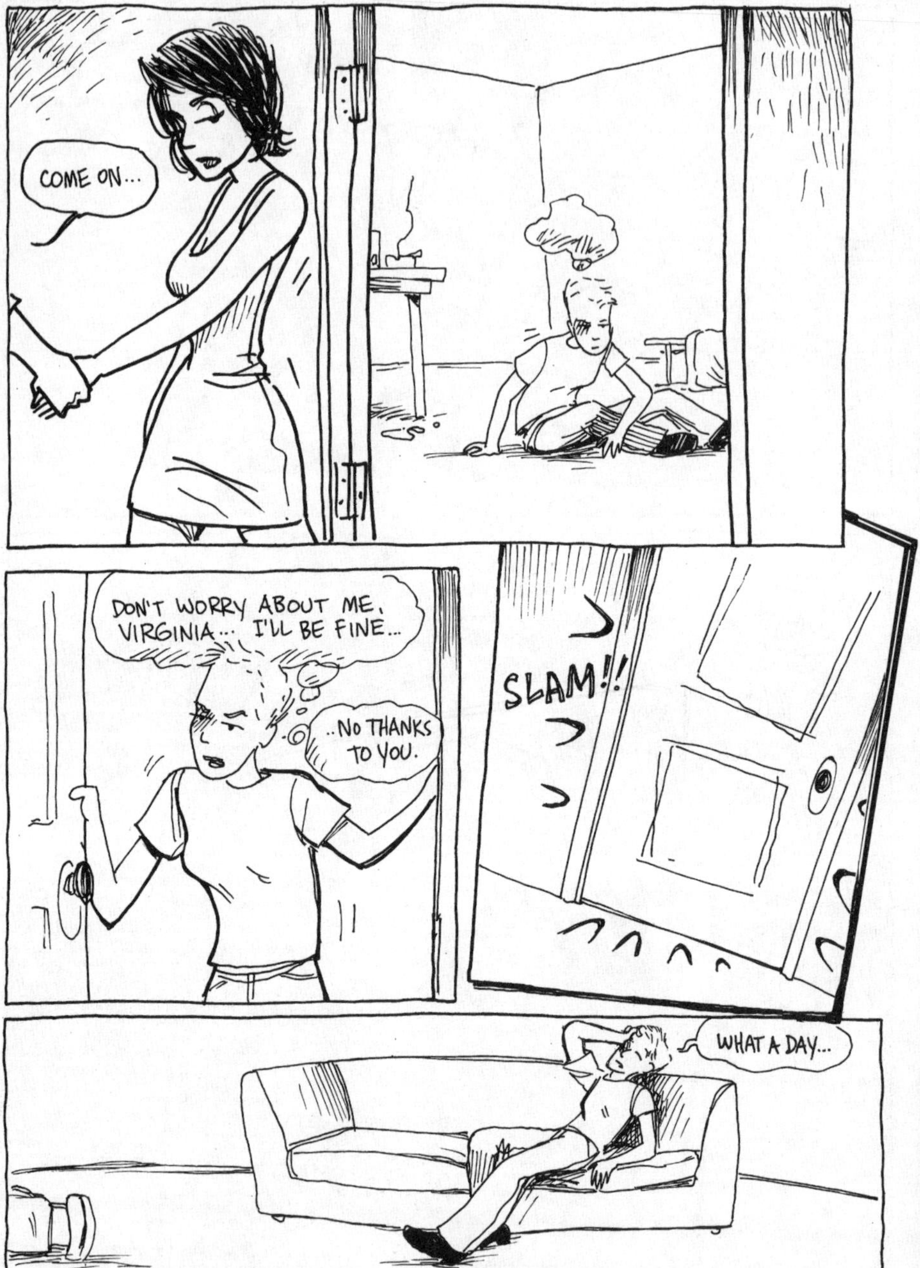
COME ON...
DON'T WORRY ABOUT ME, VIRGINIA... I'LL BE FINE...
..NO THANKS TO YOU.
SLAM!!
WHAT A DAY...

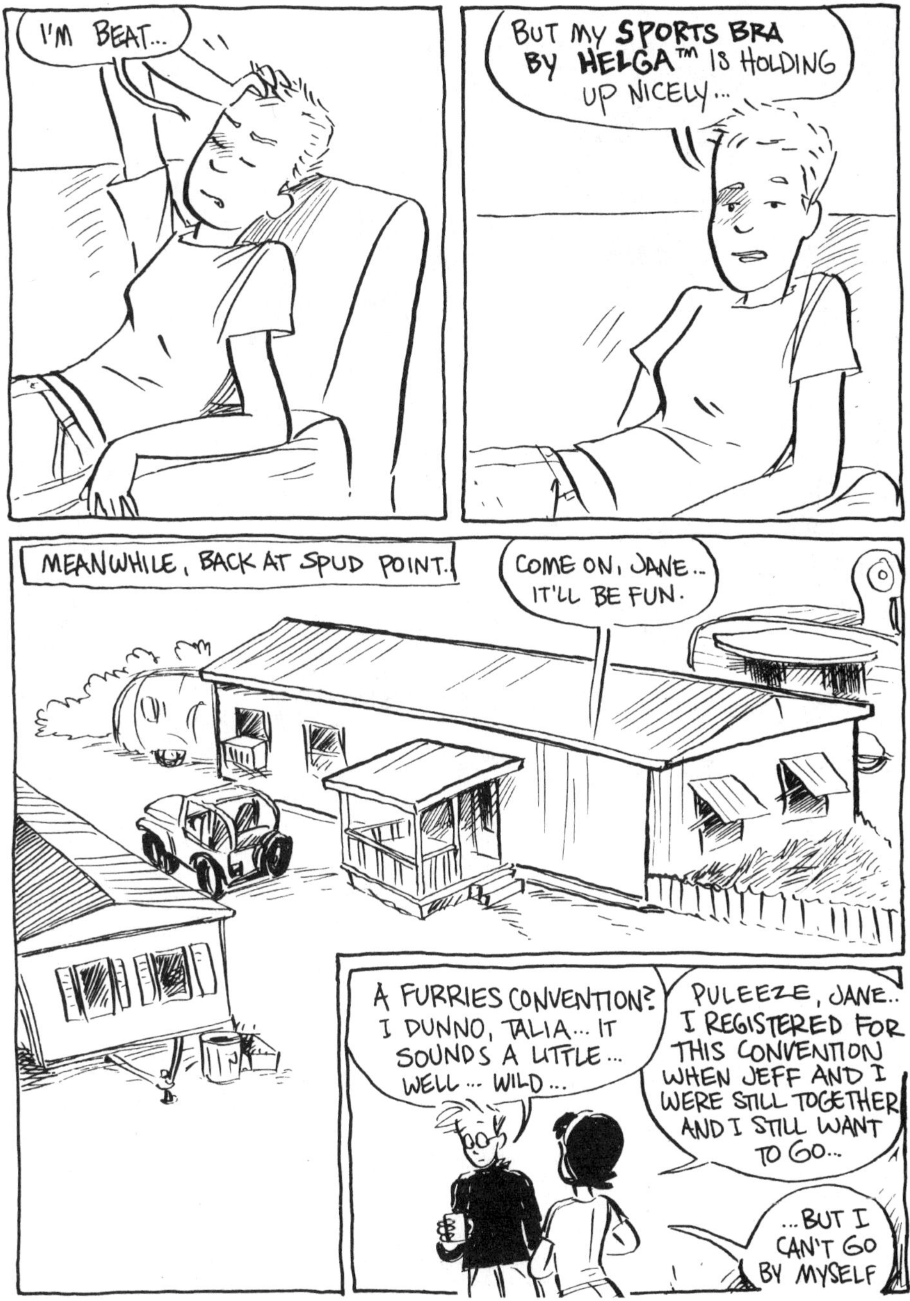
I'M BEAT...
BUT MY **SPORTS BRA BY HELGA™** IS HOLDING UP NICELY...
MEANWHILE, BACK AT SPUD POINT.
COME ON, JANE.. IT'LL BE FUN.
A FURRIES CONVENTION? I DUNNO, TALIA... IT SOUNDS A LITTLE... WELL... WILD...
PULEEZE, JANE.. I REGISTERED FOR THIS CONVENTION WHEN JEFF AND I WERE STILL TOGETHER AND I STILL WANT TO GO...
...BUT I CAN'T GO BY MYSELF

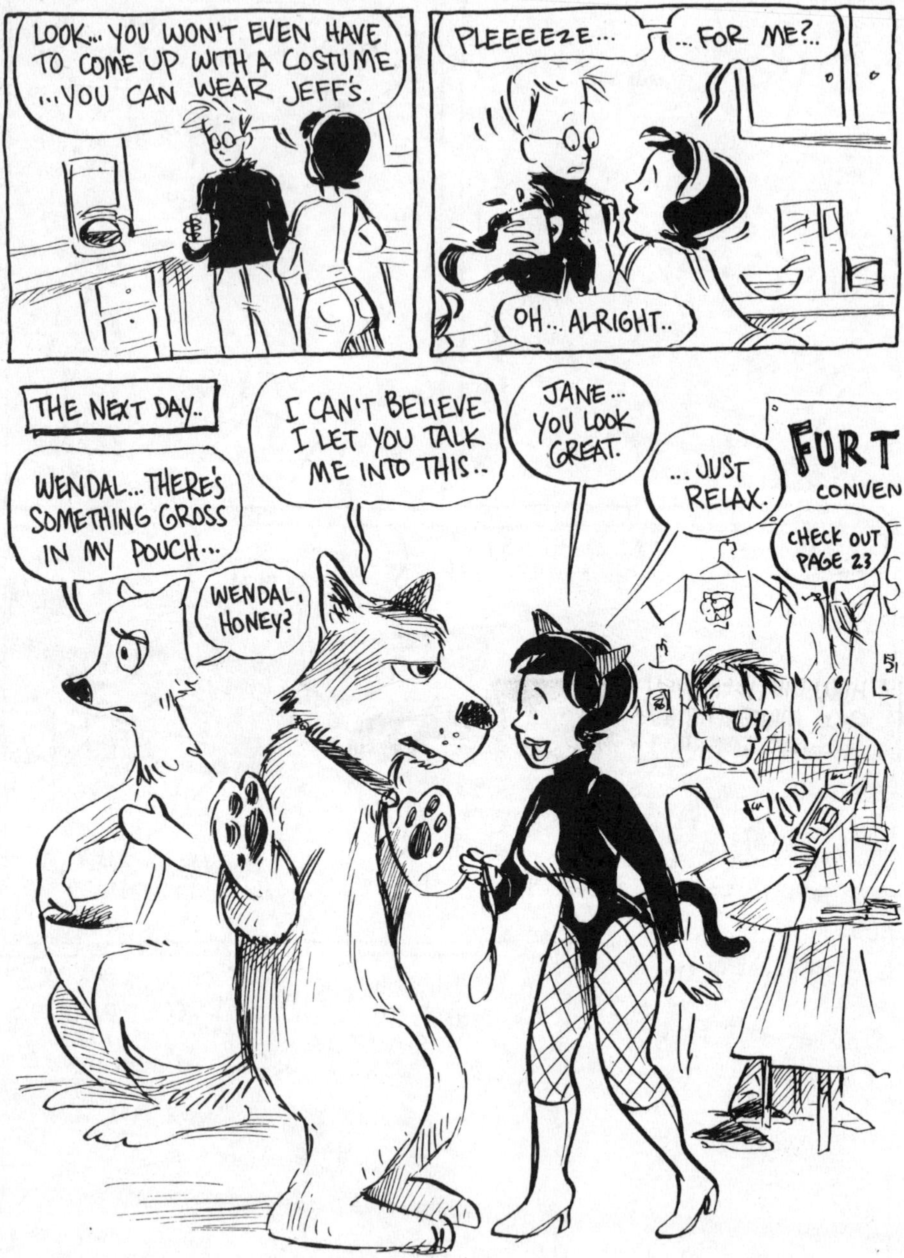
LOOK... YOU WON'T EVEN HAVE TO COME UP WITH A COSTUME ...YOU CAN WEAR JEFF'S.
PLEEEEZE...
...FOR ME?..
OH... ALRIGHT..
THE NEXT DAY..
WENDAL... THERE'S SOMETHING GROSS IN MY POUCH...
WENDAL, HONEY?
I CAN'T BELIEVE I LET YOU TALK ME INTO THIS..
JANE... YOU LOOK GREAT.
...JUST RELAX.
FURT
CONVEN
CHECK OUT PAGE 23

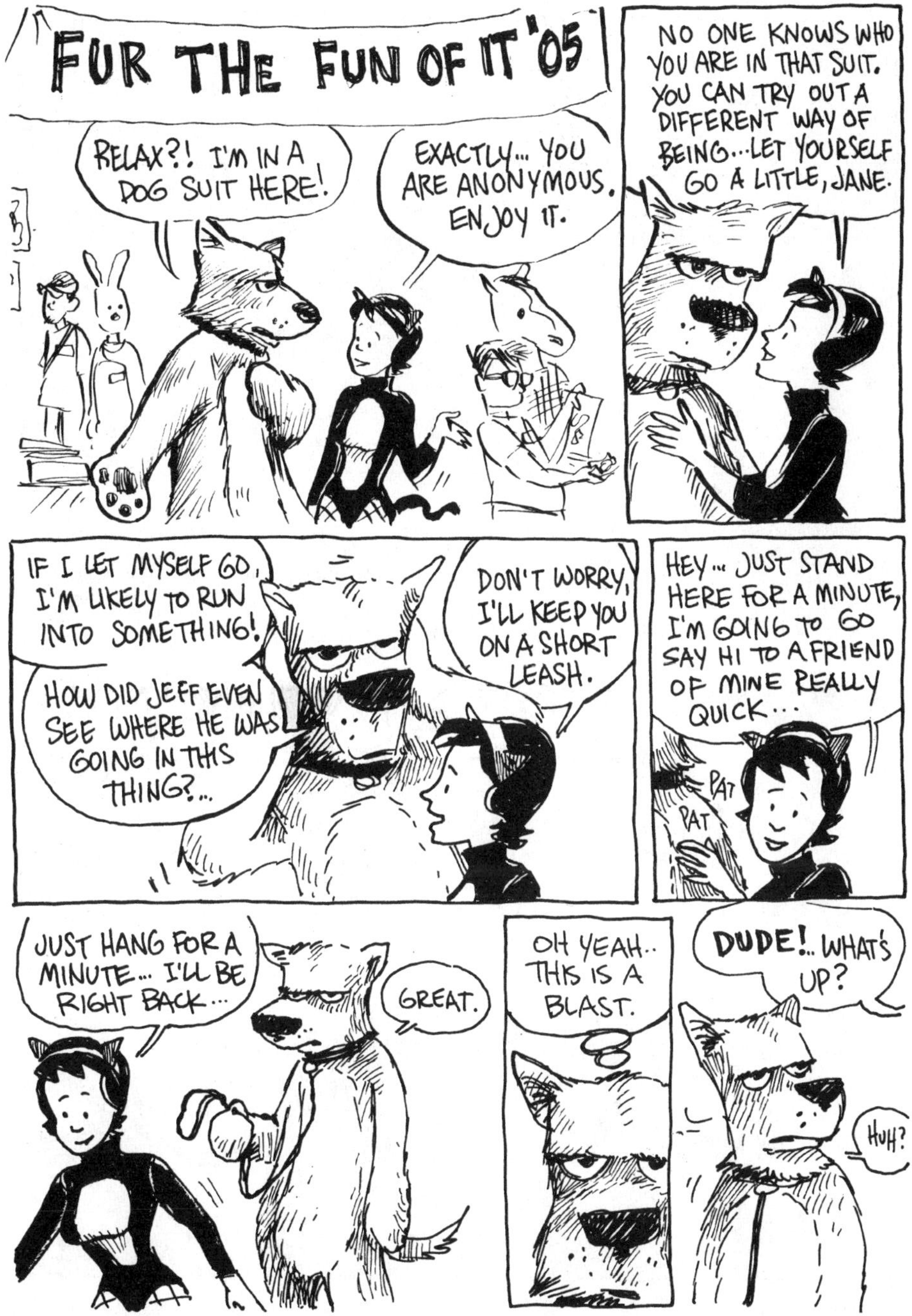
FUR THE FUN OF IT '05
RELAX?! I'M IN A DOG SUIT HERE!
EXACTLY... YOU ARE ANONYMOUS. ENJOY IT.
NO ONE KNOWS WHO YOU ARE IN THAT SUIT. YOU CAN TRY OUT A DIFFERENT WAY OF BEING...LET YOURSELF GO A LITTLE, JANE.
IF I LET MYSELF GO, I'M LIKELY TO RUN INTO SOMETHING!
HOW DID JEFF EVEN SEE WHERE HE WAS GOING IN THIS THING?...
DON'T WORRY, I'LL KEEP YOU ON A SHORT LEASH.
HEY... JUST STAND HERE FOR A MINUTE, I'M GOING TO GO SAY HI TO A FRIEND OF MINE REALLY QUICK...
PAT
PAT
JUST HANG FOR A MINUTE... I'LL BE RIGHT BACK...
GREAT.
OH YEAH.. THIS IS A BLAST.
DUDE!.. WHAT'S UP?
HUH?

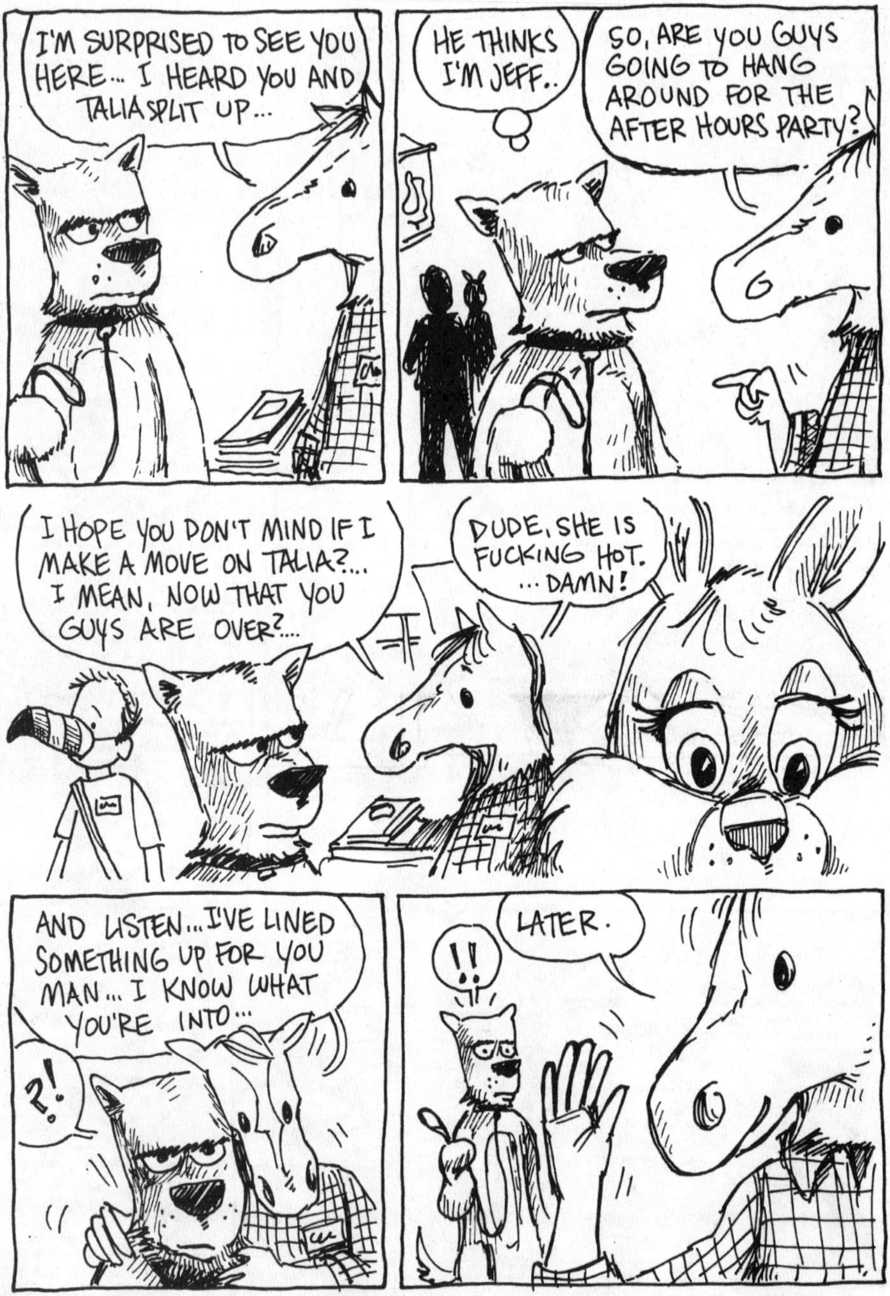
I'M SURPRISED TO SEE YOU HERE... I HEARD YOU AND TALIA SPLIT UP...
HE THINKS I'M JEFF..
SO, ARE YOU GUYS GOING TO HANG AROUND FOR THE AFTER HOURS PARTY?
I HOPE YOU DON'T MIND IF I MAKE A MOVE ON TALIA?... I MEAN, NOW THAT YOU GUYS ARE OVER?...
DUDE, SHE IS FUCKING HOT. ...DAMN!
AND LISTEN... I'VE LINED SOMETHING UP FOR YOU MAN... I KNOW WHAT YOU'RE INTO...
?!
!!
LATER.

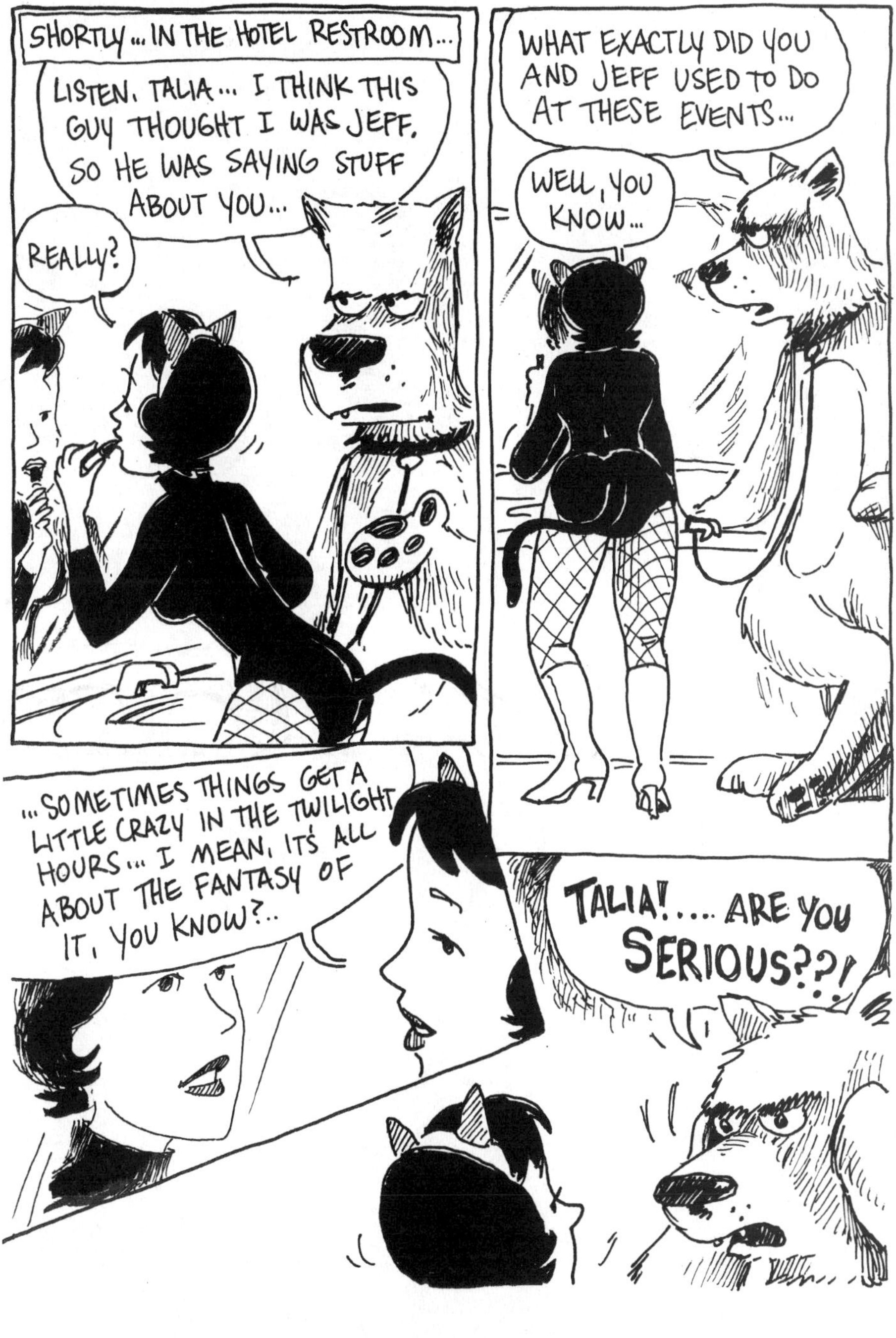
SHORTLY... IN THE HOTEL RESTROOM...
LISTEN, TALIA... I THINK THIS GUY THOUGHT I WAS JEFF, SO HE WAS SAYING STUFF ABOUT YOU...
REALLY?
WHAT EXACTLY DID YOU AND JEFF USED TO DO AT THESE EVENTS...
WELL, YOU KNOW...
...SOMETIMES THINGS GET A LITTLE CRAZY IN THE TWILIGHT HOURS... I MEAN, IT'S ALL ABOUT THE FANTASY OF IT, YOU KNOW?..
TALIA!.... ARE YOU SERIOUS??!

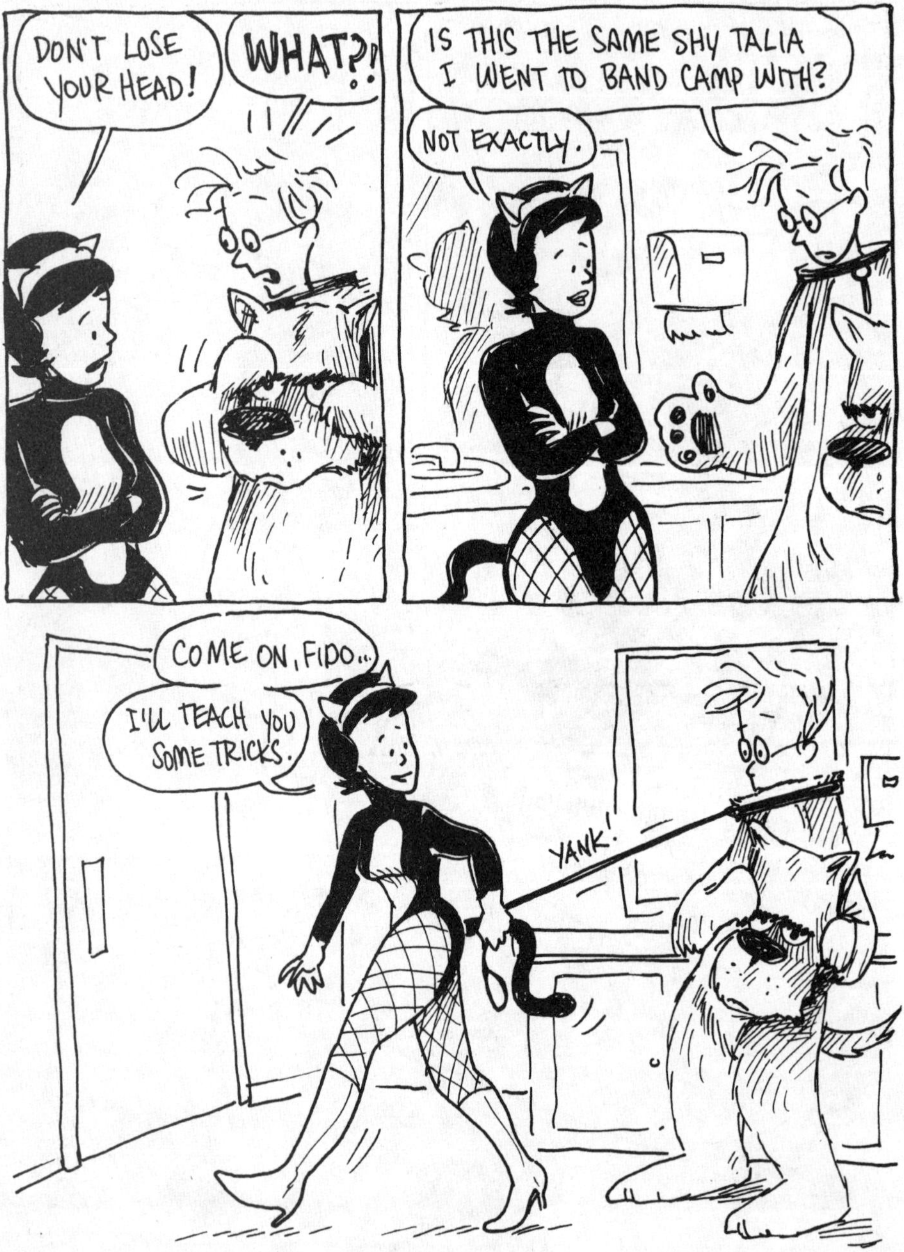
DON'T LOSE YOUR HEAD!
WHAT?!
IS THIS THE SAME SHY TALIA I WENT TO BAND CAMP WITH?
NOT EXACTLY.
COME ON, FIDO...
I'LL TEACH YOU SOME TRICKS.
YANK!

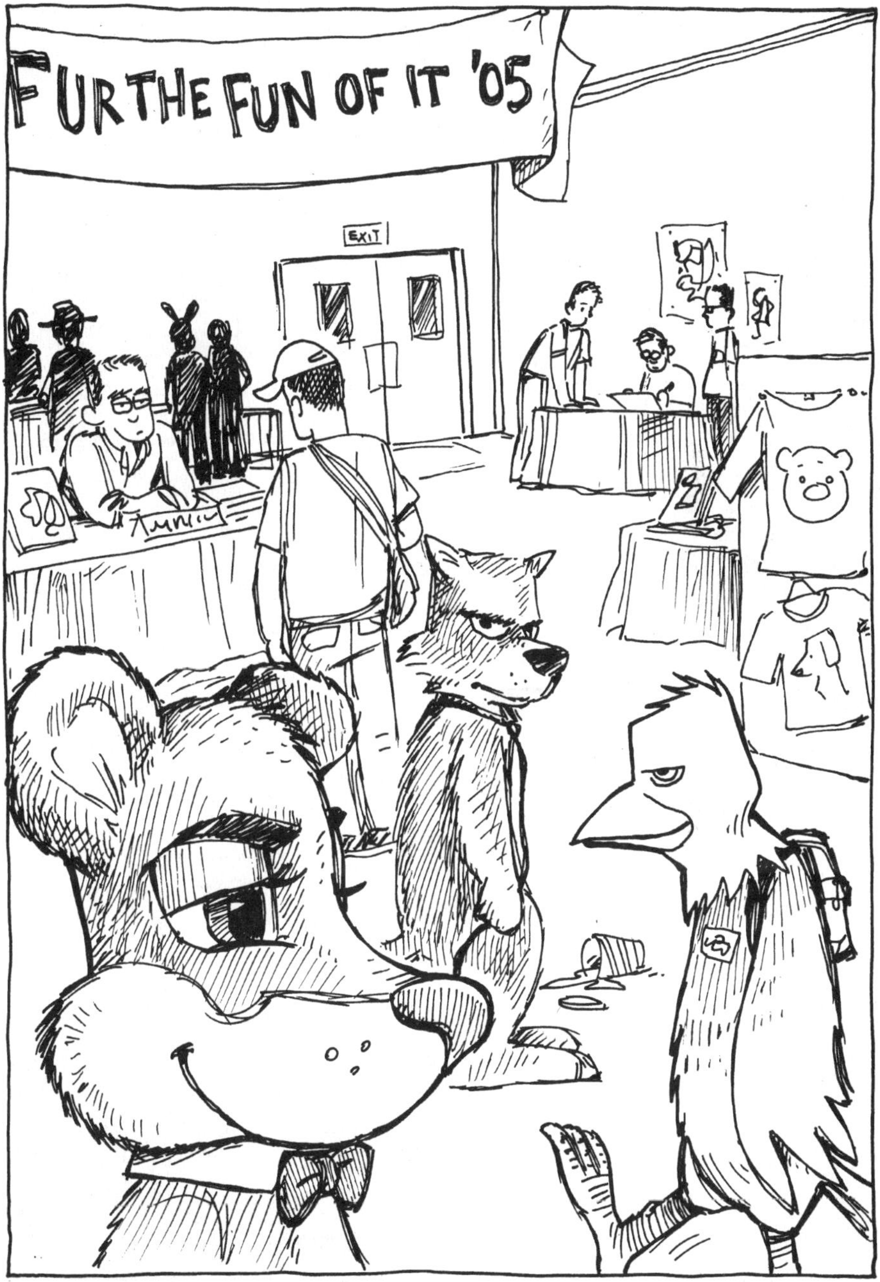
FUR THE FUN OF IT '05
EXIT

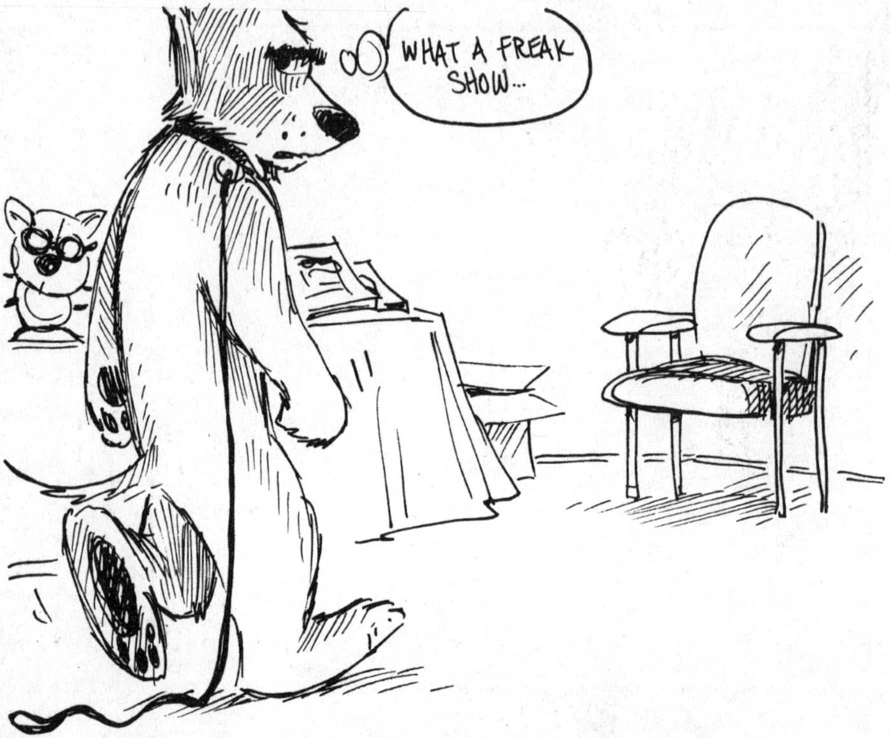
WHAT A FREAK SHOW...

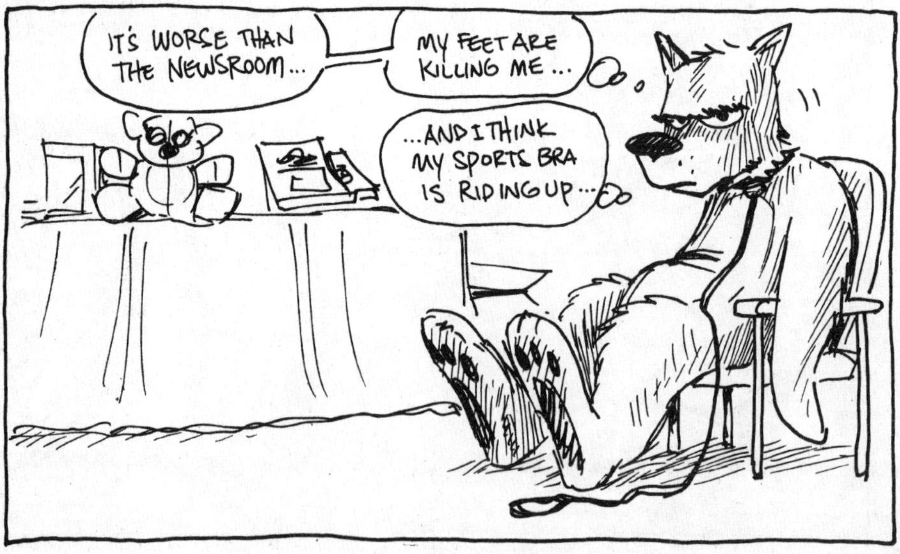
IT'S WORSE THAN THE NEWSROOM...
MY FEET ARE KILLING ME...
...AND I THINK MY SPORTS BRA IS RIDING UP...

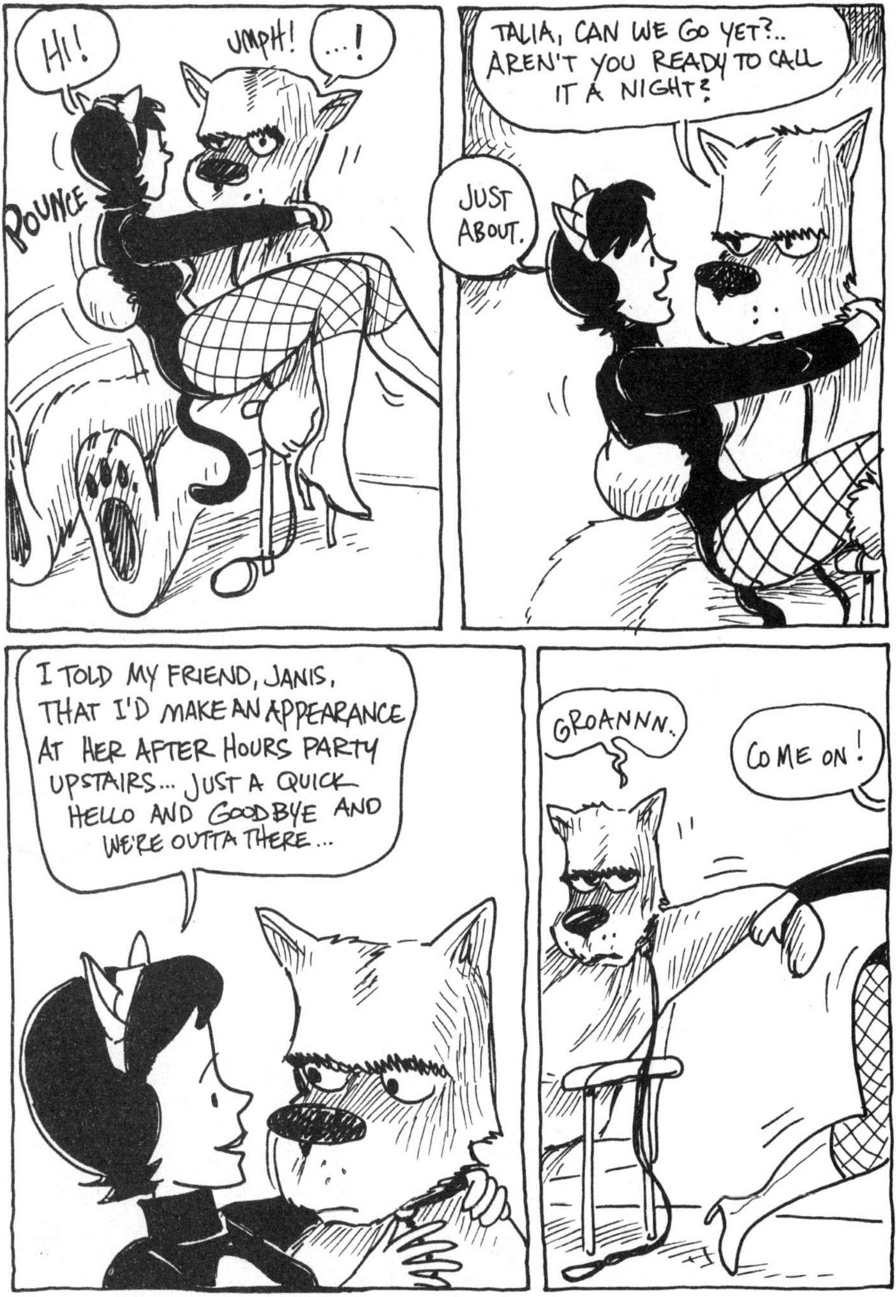
HI!
UMPH!
...!
POUNCE
TALIA, CAN WE GO YET?.. AREN'T YOU READY TO CALL IT A NIGHT?
JUST ABOUT.
I TOLD MY FRIEND, JANIS, THAT I'D MAKE AN APPEARANCE AT HER AFTER HOURS PARTY UPSTAIRS... JUST A QUICK HELLO AND GOODBYE AND WE'RE OUTTA THERE...
GROANNN..
COME ON!

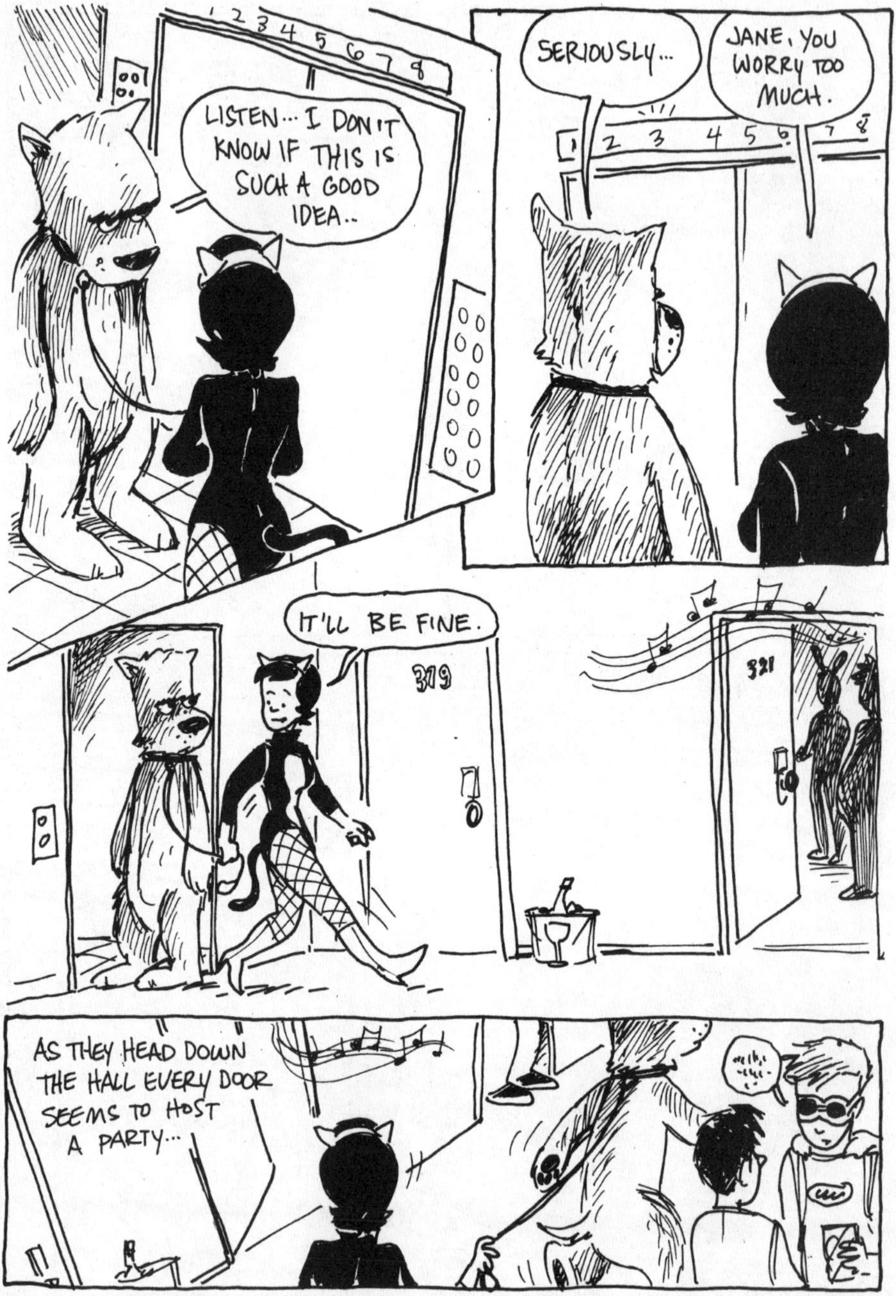
LISTEN... I DON'T KNOW IF THIS IS SUCH A GOOD IDEA..
SERIOUSLY...
JANE, YOU WORRY TOO MUCH.
IT'LL BE FINE.
379
321
AS THEY HEAD DOWN THE HALL EVERY DOOR SEEMS TO HOST A PARTY...

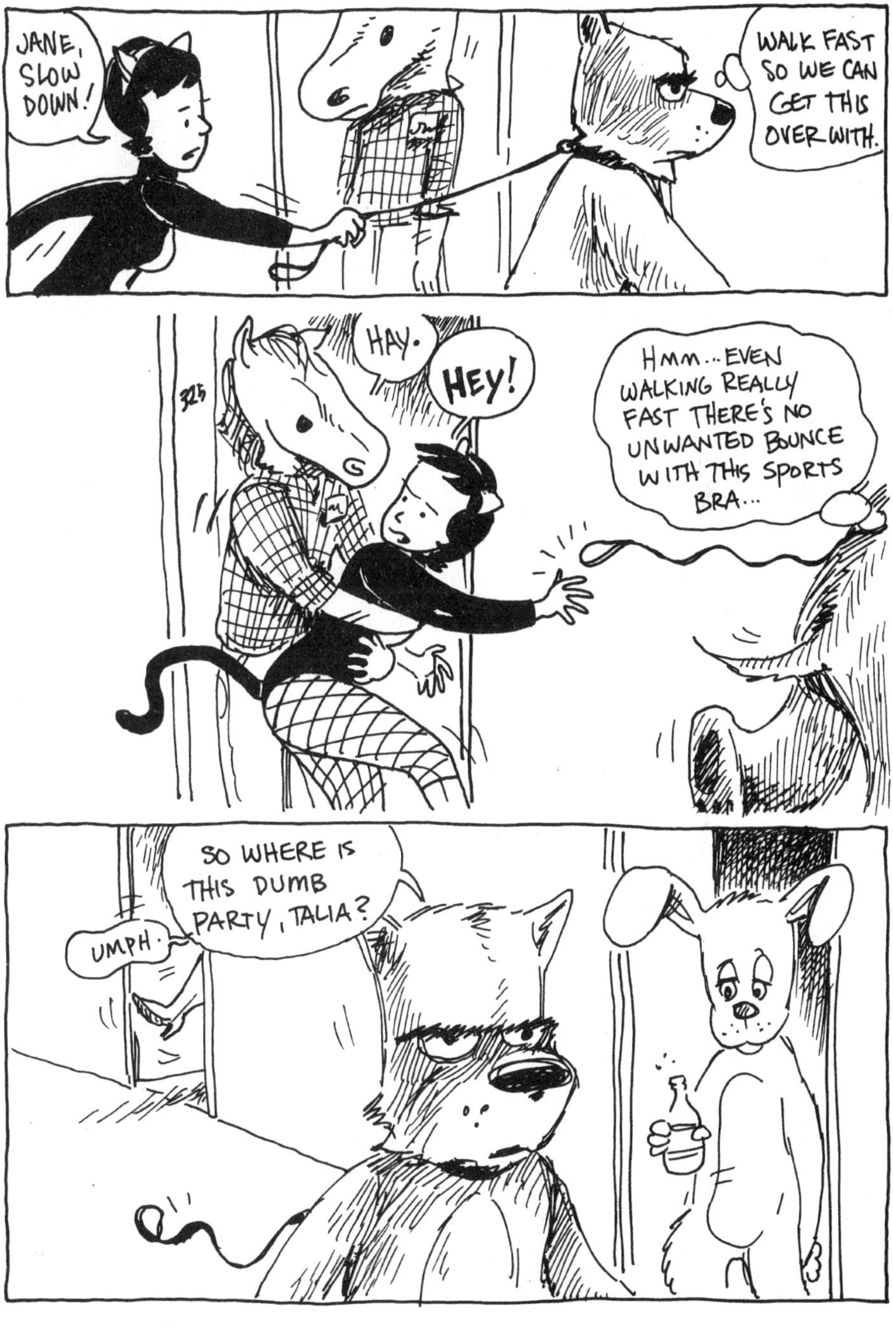
JANE, SLOW DOWN!
WALK FAST SO WE CAN GET THIS OVER WITH.
HAY.
HEY!
HMM... EVEN WALKING REALLY FAST THERE'S NO UNWANTED BOUNCE WITH THIS SPORTS BRA...
325
SO WHERE IS THIS DUMB PARTY, TALIA?
UMPH.

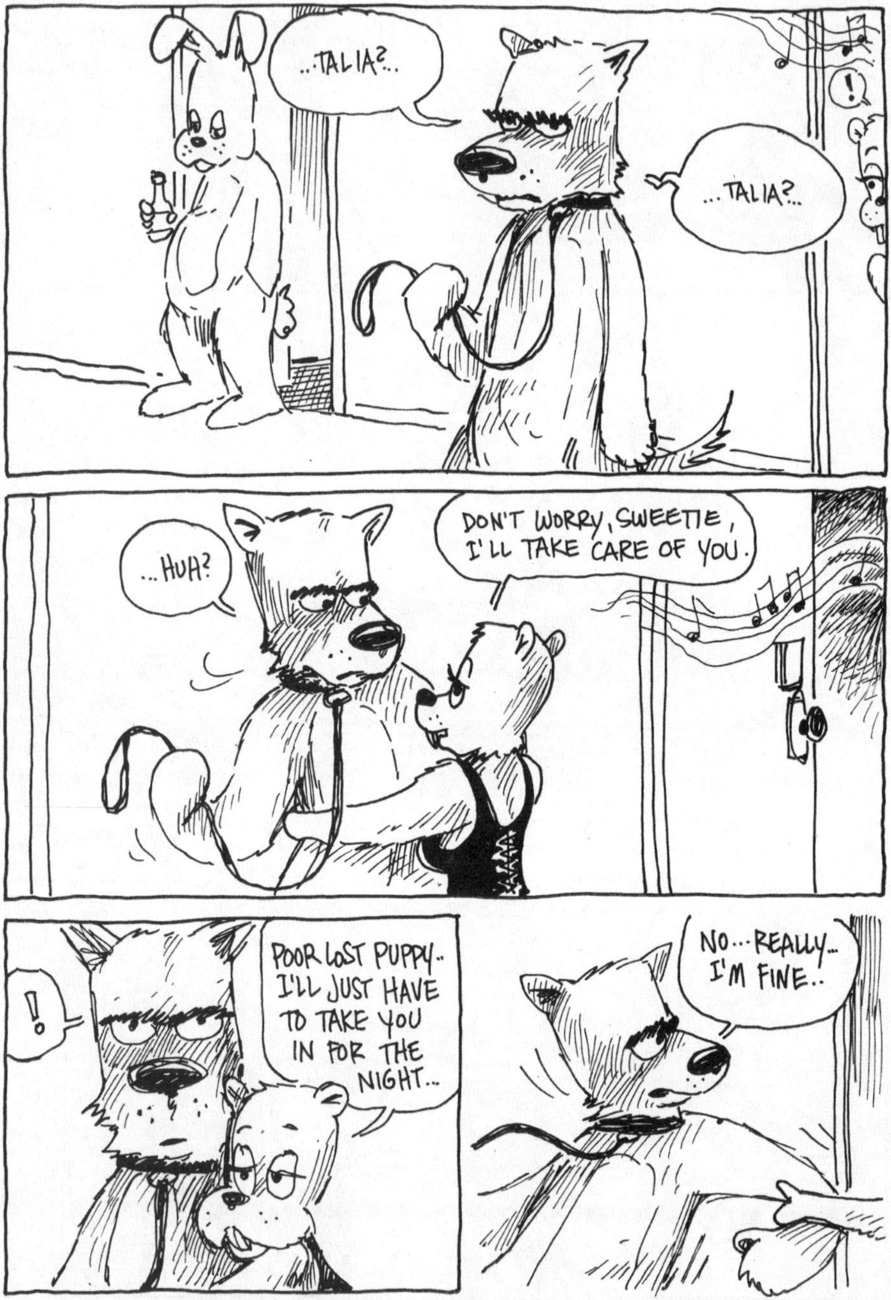

...TALIA?...
...TALIA?...
!
...HUH?
DON'T WORRY, SWEETIE, I'LL TAKE CARE OF YOU.
!
POOR LOST PUPPY.. I'LL JUST HAVE TO TAKE YOU IN FOR THE NIGHT...
NO...REALLY... I'M FINE..

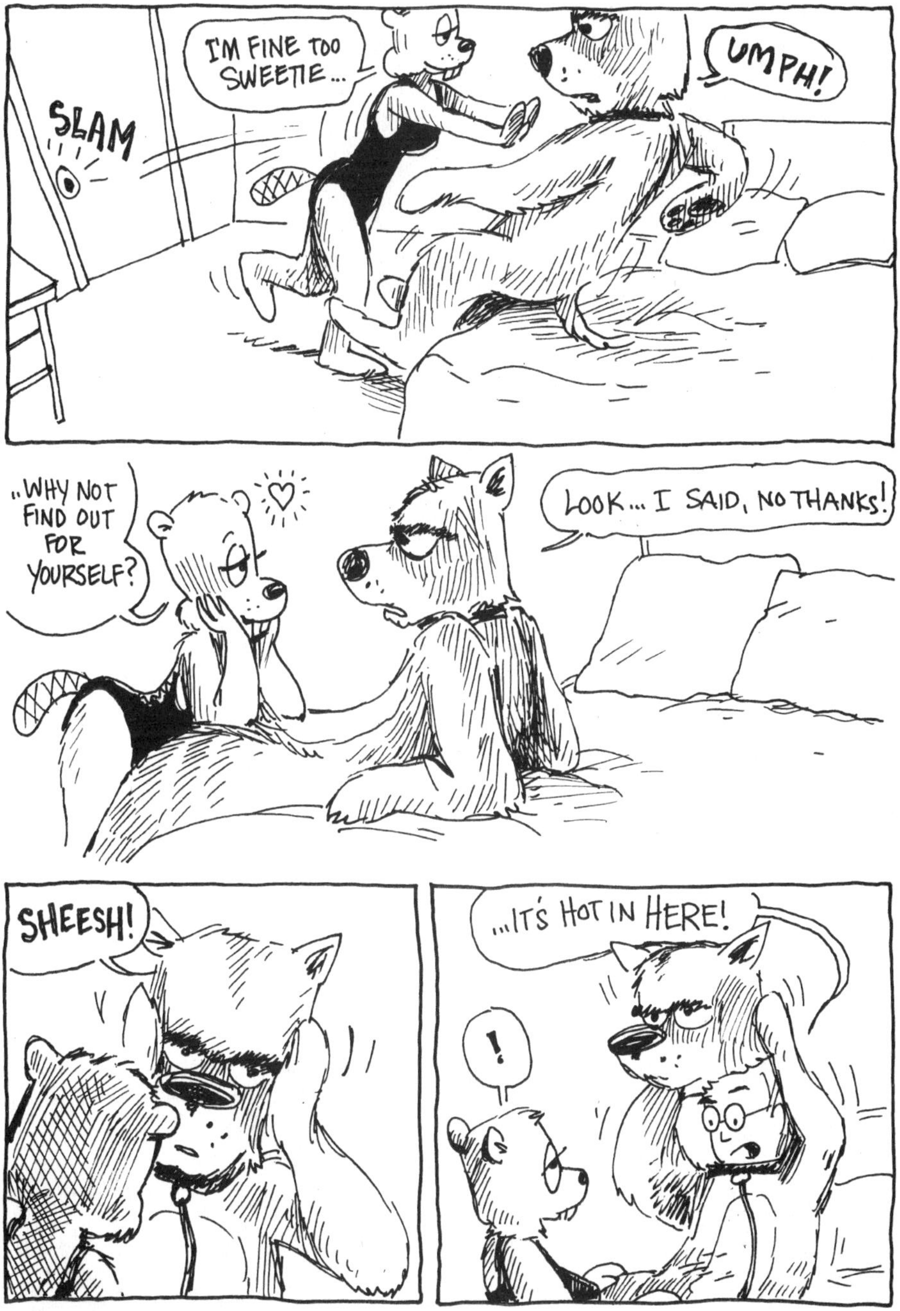
SLAM
I'M FINE TOO SWEETIE...
UMPH!
..WHY NOT FIND OUT FOR YOURSELF?
LOOK... I SAID, NO THANKS!
SHEESH!
!
...IT'S HOT IN HERE!

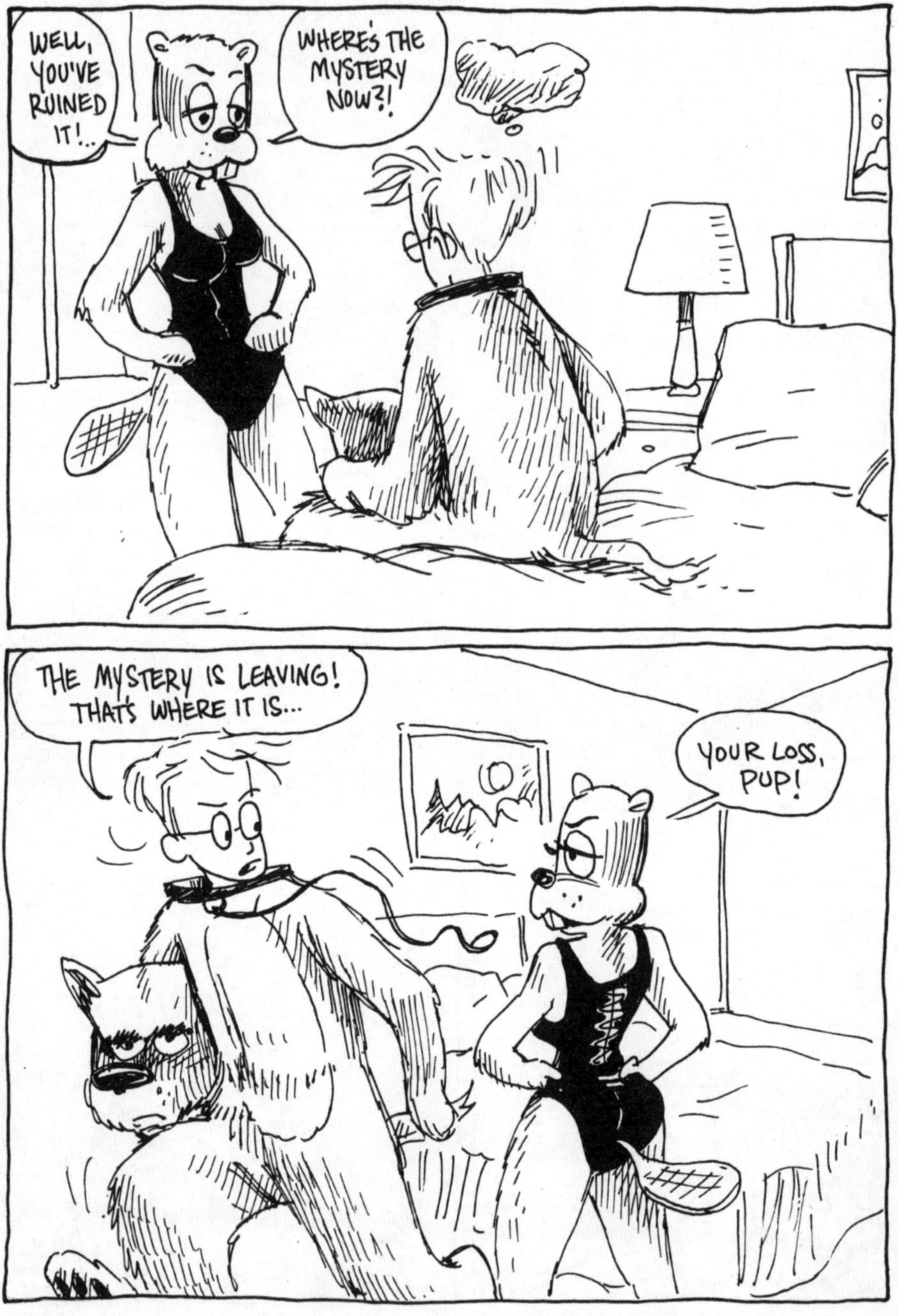
WELL, YOU'VE RUINED IT!...
WHERE'S THE MYSTERY NOW?!
THE MYSTERY IS LEAVING! THAT'S WHERE IT IS...
YOUR LOSS, PUP!

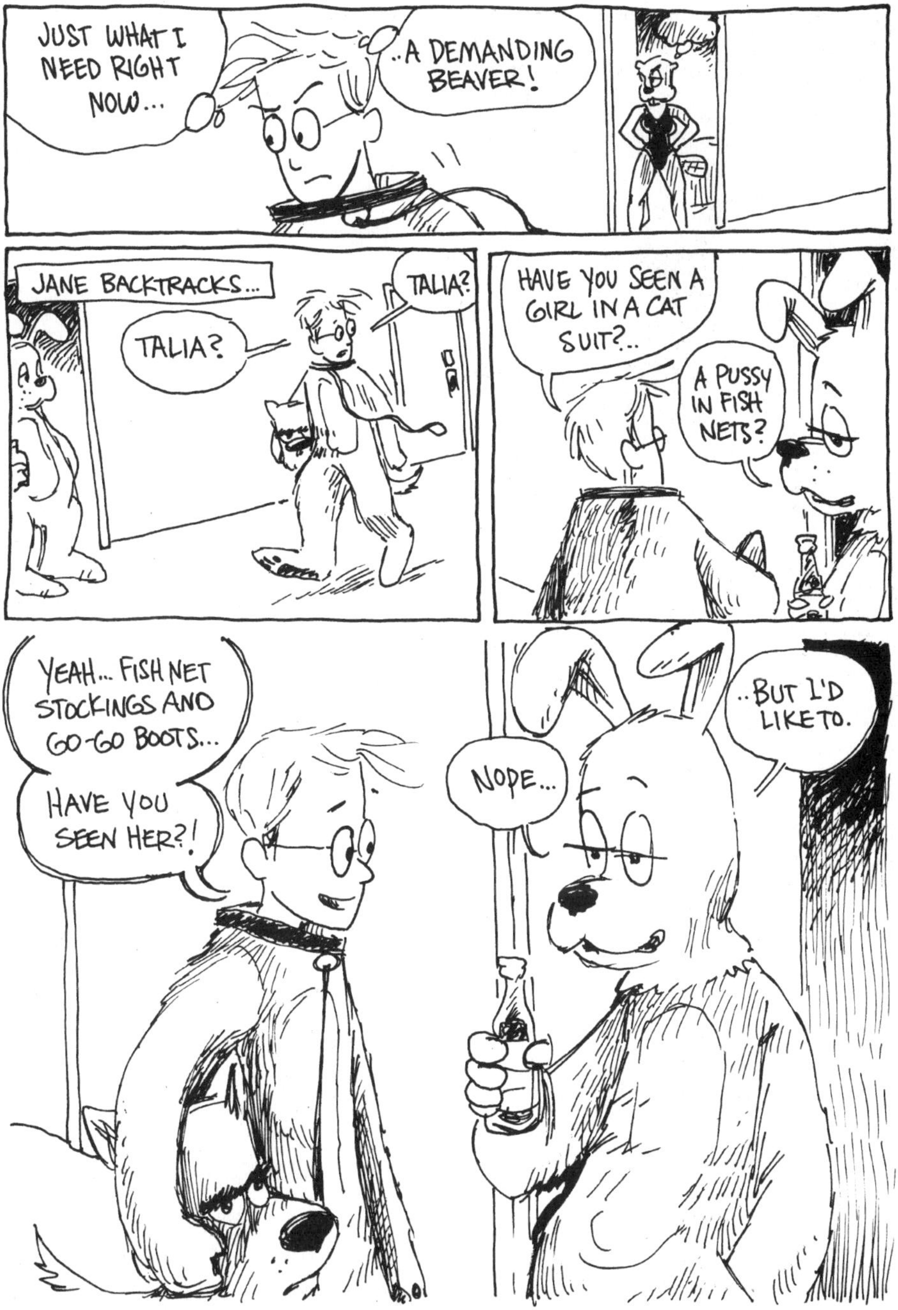
JUST WHAT I NEED RIGHT NOW...
..A DEMANDING BEAVER!
JANE BACKTRACKS...
TALIA?
TALIA?
HAVE YOU SEEN A GIRL IN A CAT SUIT?..
A PUSSY IN FISH NETS?
YEAH... FISH NET STOCKINGS AND GO-GO BOOTS...
HAVE YOU SEEN HER?!
NOPE...
..BUT I'D LIKE TO.

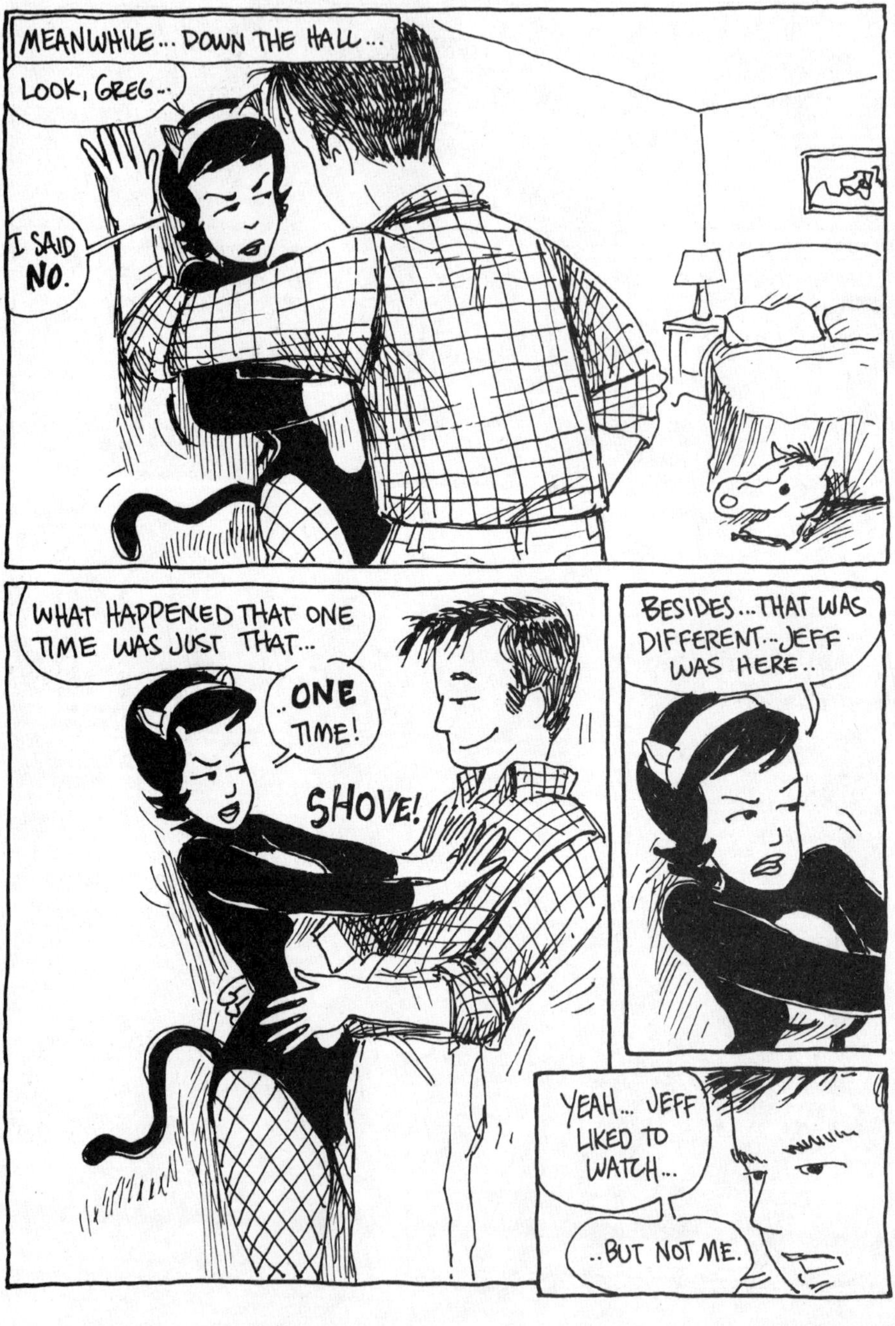
MEANWHILE... DOWN THE HALL...
LOOK, GREG..
I SAID NO.
WHAT HAPPENED THAT ONE TIME WAS JUST THAT...
..ONE TIME!
SHOVE!
BESIDES...THAT WAS DIFFERENT...JEFF WAS HERE..
YEAH... JEFF LIKED TO WATCH...
..BUT NOT ME.

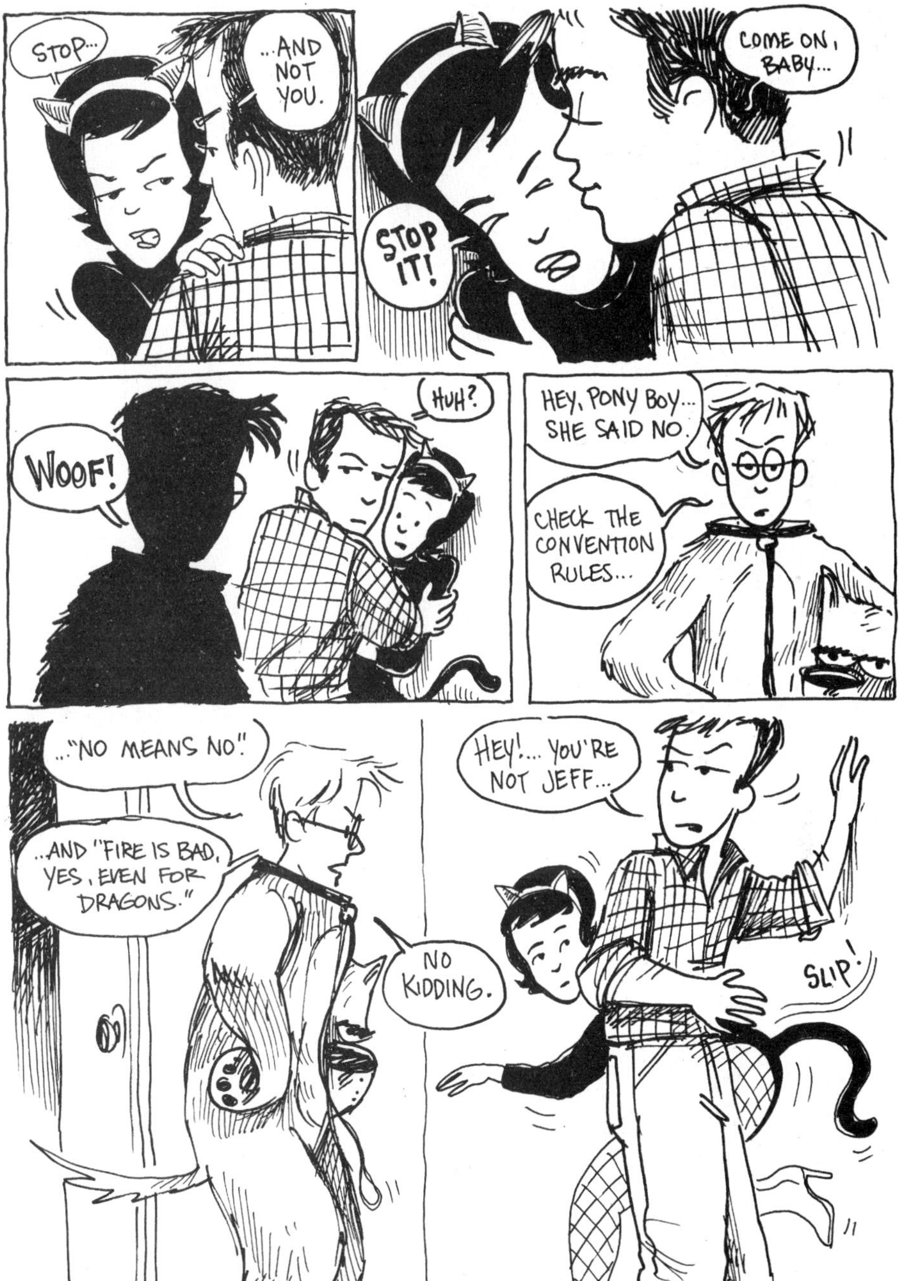
STOP...
...AND NOT YOU.
COME ON, BABY...
STOP IT!
WOOF!
HUH?
HEY, PONY BOY... SHE SAID NO.
CHECK THE CONVENTION RULES...
..."NO MEANS NO."
...AND "FIRE IS BAD, YES, EVEN FOR DRAGONS."
NO KIDDING.
HEY!... YOU'RE NOT JEFF...
SLIP!

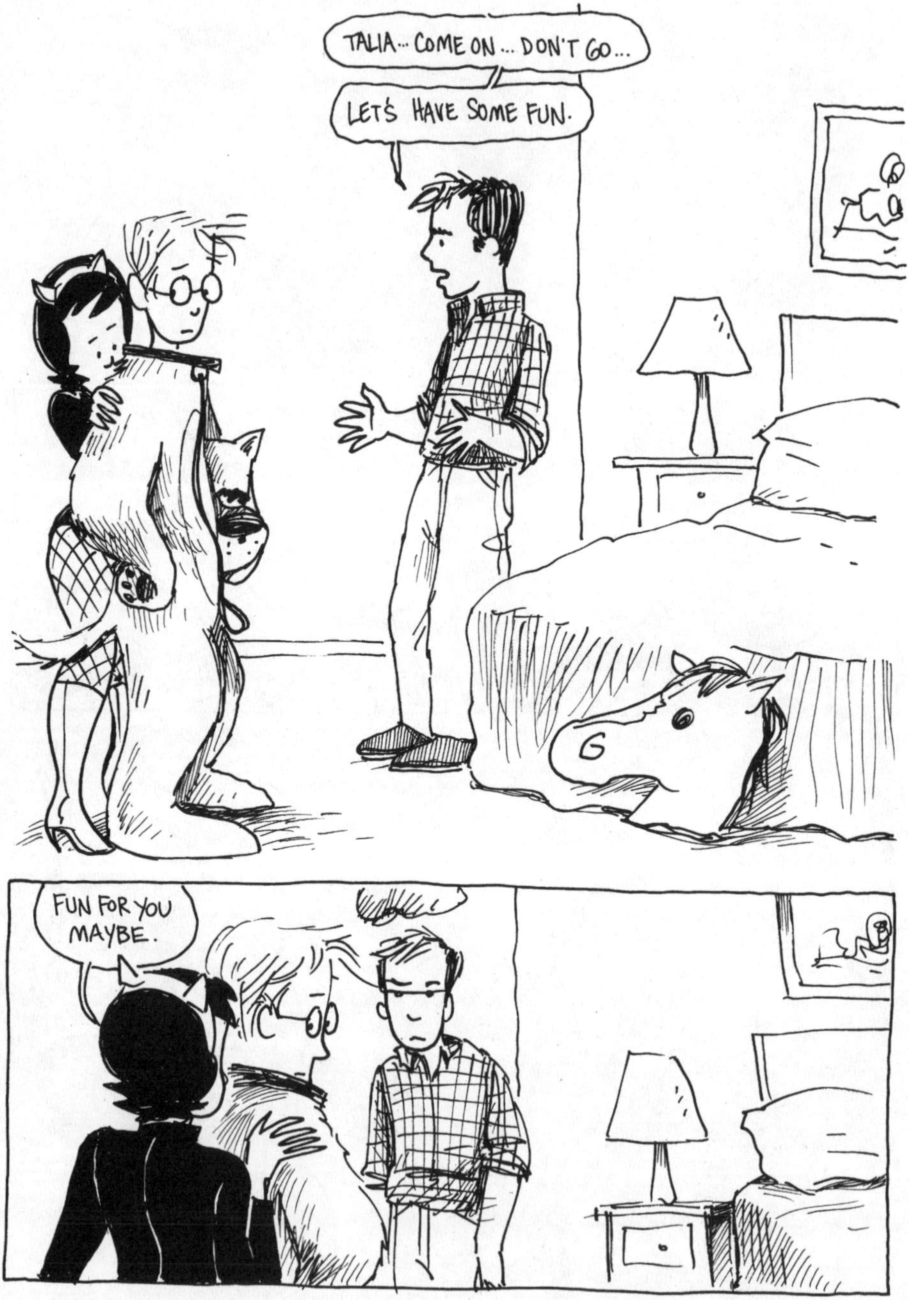
TALIA... COME ON... DON'T GO...
LET'S HAVE SOME FUN.
FUN FOR YOU MAYBE.

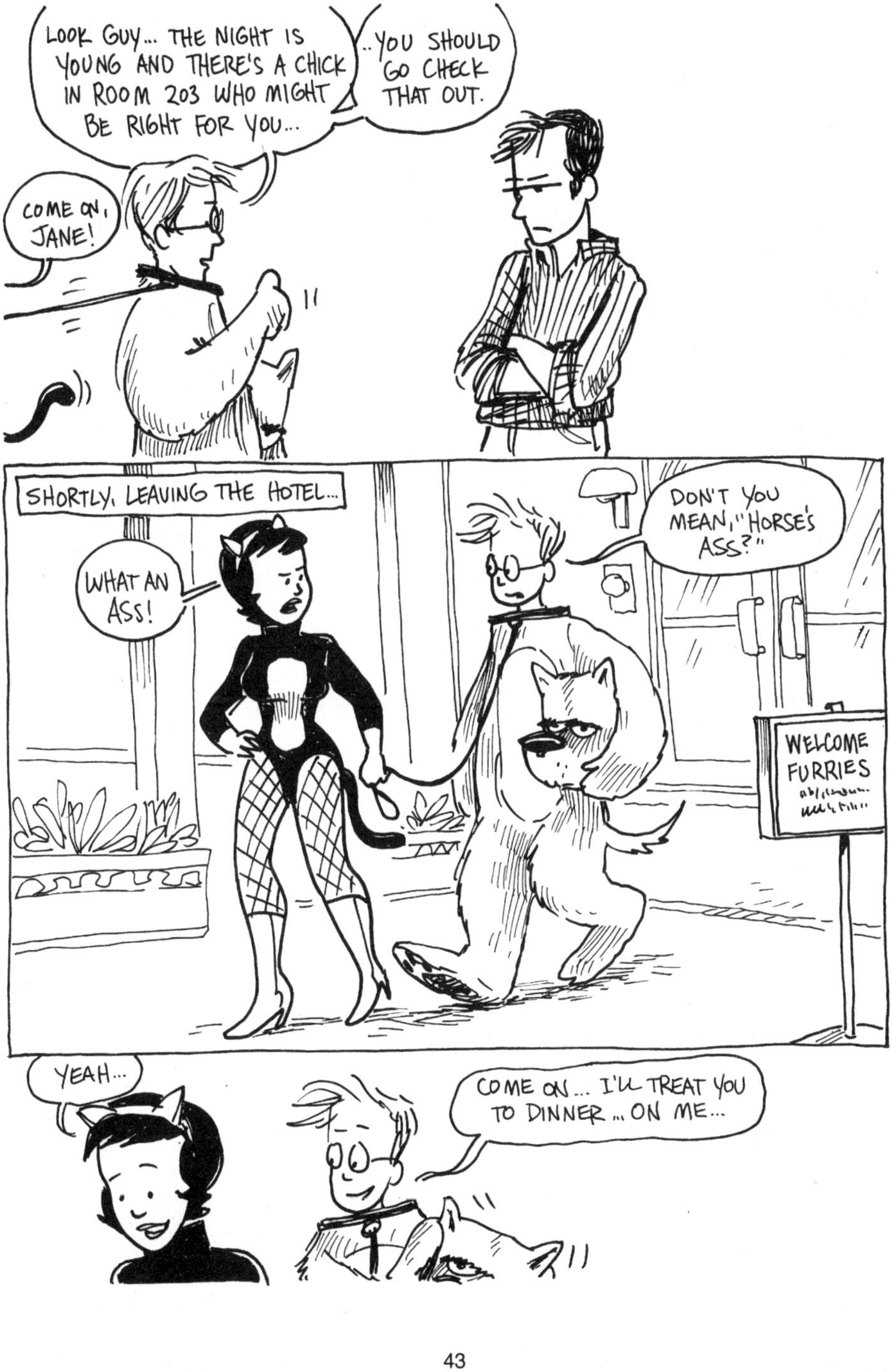
LOOK GUY... THE NIGHT IS YOUNG AND THERE'S A CHICK IN ROOM 203 WHO MIGHT BE RIGHT FOR YOU...
..YOU SHOULD GO CHECK THAT OUT.
COME ON, JANE!
SHORTLY, LEAVING THE HOTEL...
WHAT AN ASS!
DON'T YOU MEAN, "HORSE'S ASS?"
WELCOME FURRIES
YEAH...
COME ON... I'LL TREAT YOU TO DINNER... ON ME...

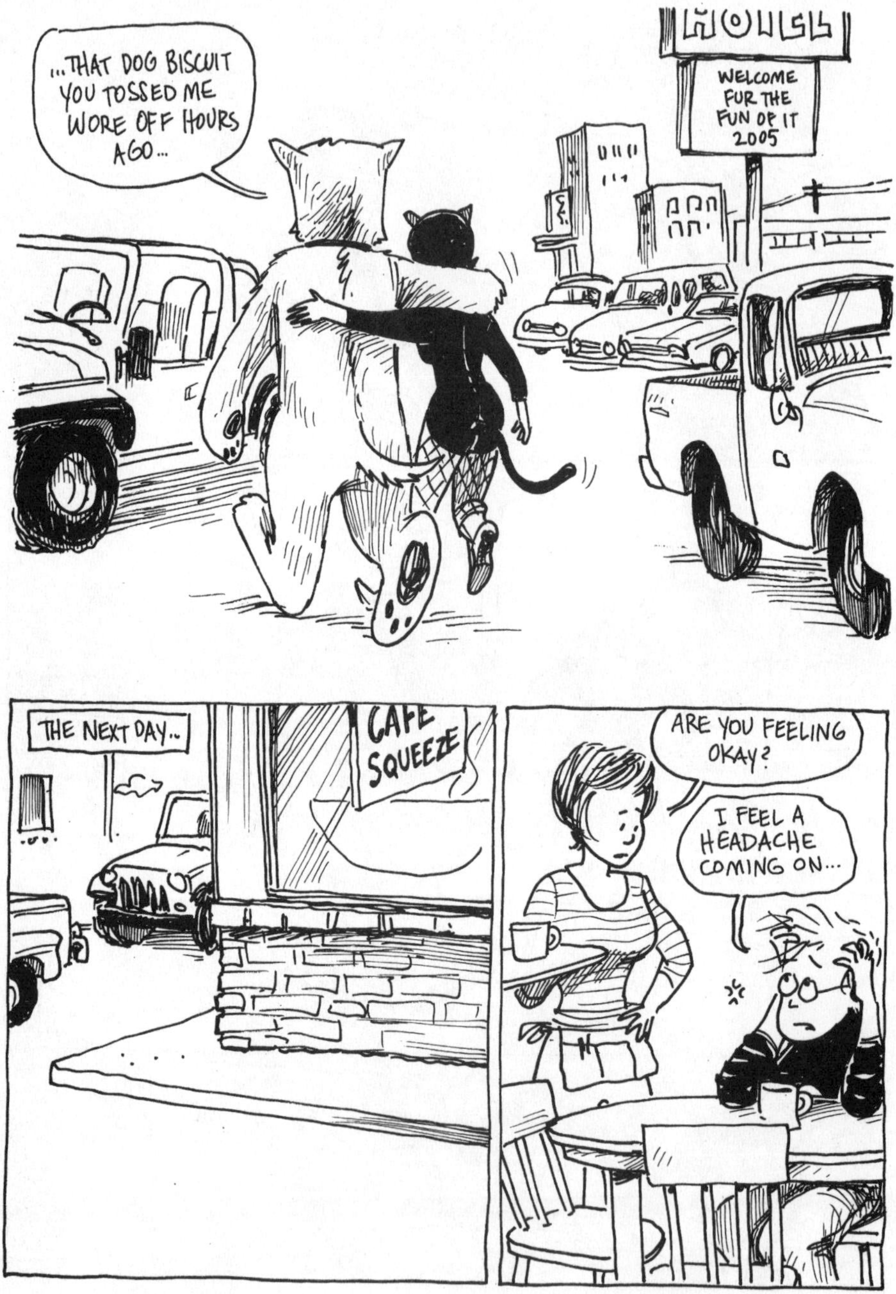
...THAT DOG BISCUIT YOU TOSSED ME WORE OFF HOURS AGO...
WELCOME FUR THE FUN OF IT 2005
THE NEXT DAY..
CAFE SQUEEZE
ARE YOU FEELING OKAY?
I FEEL A HEADACHE COMING ON...

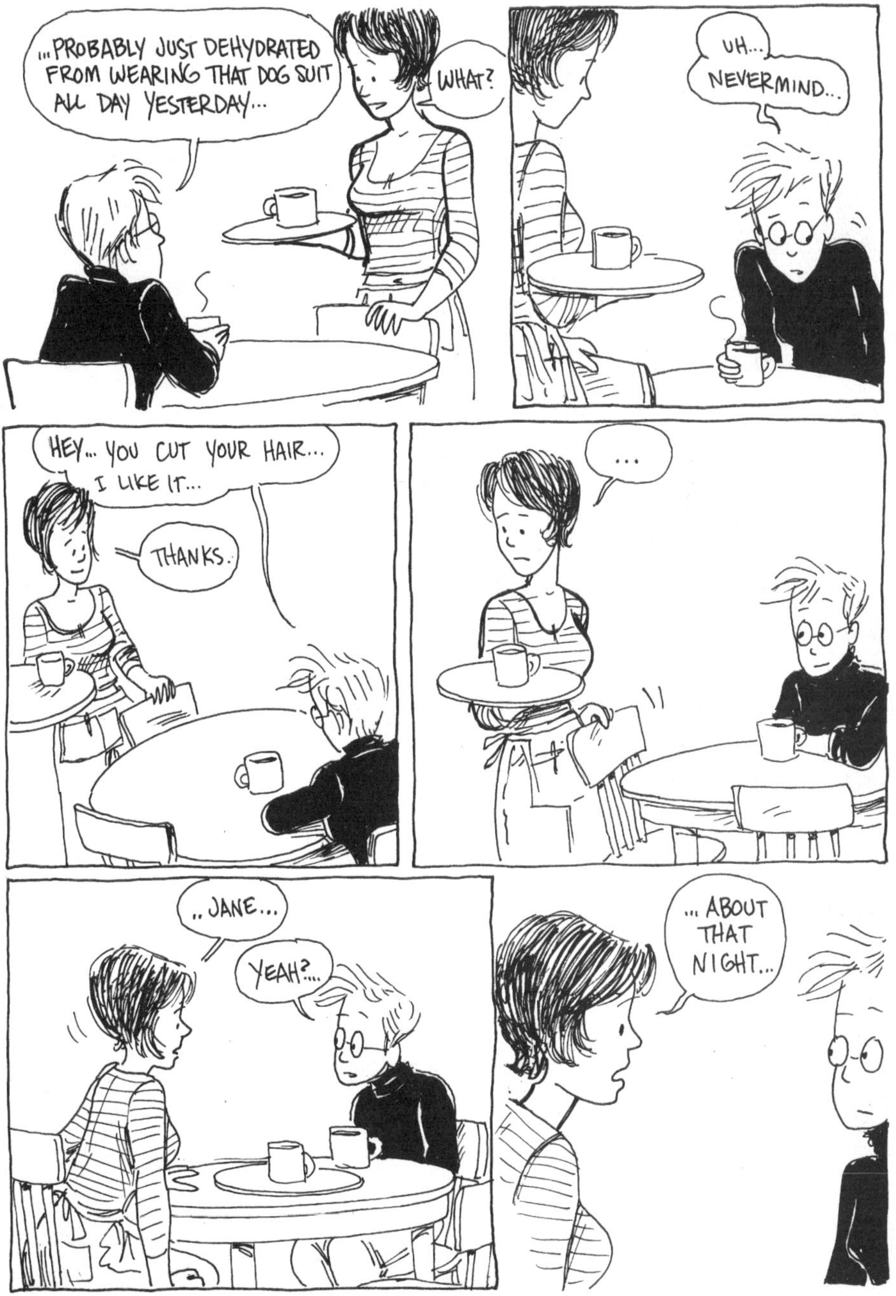
...PROBABLY JUST DEHYDRATED FROM WEARING THAT DOG SUIT ALL DAY YESTERDAY...
WHAT?
UH... NEVERMIND...
HEY... YOU CUT YOUR HAIR... I LIKE IT...
THANKS.
...
.. JANE...
YEAH?...
... ABOUT THAT NIGHT...

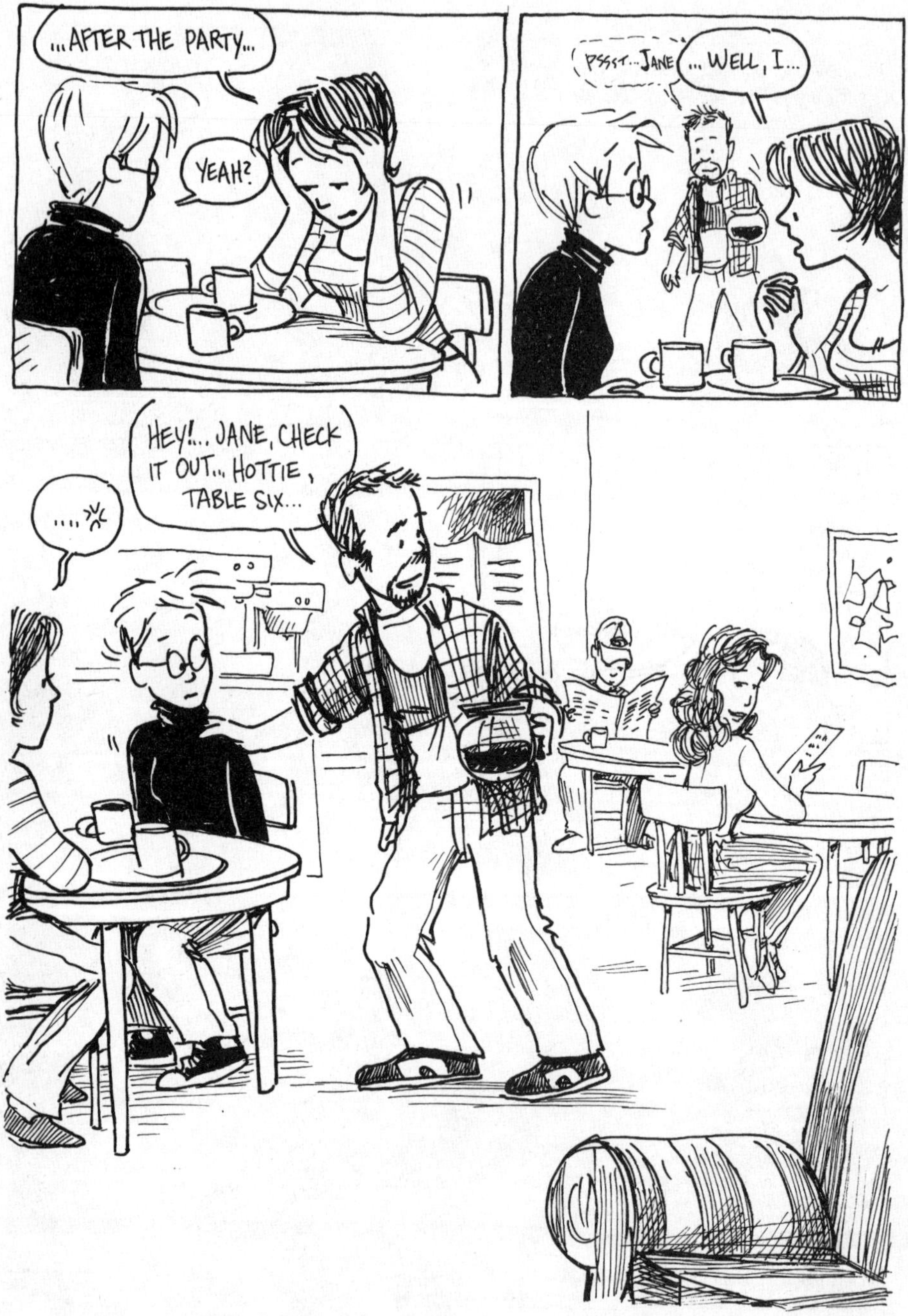
...AFTER THE PARTY...
YEAH?
PSSST... JANE
... WELL, I...
....
HEY!... JANE, CHECK IT OUT... HOTTIE, TABLE SIX...

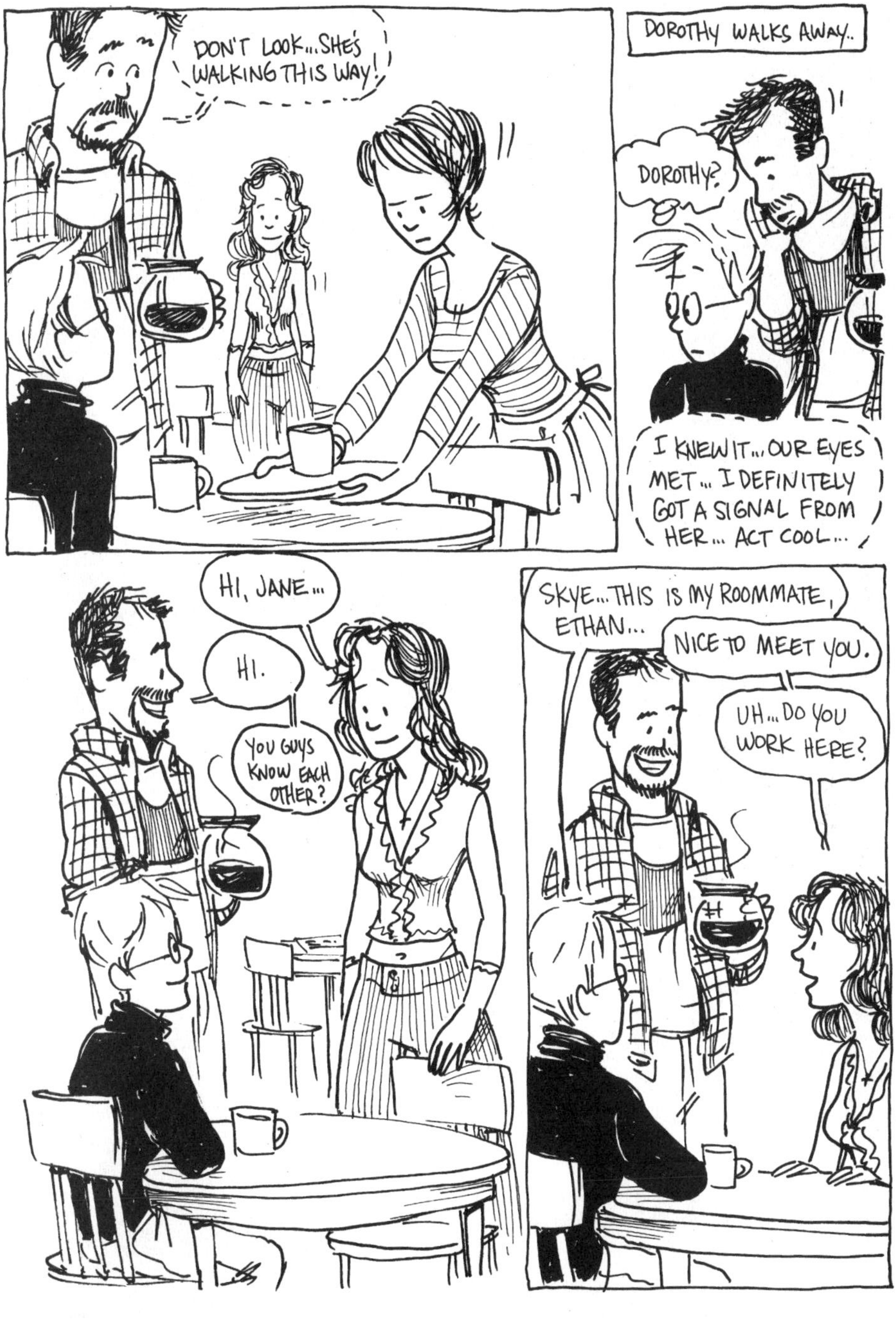
DON'T LOOK...SHE'S WALKING THIS WAY!
DOROTHY WALKS AWAY..
DOROTHY?
I KNEW IT... OUR EYES MET... I DEFINITELY GOT A SIGNAL FROM HER... ACT COOL...
HI, JANE...
HI.
YOU GUYS KNOW EACH OTHER?
SKYE...THIS IS MY ROOMMATE, ETHAN...
NICE TO MEET YOU.
UH... DO YOU WORK HERE?

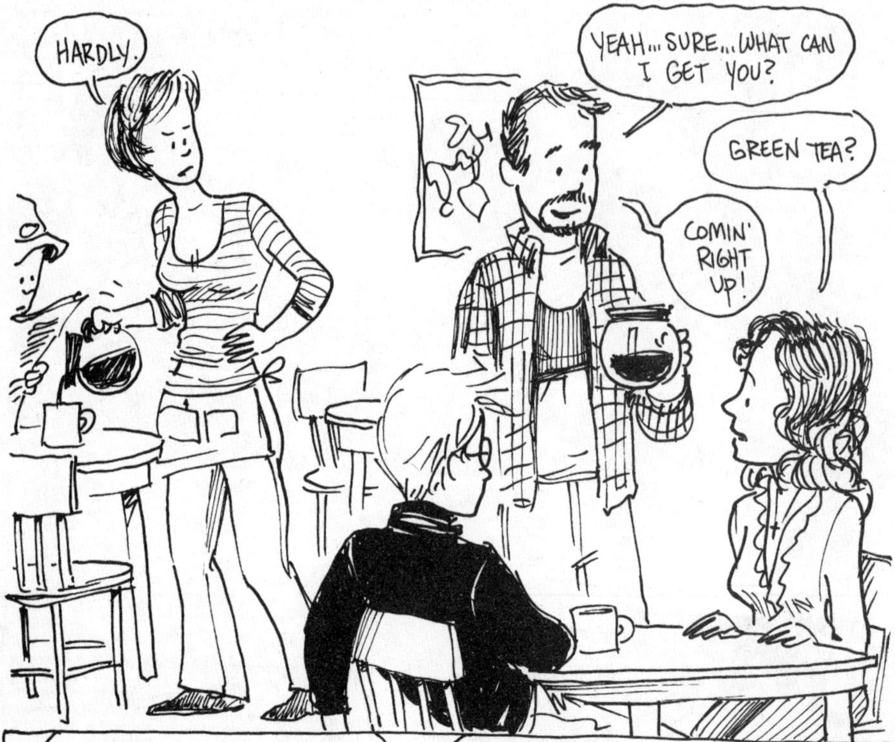
HARDLY.
YEAH... SURE... WHAT CAN I GET YOU?
GREEN TEA?
COMIN' RIGHT UP!

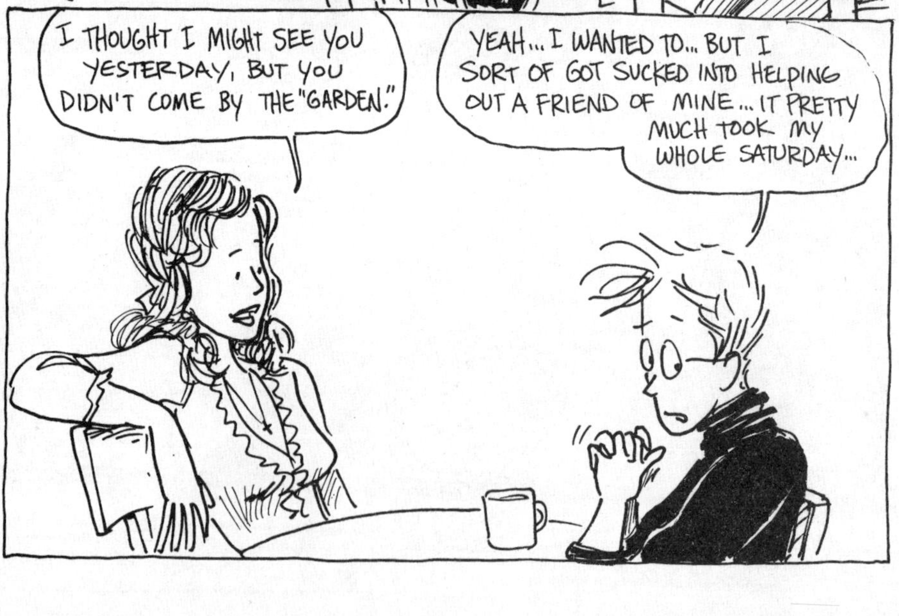
I THOUGHT I MIGHT SEE YOU YESTERDAY, BUT YOU DIDN'T COME BY THE "GARDEN."
YEAH... I WANTED TO... BUT I SORT OF GOT SUCKED INTO HELPING OUT A FRIEND OF MINE... IT PRETTY MUCH TOOK MY WHOLE SATURDAY...

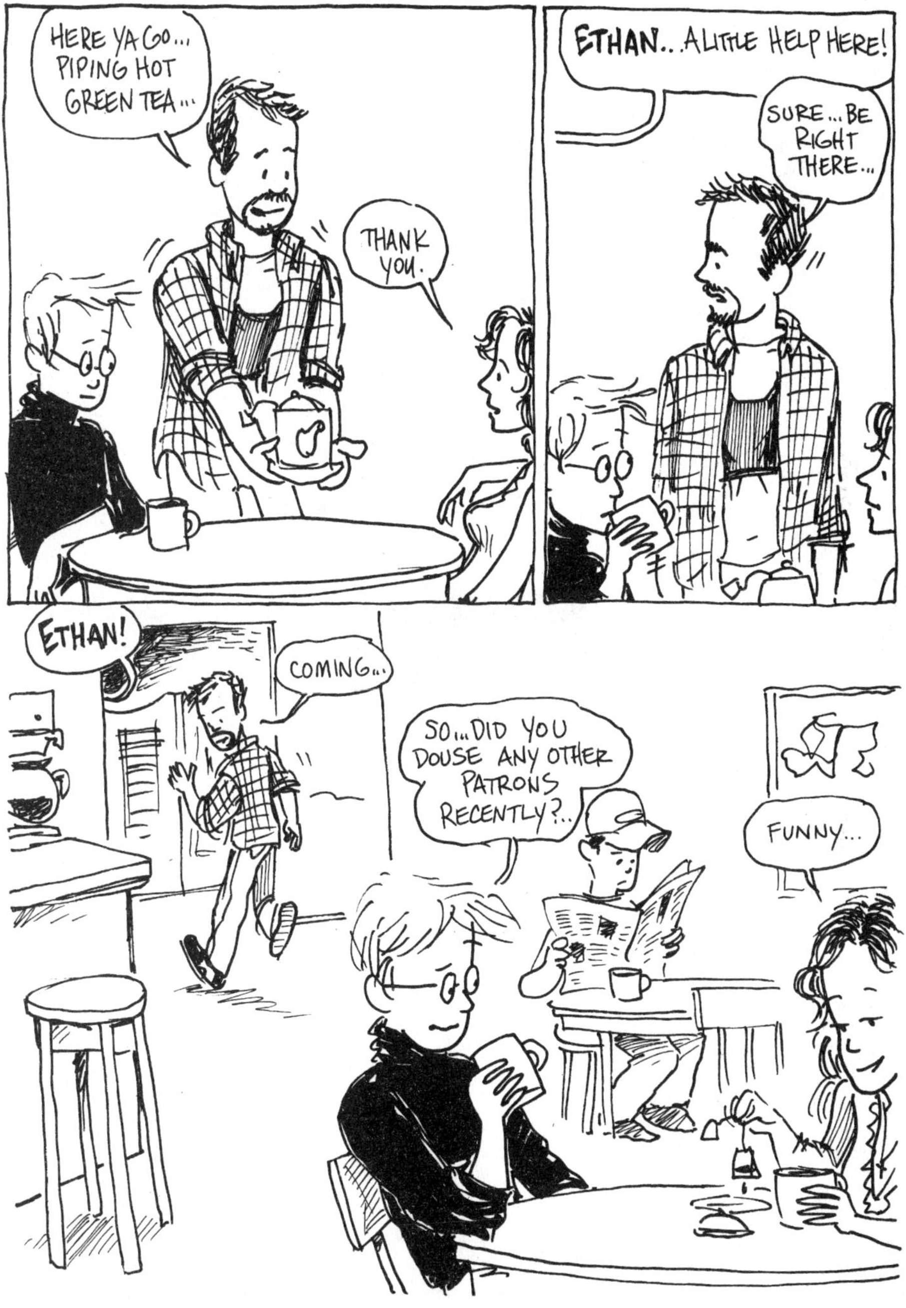
HERE YA GO... PIPING HOT GREEN TEA...
THANK YOU.
ETHAN... A LITTLE HELP HERE!
SURE... BE RIGHT THERE...
ETHAN!
COMING...
SO... DID YOU DOUSE ANY OTHER PATRONS RECENTLY?..
FUNNY...

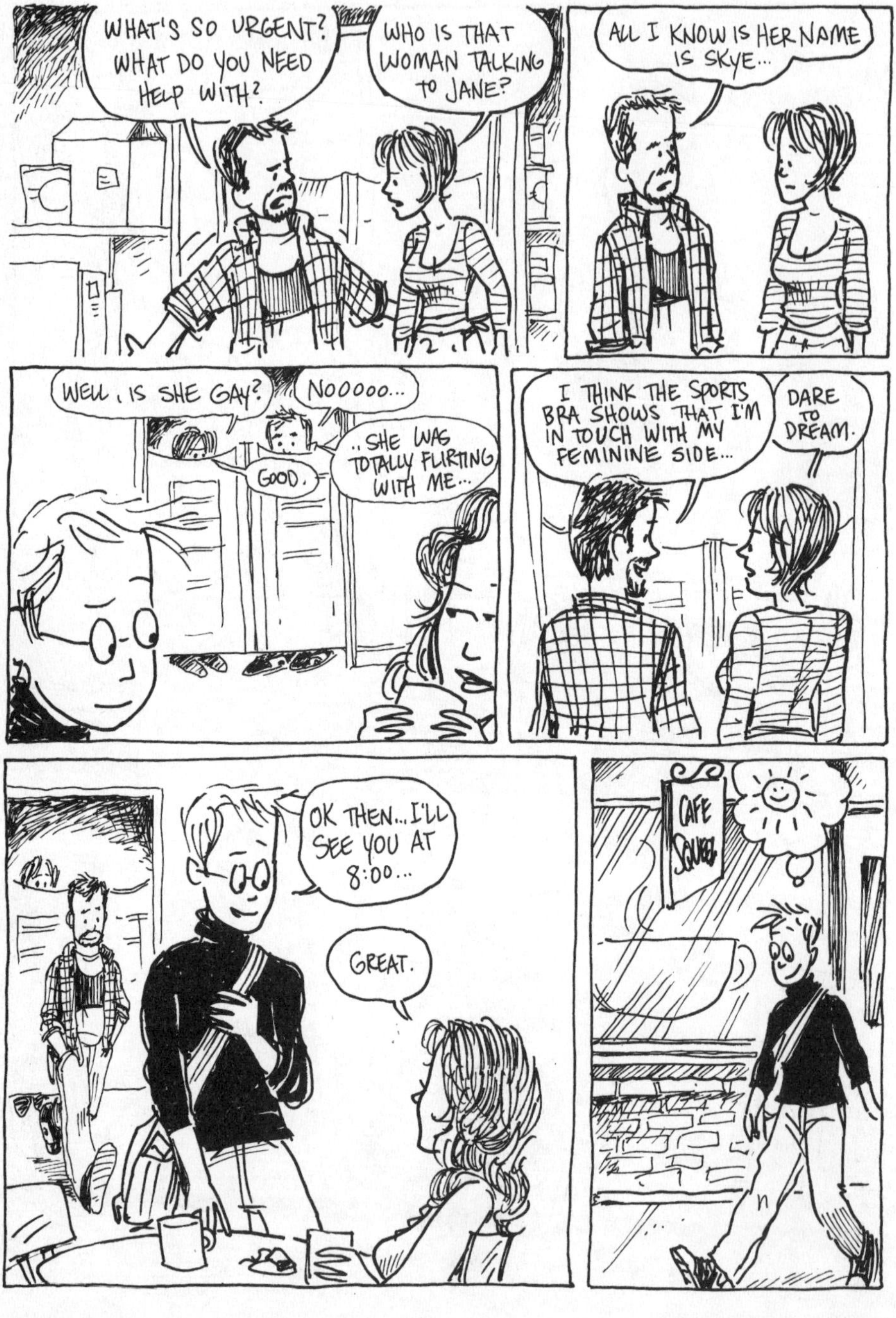
WHAT'S SO URGENT? WHAT DO YOU NEED HELP WITH?
WHO IS THAT WOMAN TALKING TO JANE?
ALL I KNOW IS HER NAME IS SKYE...
WELL, IS SHE GAY?
NOOOOO...
GOOD.
..SHE WAS TOTALLY FLIRTING WITH ME...
I THINK THE SPORTS BRA SHOWS THAT I'M IN TOUCH WITH MY FEMININE SIDE...
DARE TO DREAM.
OK THEN... I'LL SEE YOU AT 8:00...
GREAT.
CAFE SQUEEZ

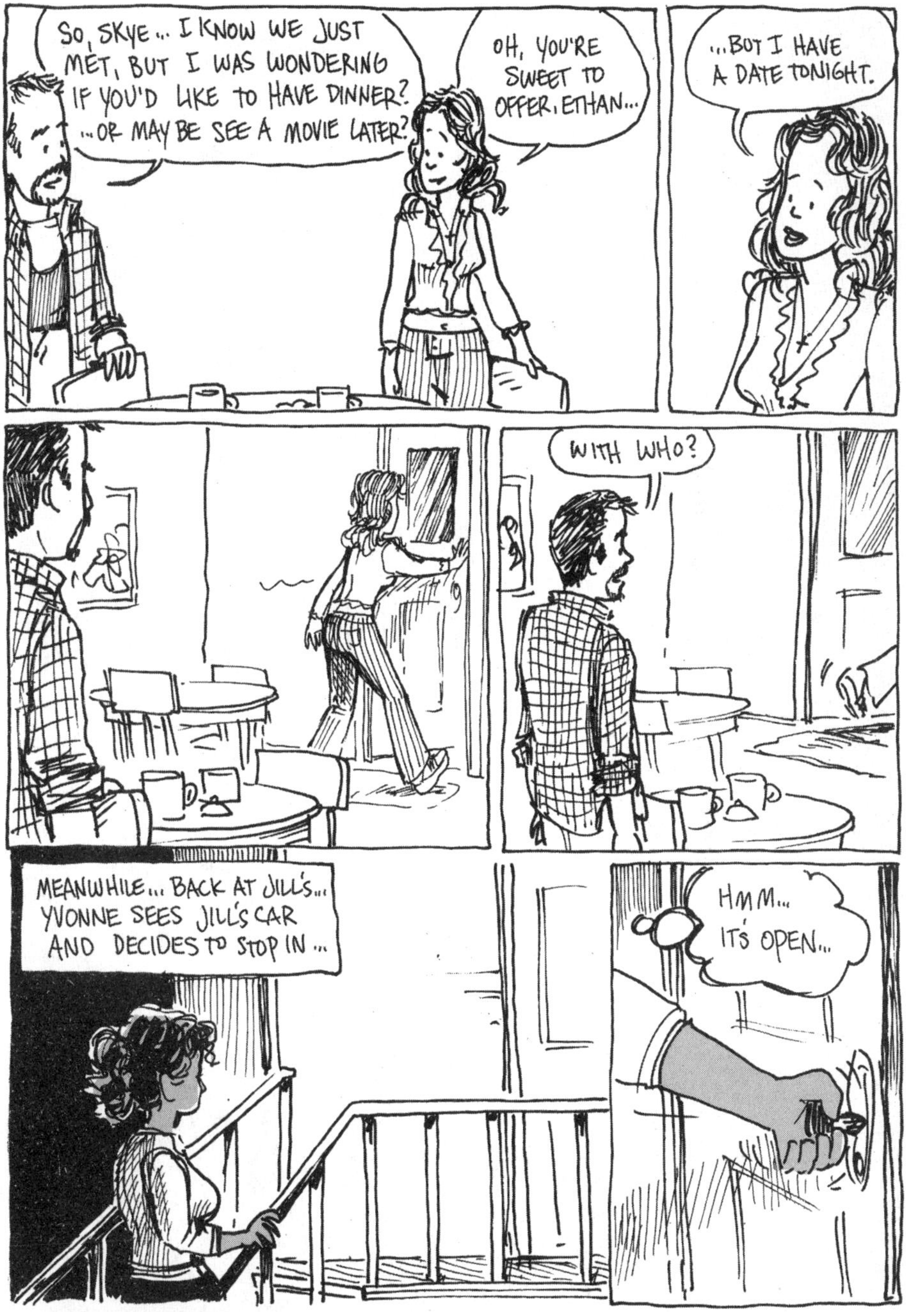

SO, SKYE... I KNOW WE JUST MET, BUT I WAS WONDERING IF YOU'D LIKE TO HAVE DINNER? ...OR MAYBE SEE A MOVIE LATER?
OH, YOU'RE SWEET TO OFFER, ETHAN...
...BUT I HAVE A DATE TONIGHT.
WITH WHO?
MEANWHILE... BACK AT JILL'S... YVONNE SEES JILL'S CAR AND DECIDES TO STOP IN...
HMM... IT'S OPEN...

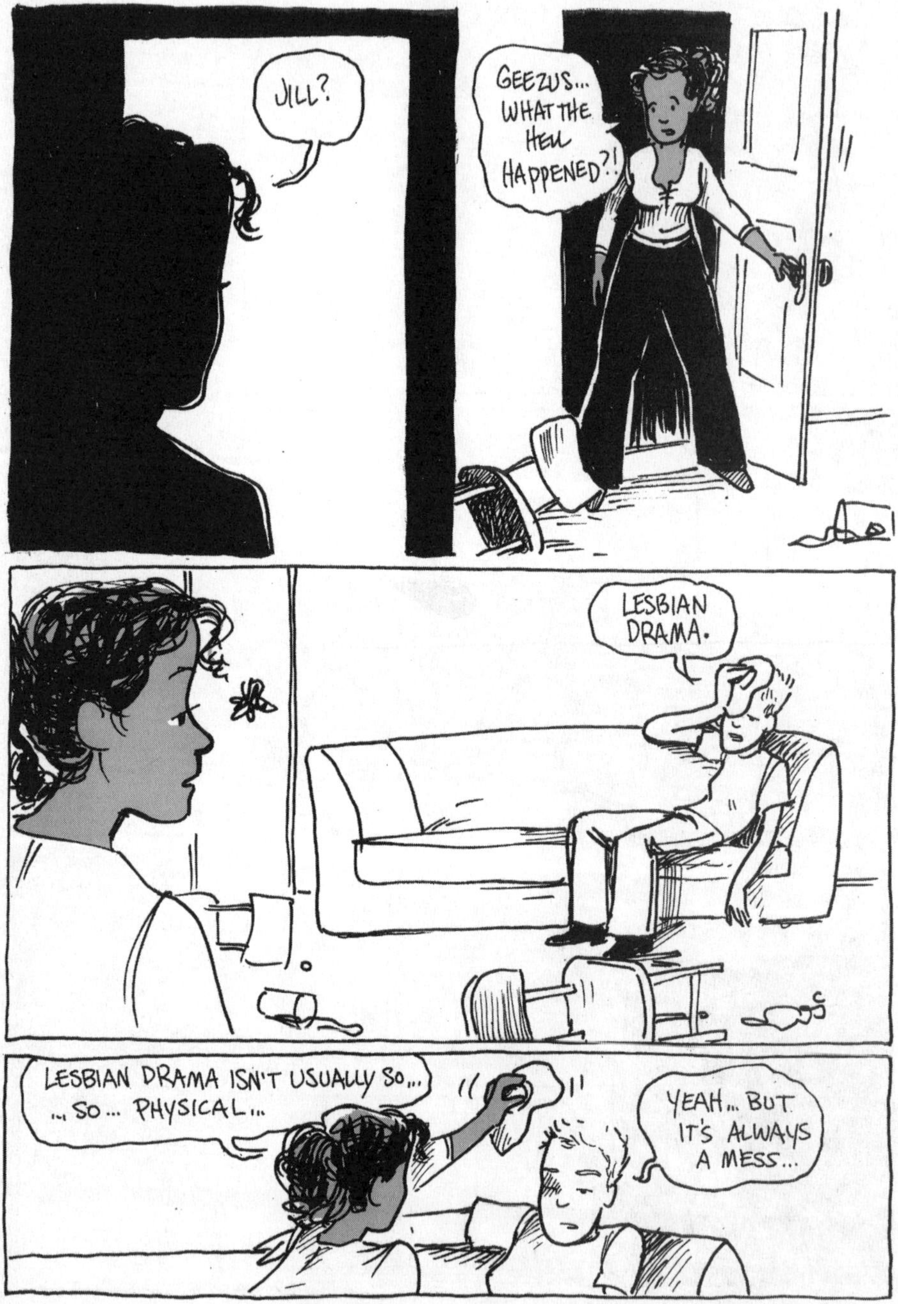
JILL?
GEEZUS... WHAT THE HELL HAPPENED?!
LESBIAN DRAMA.
LESBIAN DRAMA ISN'T USUALLY SO... ...SO... PHYSICAL...
YEAH... BUT IT'S ALWAYS A MESS...

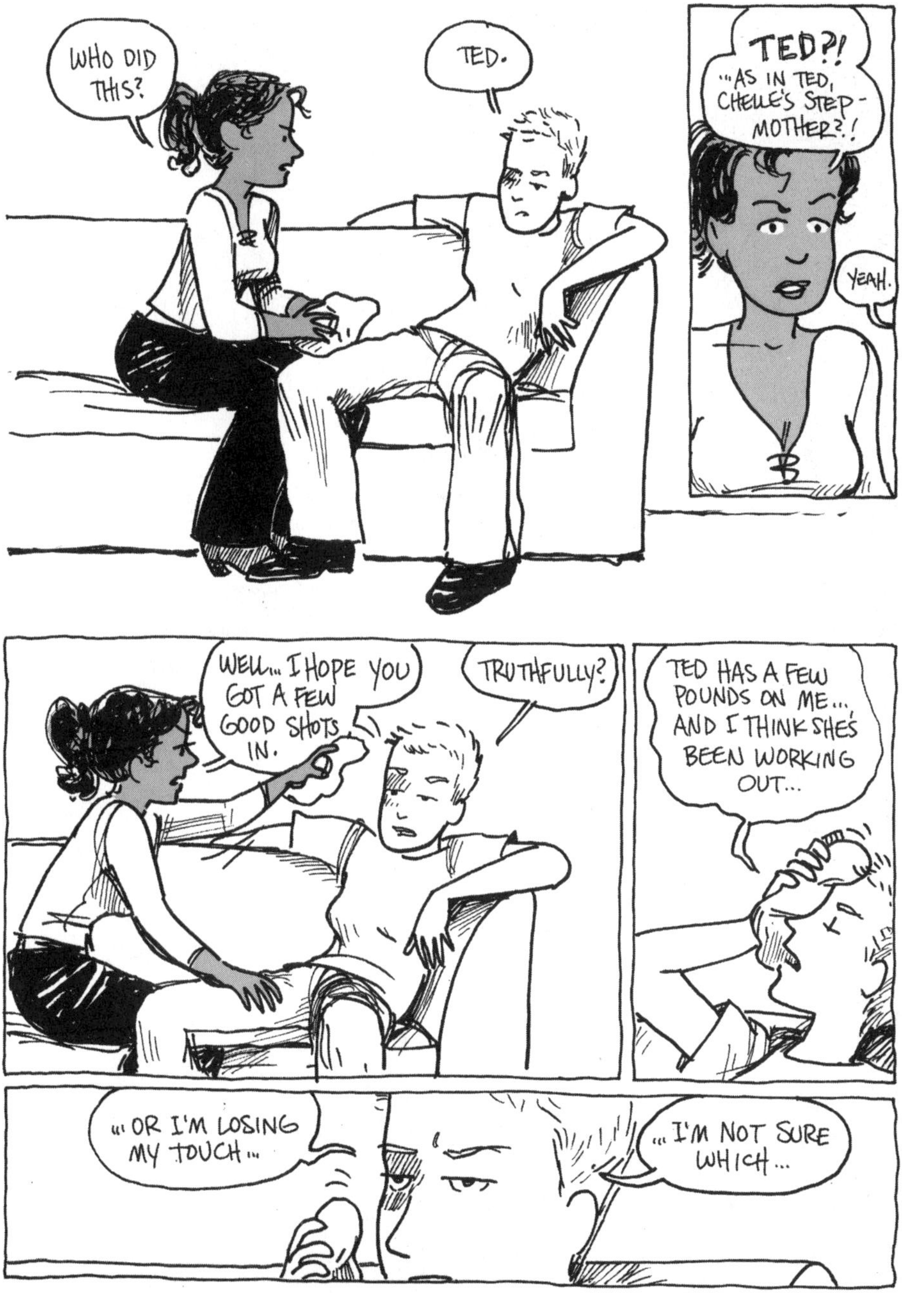
WHO DID THIS?
TED.
TED?! ...AS IN TED, CHELLE'S STEP-MOTHER?!
YEAH.
WELL... I HOPE YOU GOT A FEW GOOD SHOTS IN.
TRUTHFULLY?
TED HAS A FEW POUNDS ON ME... AND I THINK SHE'S BEEN WORKING OUT...
...OR I'M LOSING MY TOUCH...
...I'M NOT SURE WHICH...

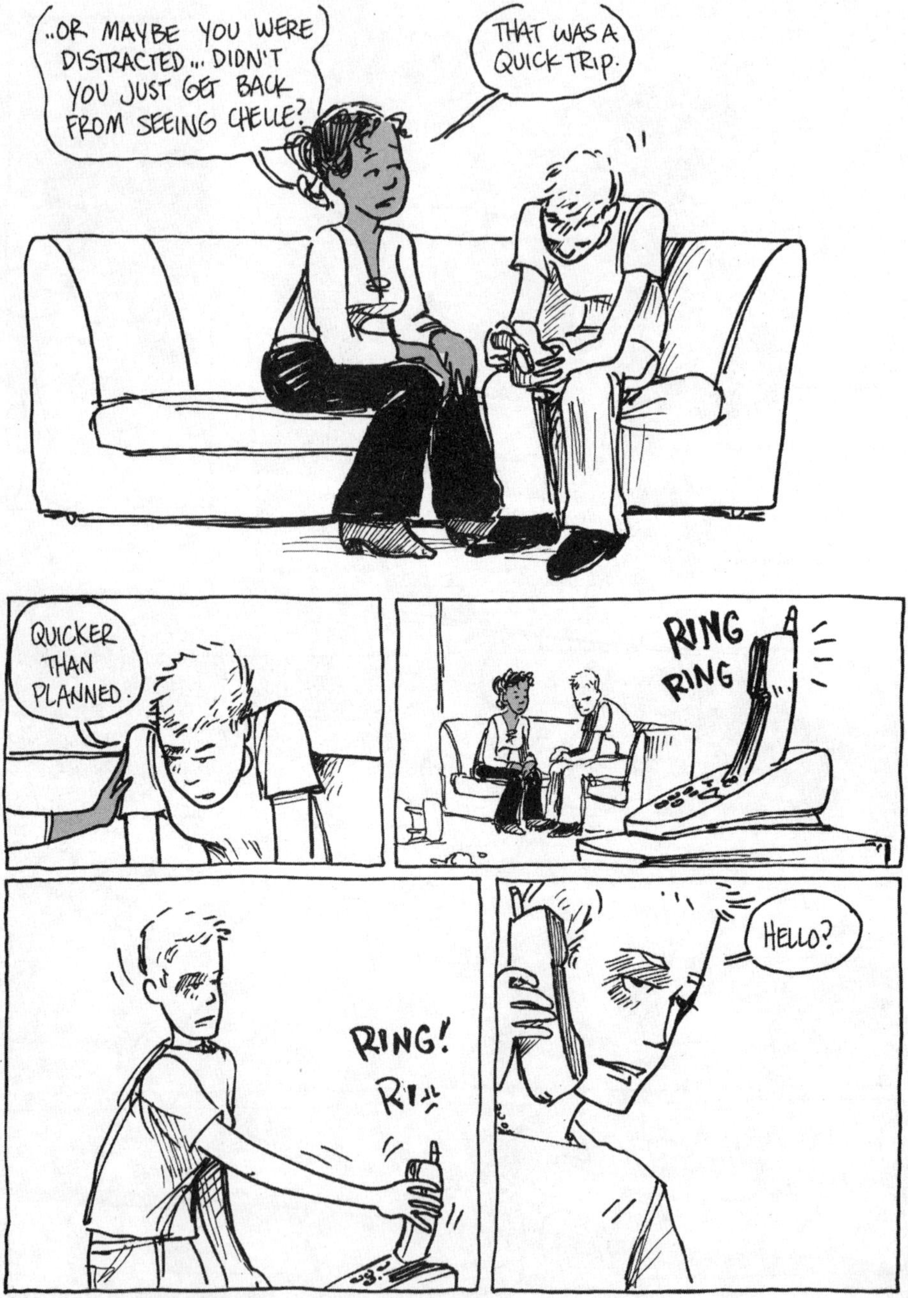
..OR MAYBE YOU WERE DISTRACTED... DIDN'T YOU JUST GET BACK FROM SEEING CHELLE?
THAT WAS A QUICK TRIP.
QUICKER THAN PLANNED.
RING RING
RING!
HELLO?

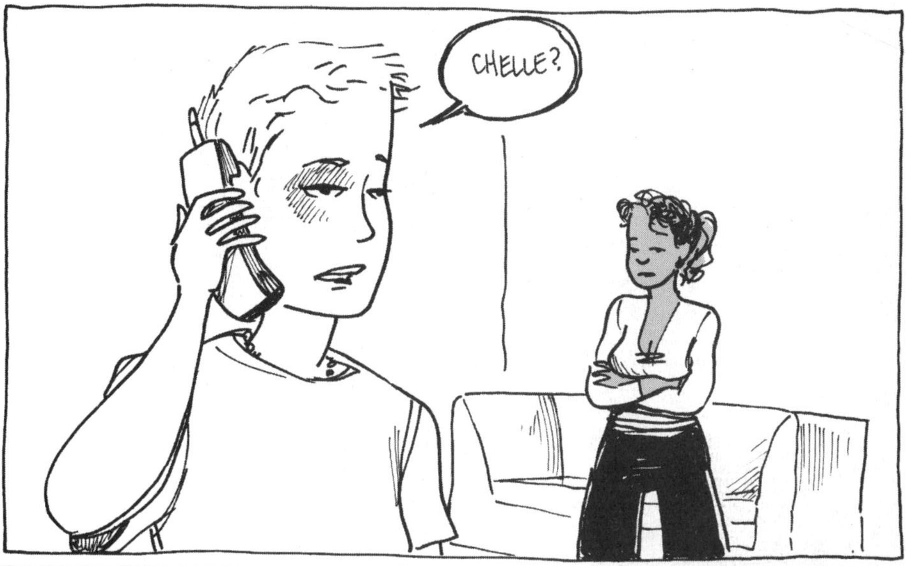
CHELLE?

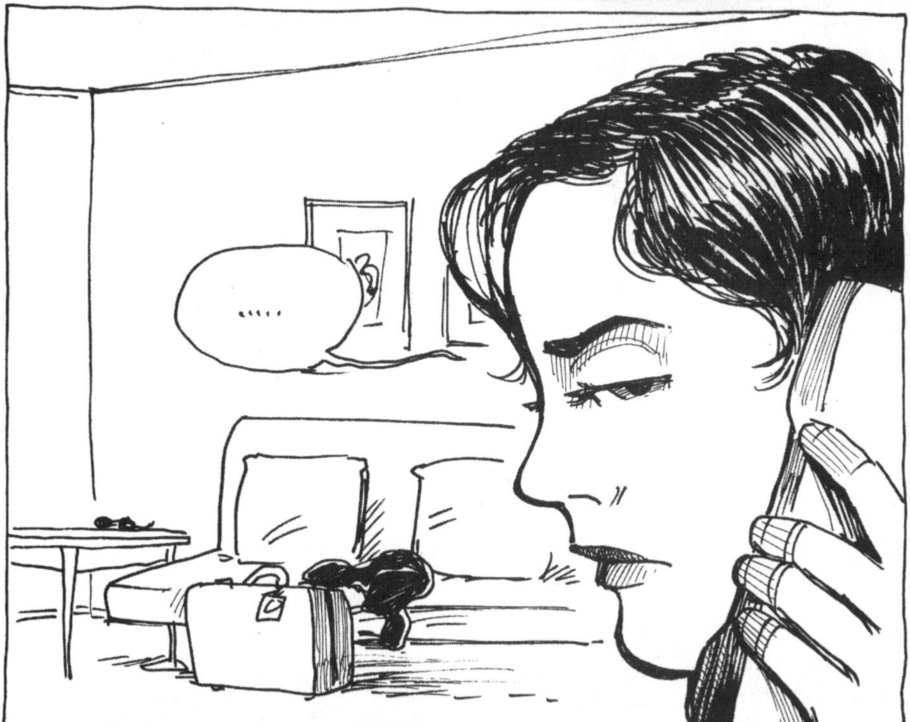
.....

Chapter Two

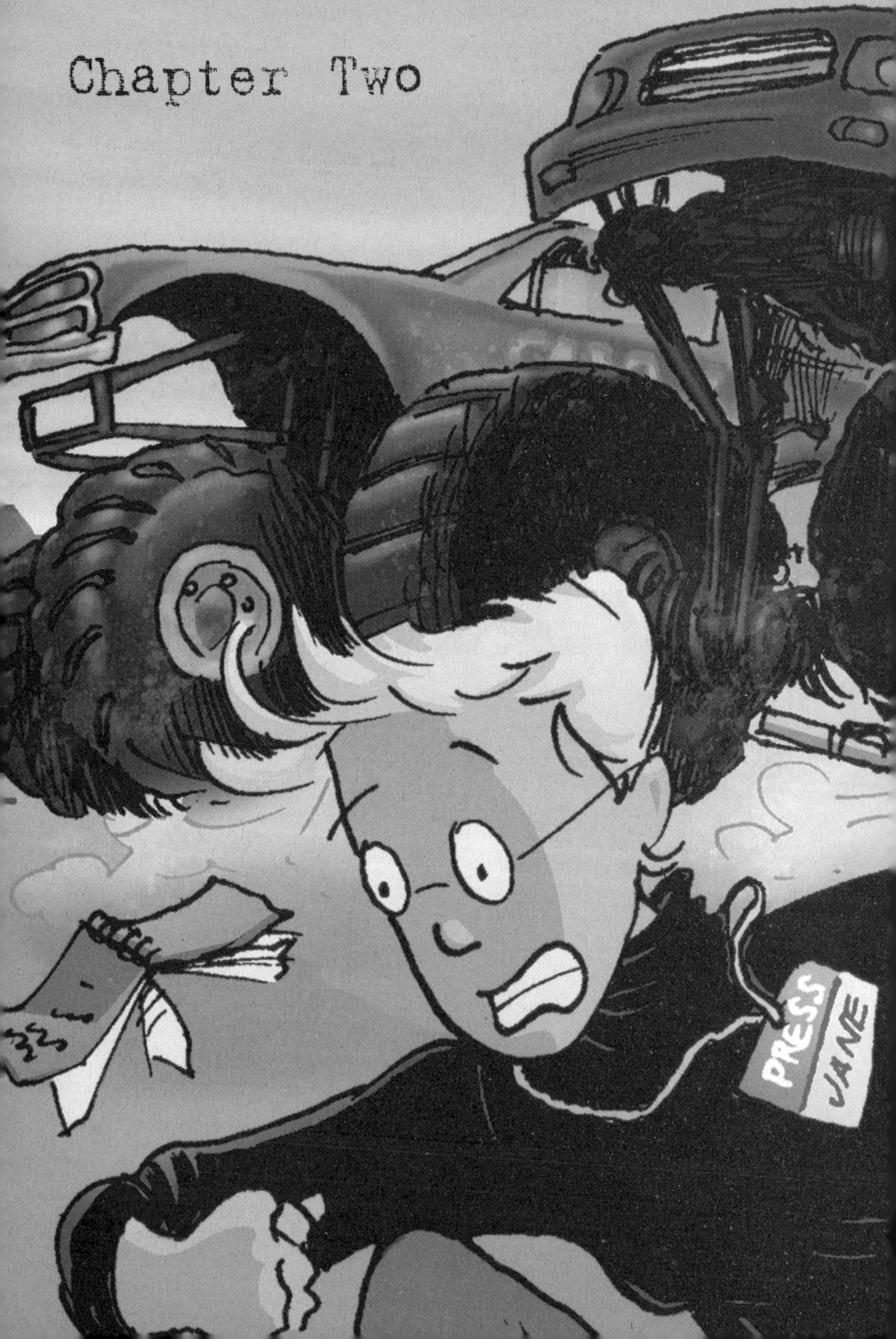
PRESS
JANE

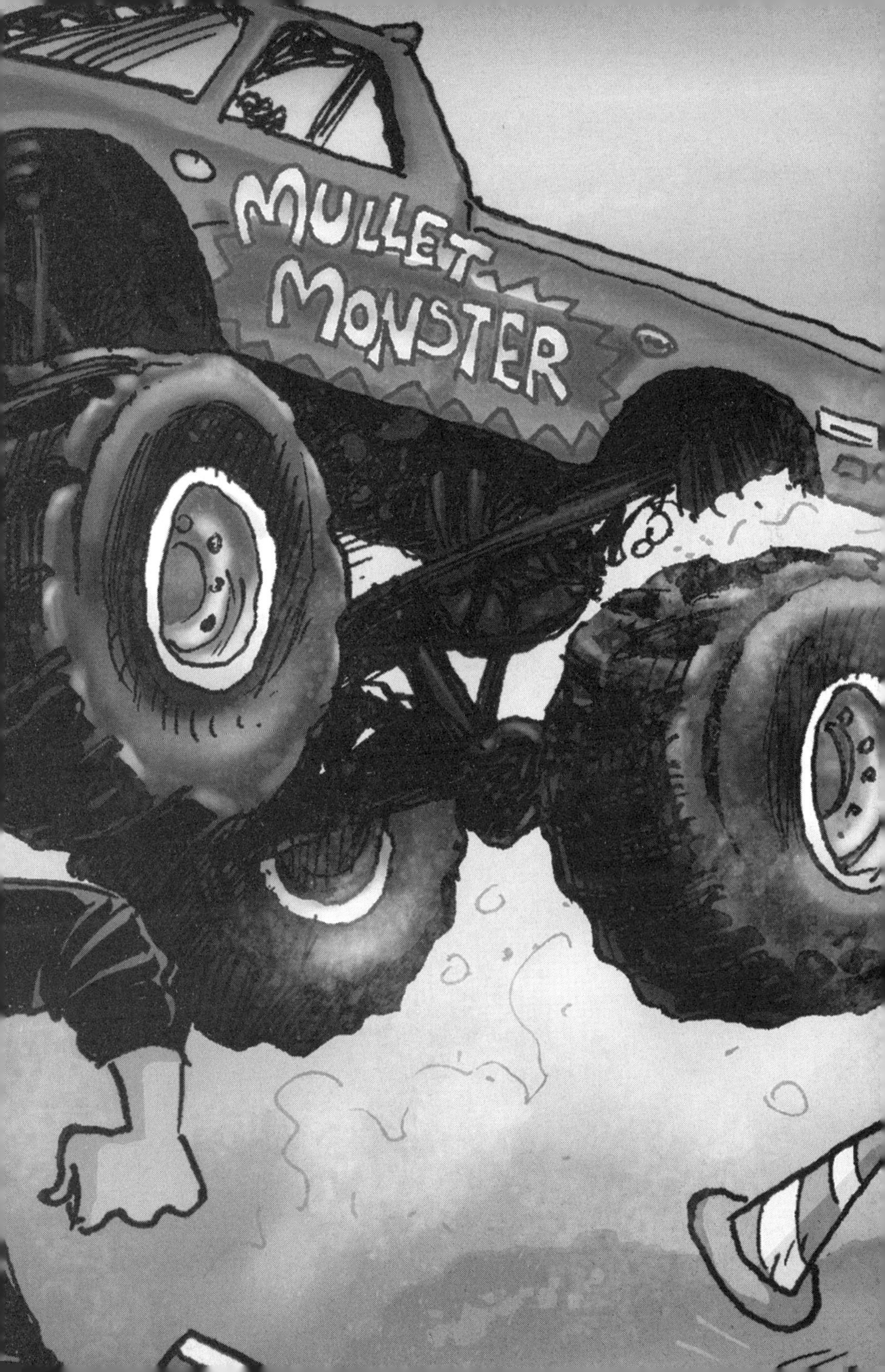
MULLET MONSTER

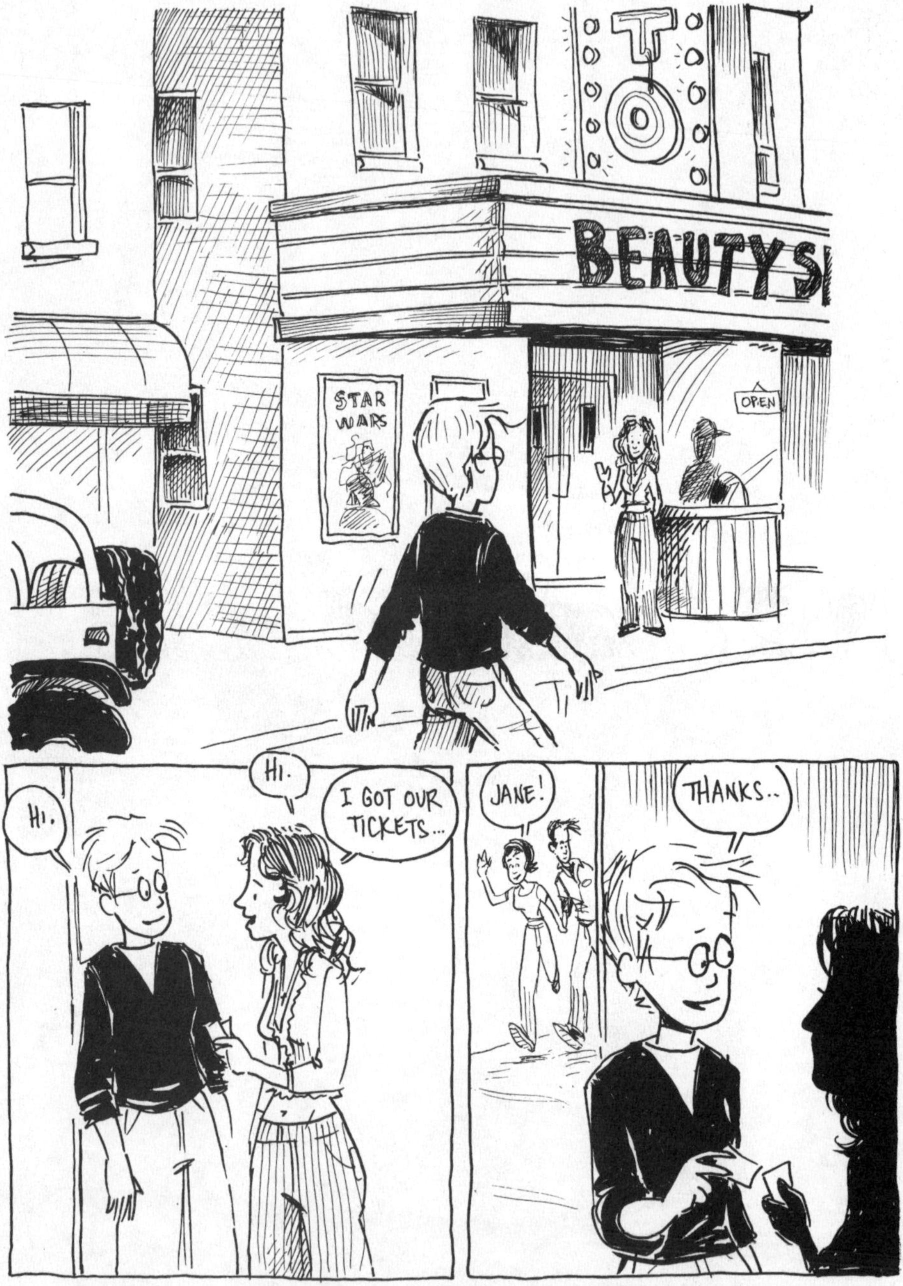

STAR WARS
BEAUTY S
OPEN
HI.
HI.
I GOT OUR TICKETS...
JANE!
THANKS..

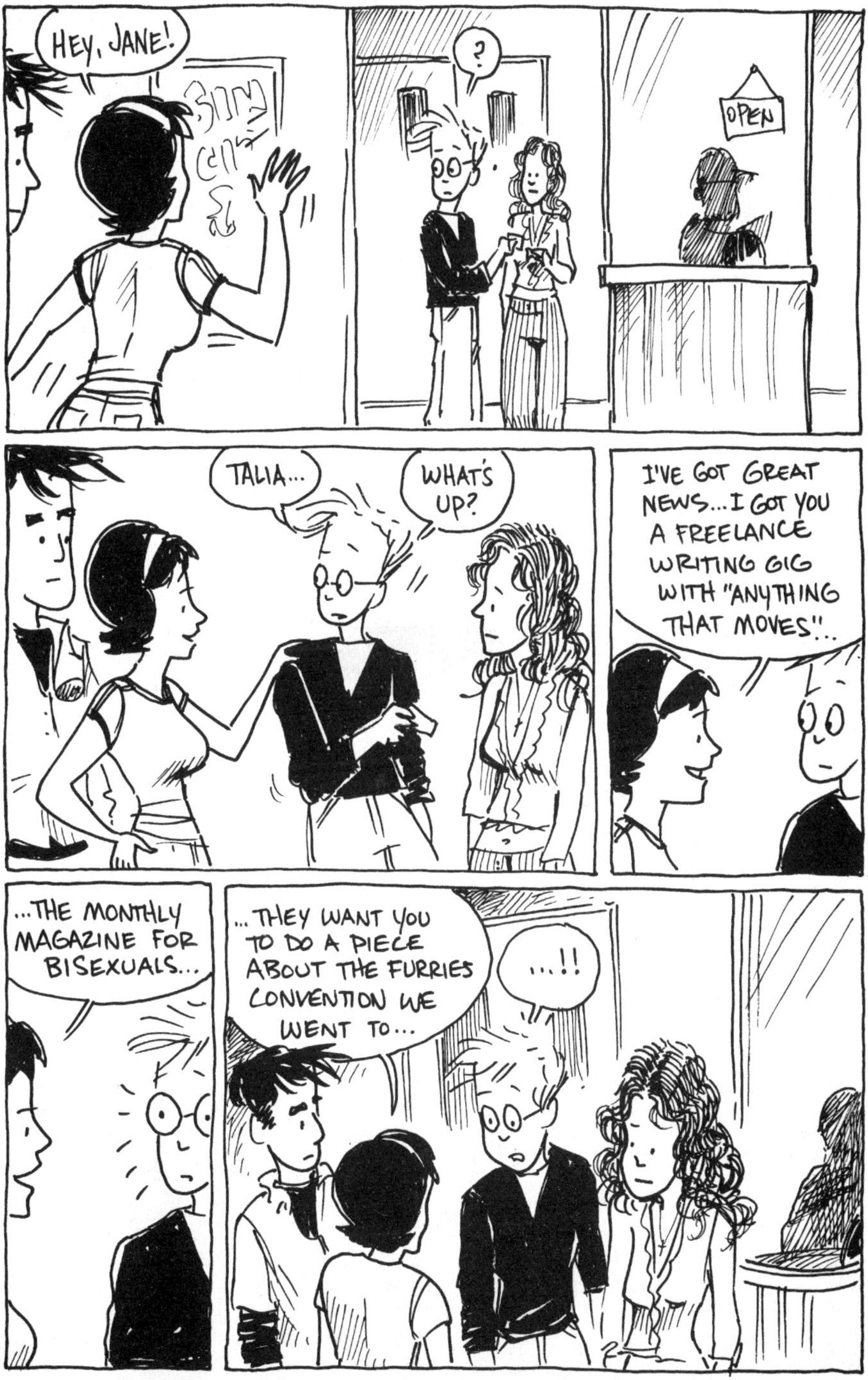
HEY, JANE!
?
OPEN
TALIA...
WHAT'S UP?
I'VE GOT GREAT NEWS... I GOT YOU A FREELANCE WRITING GIG WITH "ANYTHING THAT MOVES"...
...THE MONTHLY MAGAZINE FOR BISEXUALS...
...THEY WANT YOU TO DO A PIECE ABOUT THE FURRIES CONVENTION WE WENT TO...
...!!

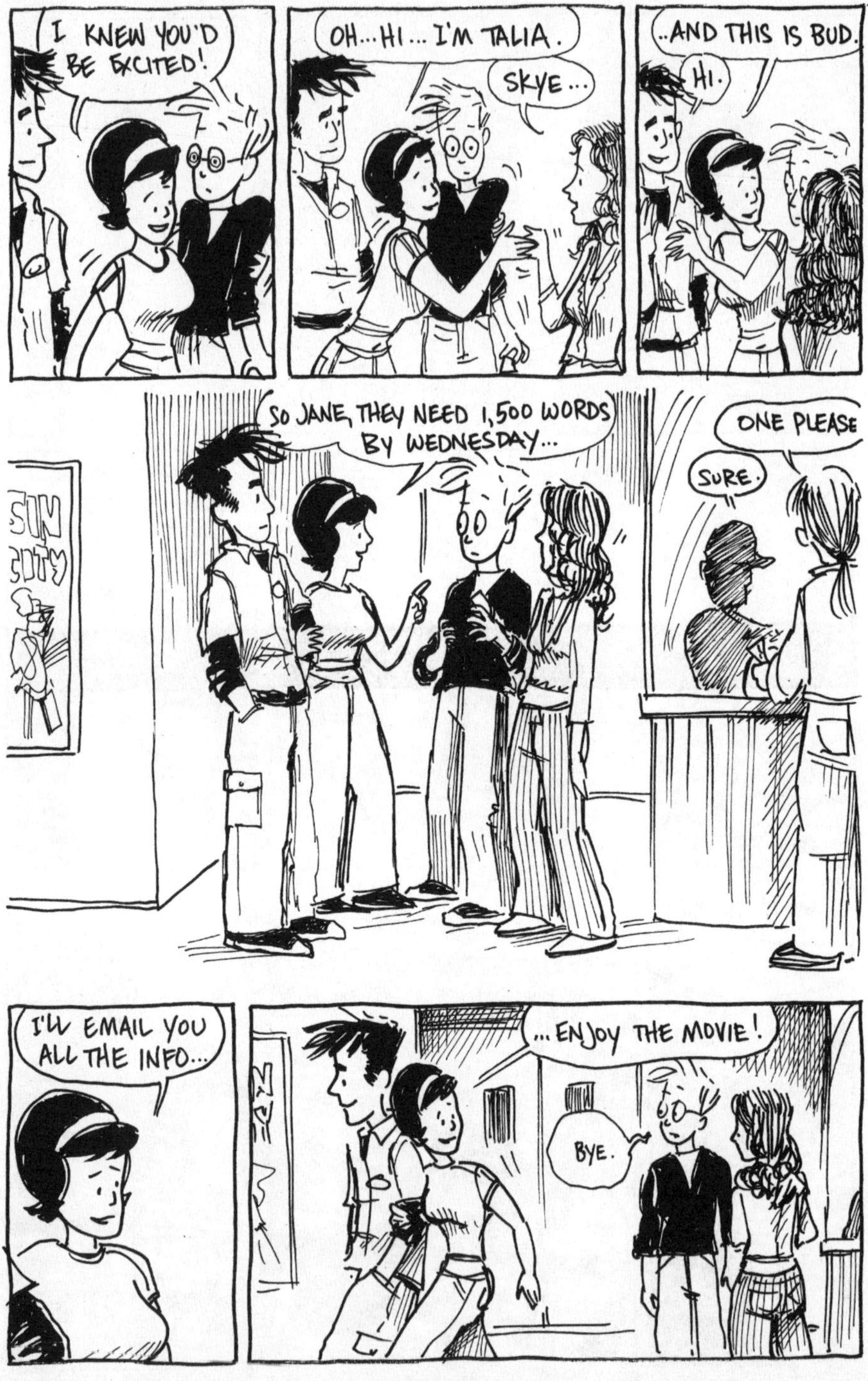
I KNEW YOU'D BE EXCITED!
OH... HI... I'M TALIA.
SKYE...
..AND THIS IS BUD.
HI.
SO JANE, THEY NEED 1,500 WORDS BY WEDNESDAY...
ONE PLEASE
SURE.
I'LL EMAIL YOU ALL THE INFO...
... ENJOY THE MOVIE!
BYE.

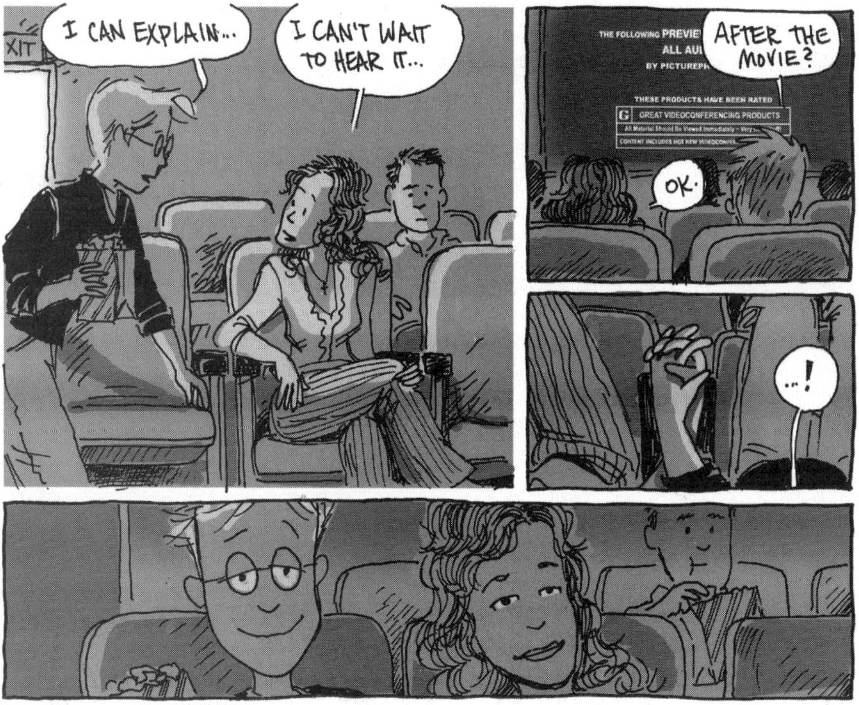
I CAN EXPLAIN...
I CAN'T WAIT TO HEAR IT...
THESE PRODUCTS HAVE BEEN RATED
GREAT VIDEOCONFERENCING PRODUCTS
AFTER THE MOVIE?
OK.
...!

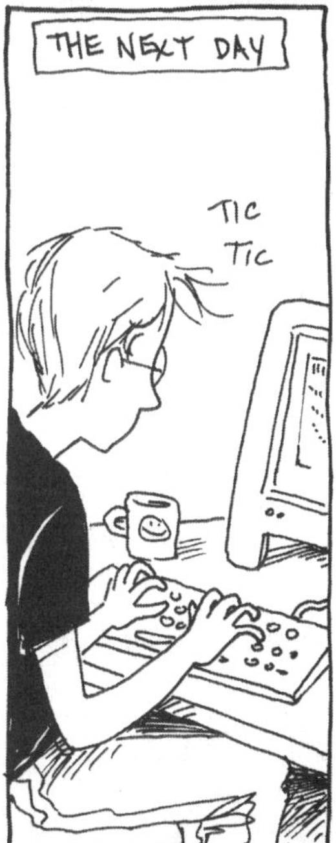
THE NEXT DAY
TIC
TIC

Jane: So now you're my agent?! You know, I'd rather write for publications that I can actually list on my resume... or better yet, things that I can show my mother... I can't show a clip from "Anything That Moves" to anything that moves!

Talia: Well, you're always complaining that you're broke. This is a good, paying gig I got for you. You're sooooo uptight.

Jane: I'm not that broke (or uptight!)... I'm lowering my overhead so that someday I can live off the proceeds from my novel.

Talia: Novel?

Jane: Yes... the one that isn't written yet.

Talia: Oh, that novel.

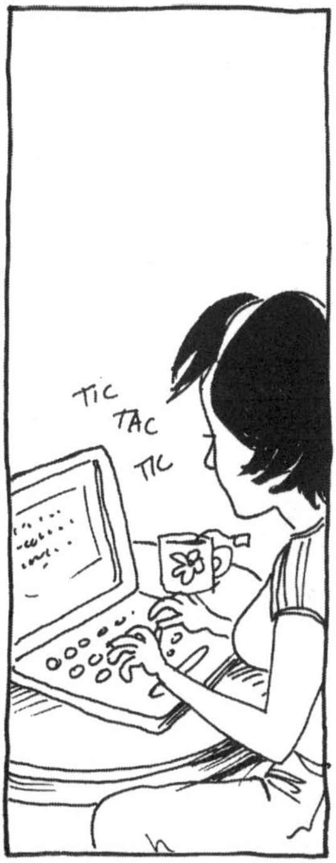
TIC
TAC
TIC

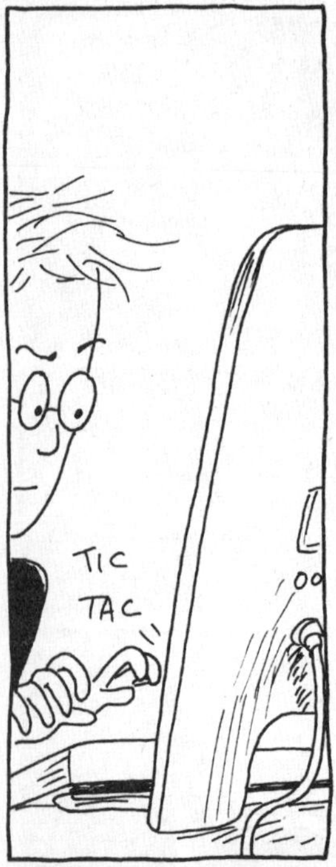
TIC
TAC

Jane: and besides!!!... You made it sound like I'M BISEXUAL... You almost scared Skye off! I'd like to have at least a couple of dates before I screw things up on my own... thank you VERY MUCH.

Talia: She probably just thinks you're more interesting now... that cross she wears isn't fooling me... that girl has a wild side... she's probably too much for you.

Jane: Thanks for that vote of confidence!... what were you doing with Bud anyway? It creeps me out to see my ex girlfriend looking like she's out on a date with my cousin.

Talia: Well, if you can't date the one you love, love their cousin.

Jane: What?... What does that mean??

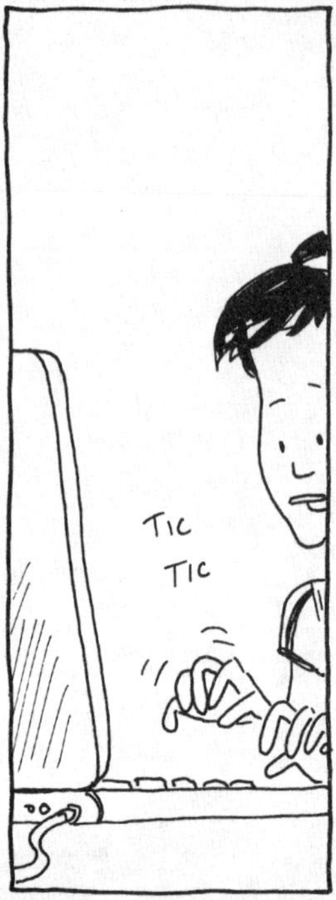
TIC
TIC

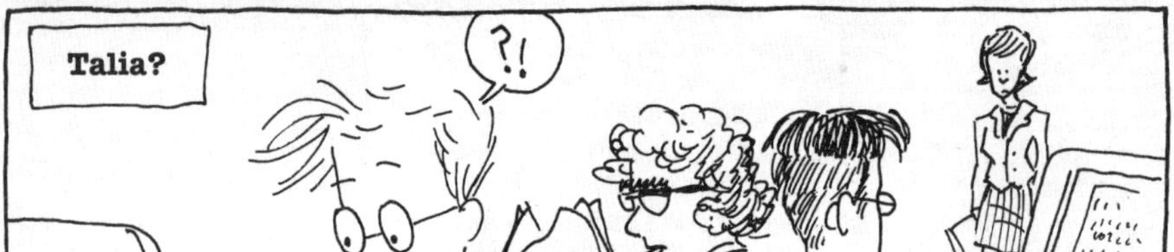
Talia?
?!

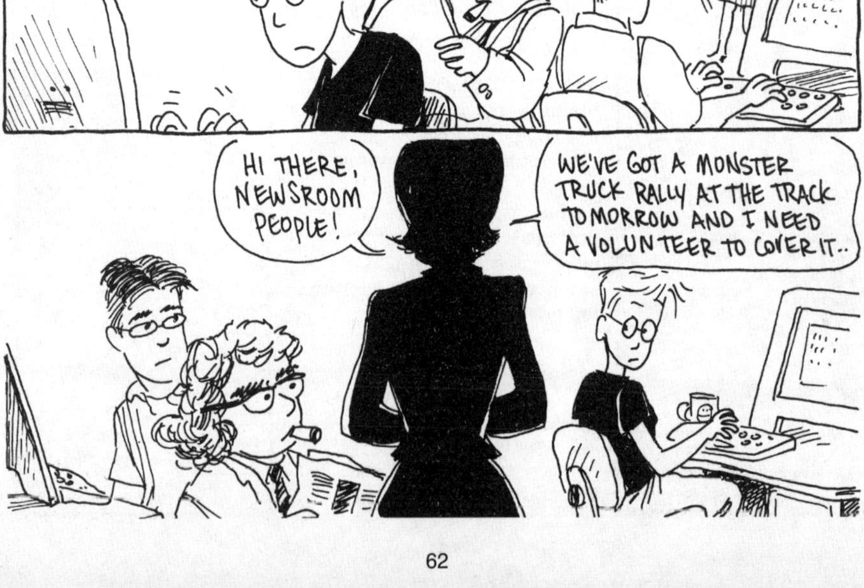
HI THERE, NEWSROOM PEOPLE!
WE'VE GOT A MONSTER TRUCK RALLY AT THE TRACK TOMORROW AND I NEED A VOLUNTEER TO COVER IT..

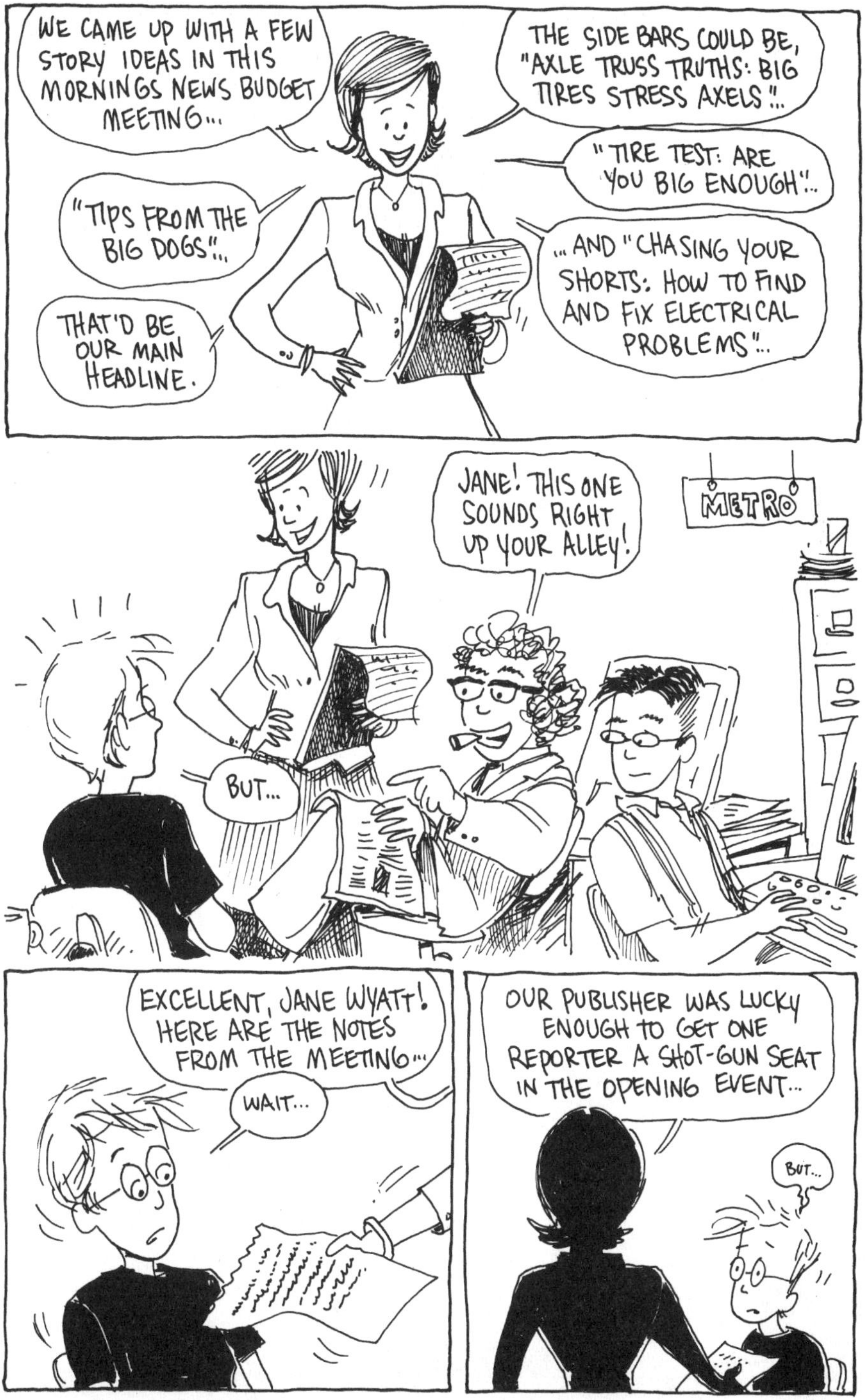
WE CAME UP WITH A FEW STORY IDEAS IN THIS MORNINGS NEWS BUDGET MEETING...
THE SIDE BARS COULD BE, "AXLE TRUSS TRUTHS: BIG TIRES STRESS AXELS"...
"TIRE TEST: ARE YOU BIG ENOUGH"...
"TIPS FROM THE BIG DOGS"...
...AND "CHASING YOUR SHORTS: HOW TO FIND AND FIX ELECTRICAL PROBLEMS"...
THAT'D BE OUR MAIN HEADLINE.
JANE! THIS ONE SOUNDS RIGHT UP YOUR ALLEY!
METRO
BUT...
EXCELLENT, JANE WYATT! HERE ARE THE NOTES FROM THE MEETING...
WAIT...
OUR PUBLISHER WAS LUCKY ENOUGH TO GET ONE REPORTER A SHOT-GUN SEAT IN THE OPENING EVENT...
BUT...

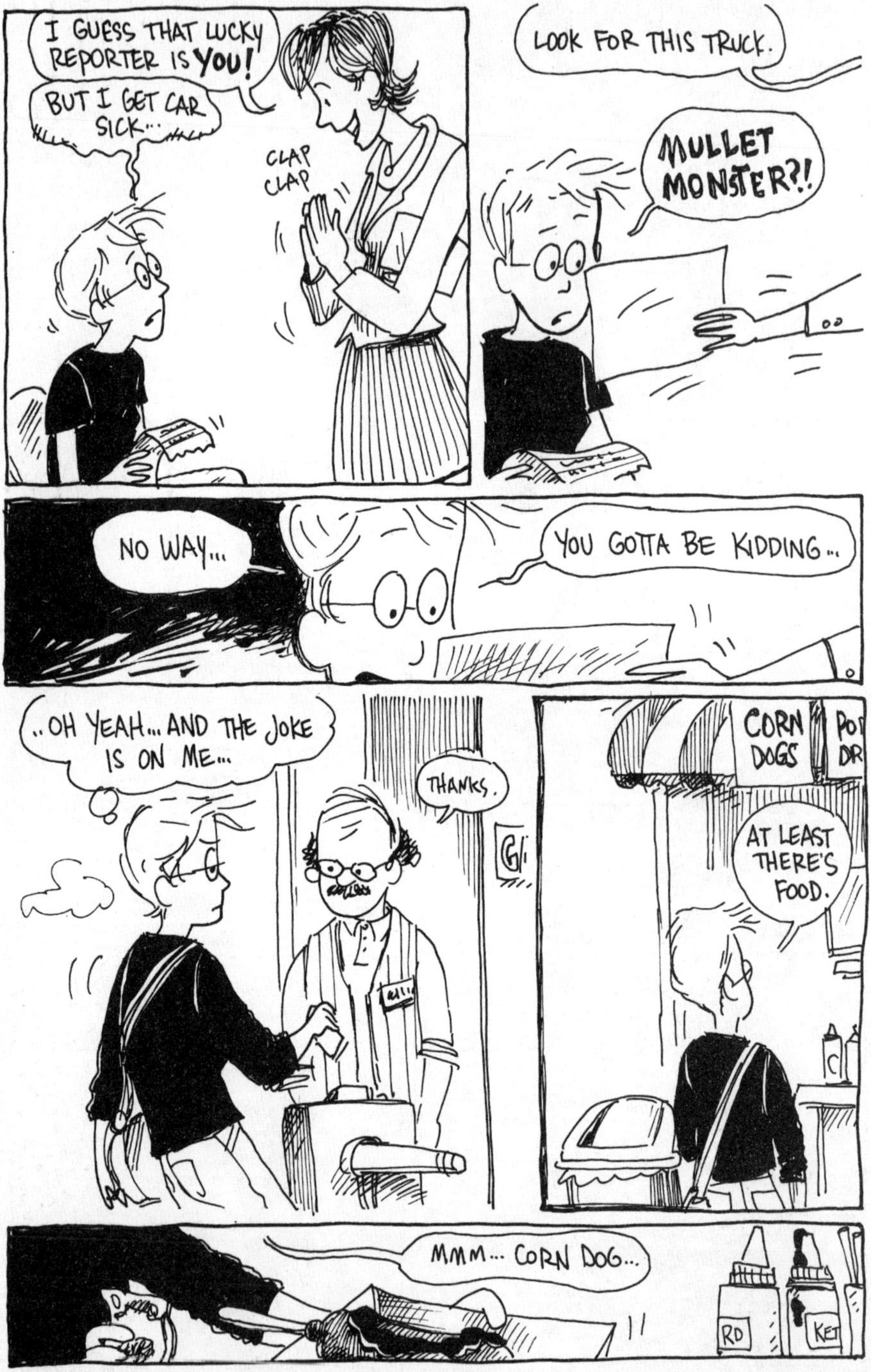
I GUESS THAT LUCKY REPORTER IS YOU!
BUT I GET CAR SICK...
CLAP CLAP
LOOK FOR THIS TRUCK.
MULLET MONSTER?!
NO WAY...
YOU GOTTA BE KIDDING...
..OH YEAH... AND THE JOKE IS ON ME...
THANKS.
CORN DOGS
AT LEAST THERE'S FOOD.
MMM... CORN DOG...

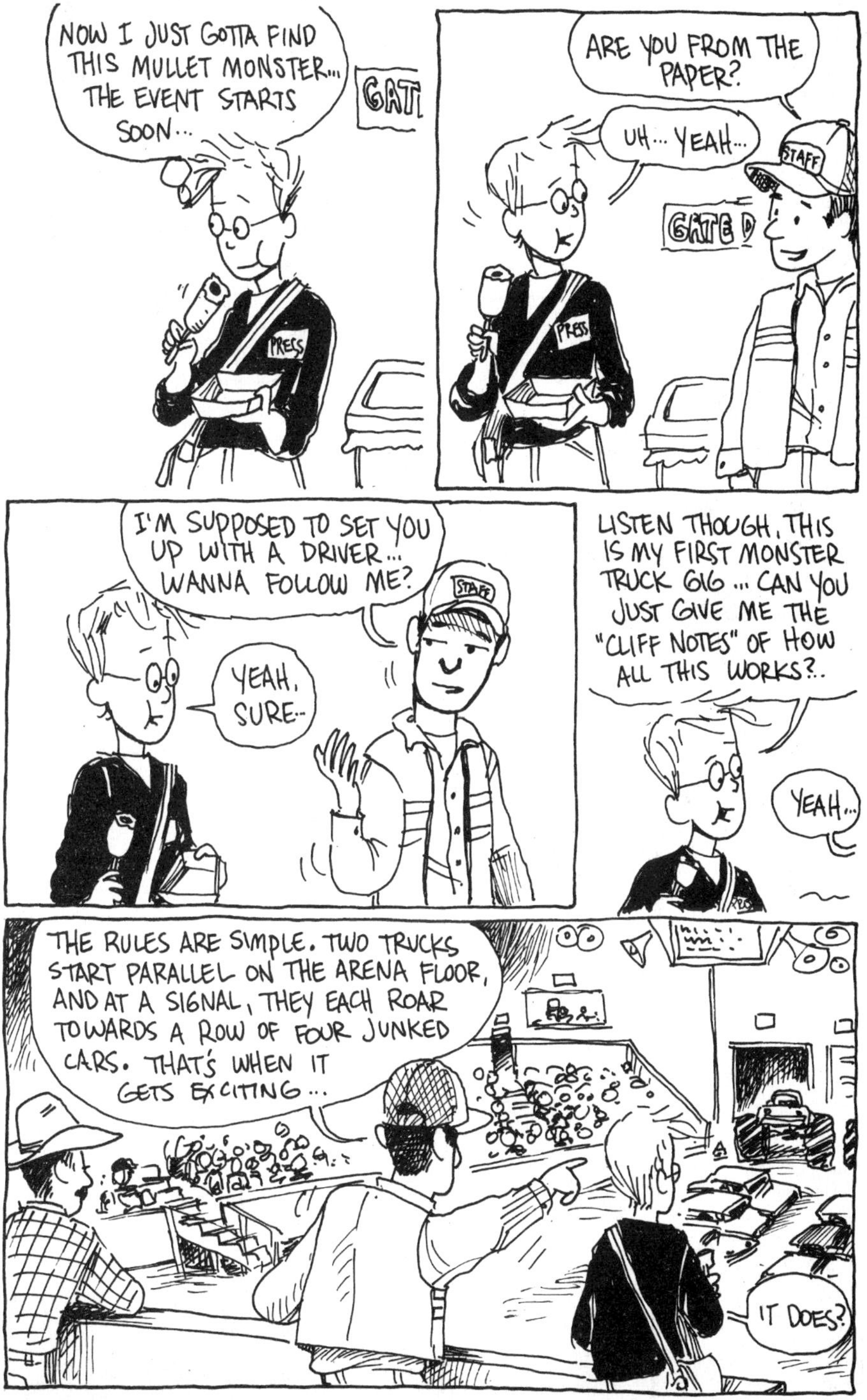
NOW I JUST GOTTA FIND THIS MULLET MONSTER... THE EVENT STARTS SOON...
GAT
PRESS
ARE YOU FROM THE PAPER?
UH... YEAH...
STAFF
GATE D
PRESS
I'M SUPPOSED TO SET YOU UP WITH A DRIVER... WANNA FOLLOW ME?
STAFF
YEAH, SURE...
LISTEN THOUGH, THIS IS MY FIRST MONSTER TRUCK GIG... CAN YOU JUST GIVE ME THE "CLIFF NOTES" OF HOW ALL THIS WORKS?..
YEAH...
THE RULES ARE SIMPLE. TWO TRUCKS START PARALLEL ON THE ARENA FLOOR, AND AT A SIGNAL, THEY EACH ROAR TOWARDS A ROW OF FOUR JUNKED CARS. THAT'S WHEN IT GETS EXCITING...
IT DOES?

YEAH... THE TRUCKS DRIVE OVER THE CARS... CRUSHING THEM... ON THEIR WAY TO THE FINISH LINE. WHICHEVER TRUCK REACHES THE END OF THE ROW OF CARS FIRST WINS.

RIVETING.

AND THEY'RE REALLY LOUD.

SO THAT'S IT? BIG THINGS GET SMASHED BY BIGGER THINGS AND WHOEVER FINISHES FIRST WINS?

...AND THEY'RE REALLY LOUD.

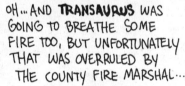

OH... AND **TRANSAURUS** WAS GOING TO BREATHE SOME FIRE TOO, BUT UNFORTUNATELY THAT WAS OVERRULED BY THE COUNTY FIRE MARSHAL...

YOU ALSO JUST MISSED **GALACTON.** THAT'S A MINIVAN THAT TURNS INTO AN ALIEN ROBOT...

LET ME GUESS...

...IT WAS DRIVEN BY A SOCCER MOM...

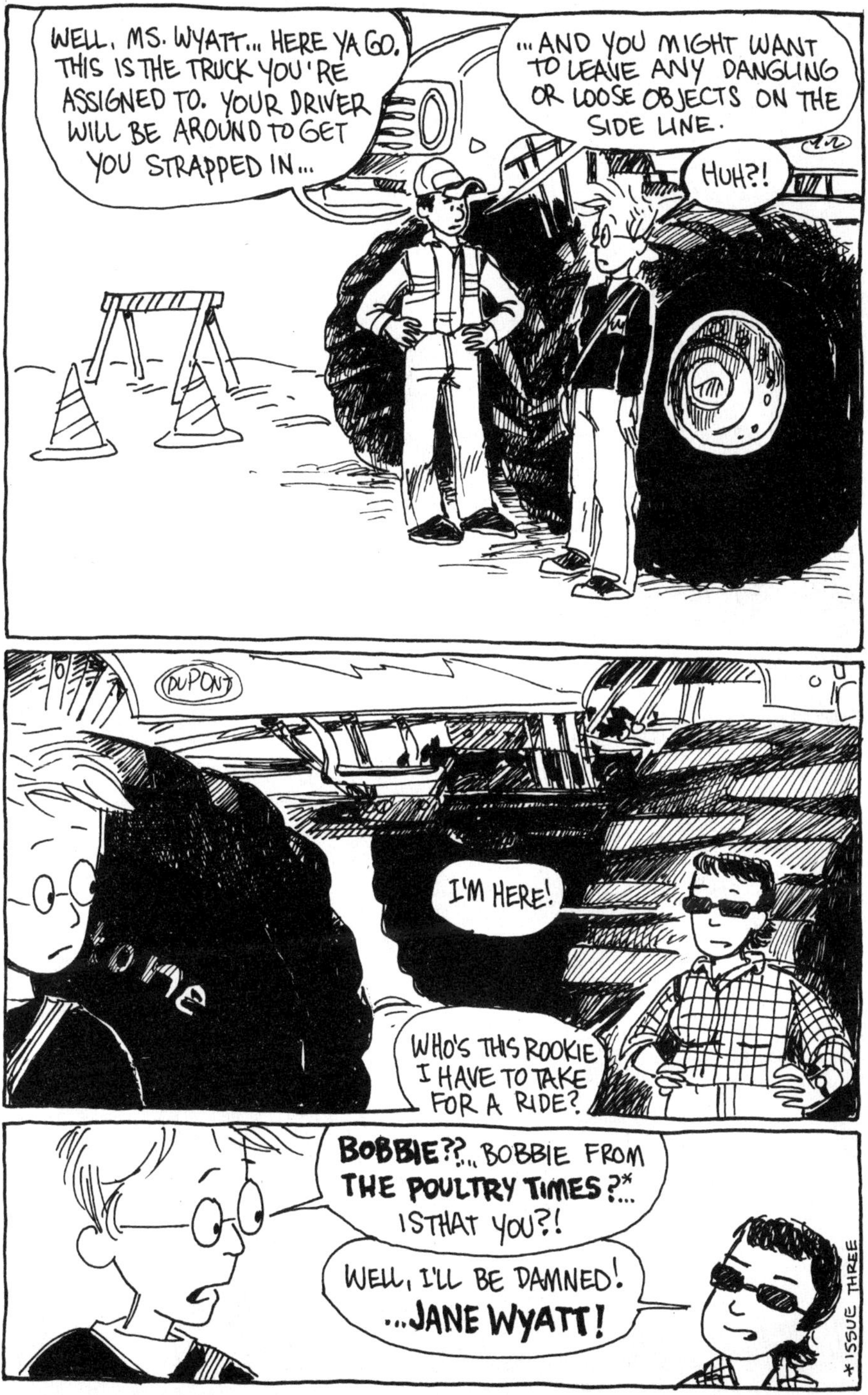
WELL, MS. WYATT... HERE YA GO. THIS IS THE TRUCK YOU'RE ASSIGNED TO. YOUR DRIVER WILL BE AROUND TO GET YOU STRAPPED IN...
...AND YOU MIGHT WANT TO LEAVE ANY DANGLING OR LOOSE OBJECTS ON THE SIDE LINE.
HUH?!
DUPONT
I'M HERE!
WHO'S THIS ROOKIE I HAVE TO TAKE FOR A RIDE?
BOBBIE??... BOBBIE FROM **THE POULTRY TIMES**?*... IS THAT YOU?!
WELL, I'LL BE DAMNED! ...**JANE WYATT**!

*ISSUE THREE

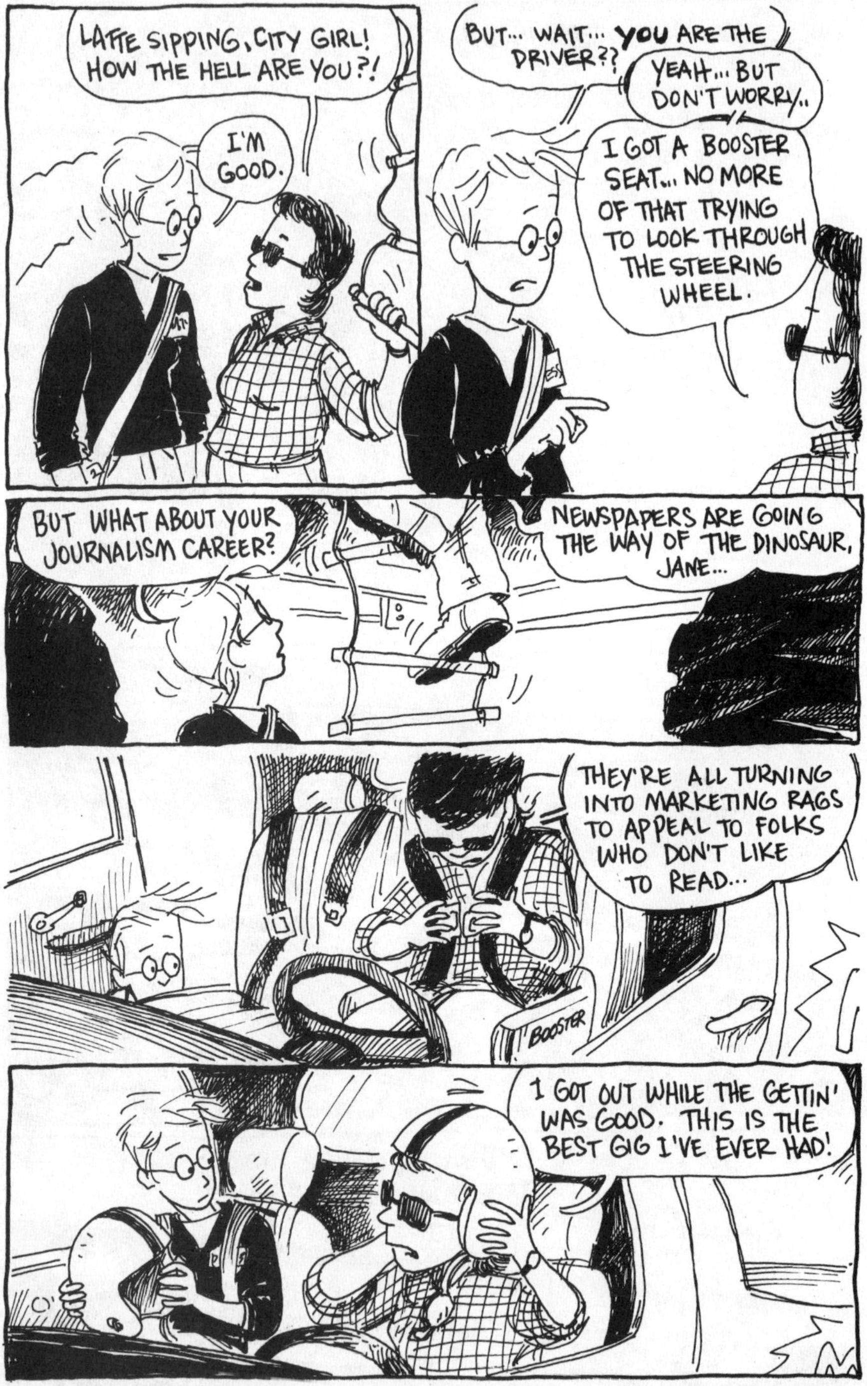
LATTE SIPPING, CITY GIRL! HOW THE HELL ARE YOU?!
I'M GOOD.
BUT... WAIT... YOU ARE THE DRIVER??
YEAH... BUT DON'T WORRY..
I GOT A BOOSTER SEAT... NO MORE OF THAT TRYING TO LOOK THROUGH THE STEERING WHEEL.
BUT WHAT ABOUT YOUR JOURNALISM CAREER?
NEWSPAPERS ARE GOING THE WAY OF THE DINOSAUR, JANE...
THEY'RE ALL TURNING INTO MARKETING RAGS TO APPEAL TO FOLKS WHO DON'T LIKE TO READ...
BOOSTER
I GOT OUT WHILE THE GETTIN' WAS GOOD. THIS IS THE BEST GIG I'VE EVER HAD!

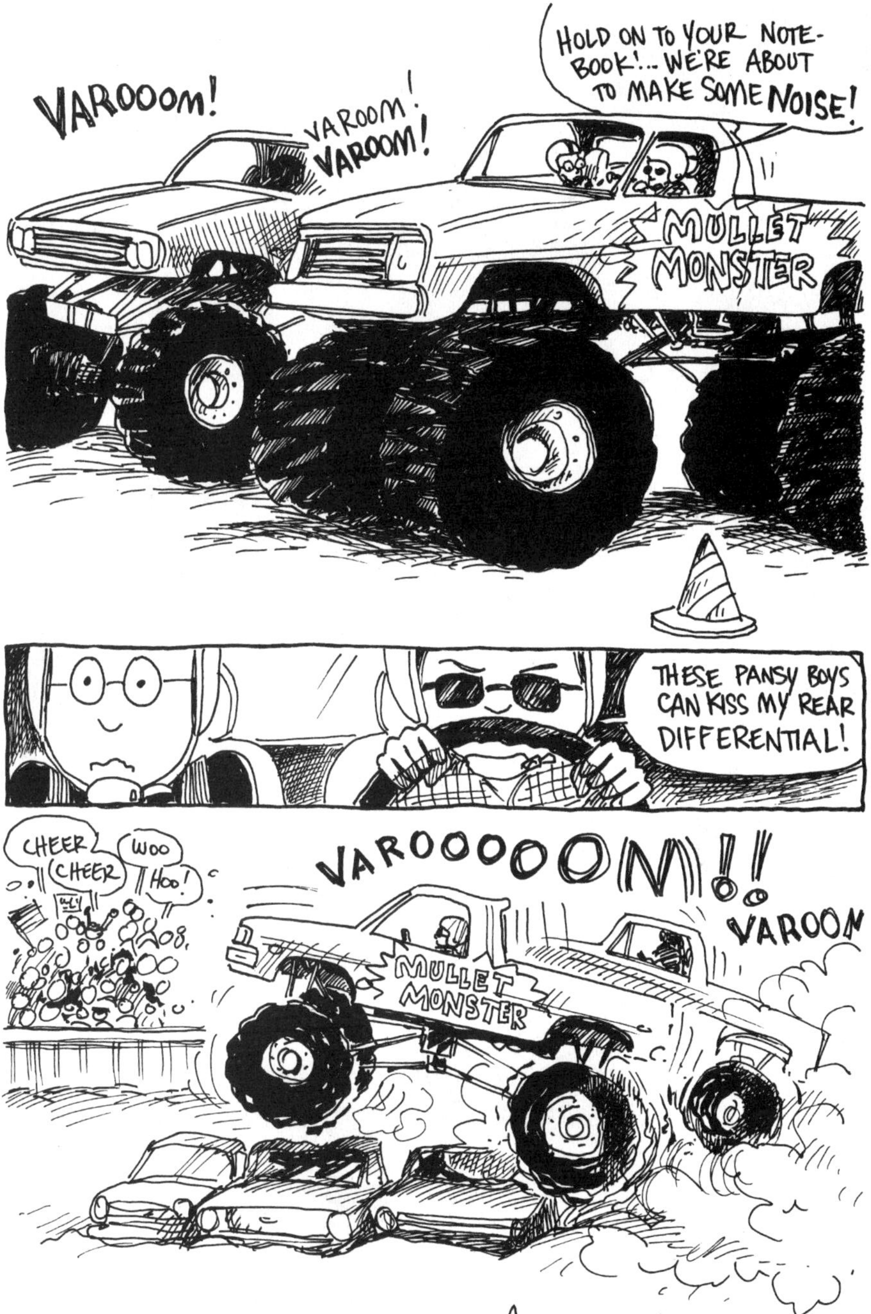
VAROOOM!
VAROOM! VAROOM!
HOLD ON TO YOUR NOTE-BOOK!... WE'RE ABOUT TO MAKE SOME NOISE!
MULLET MONSTER
THESE PANSY BOYS CAN KISS MY REAR DIFFERENTIAL!
CHEER CHEER
WOO HOO!
VAROOOOOOM!!
VAROOM
MULLET MONSTER

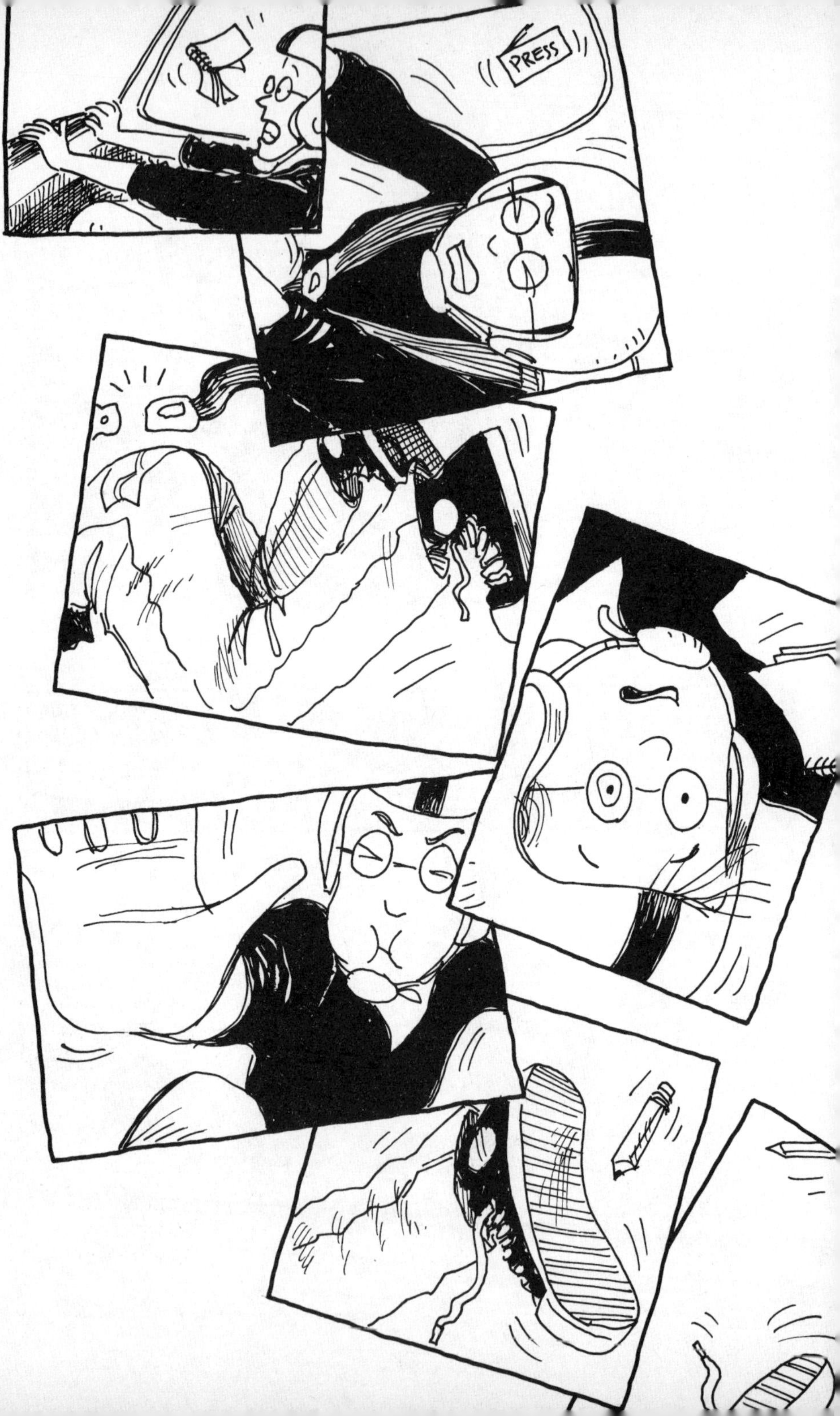
PRESS

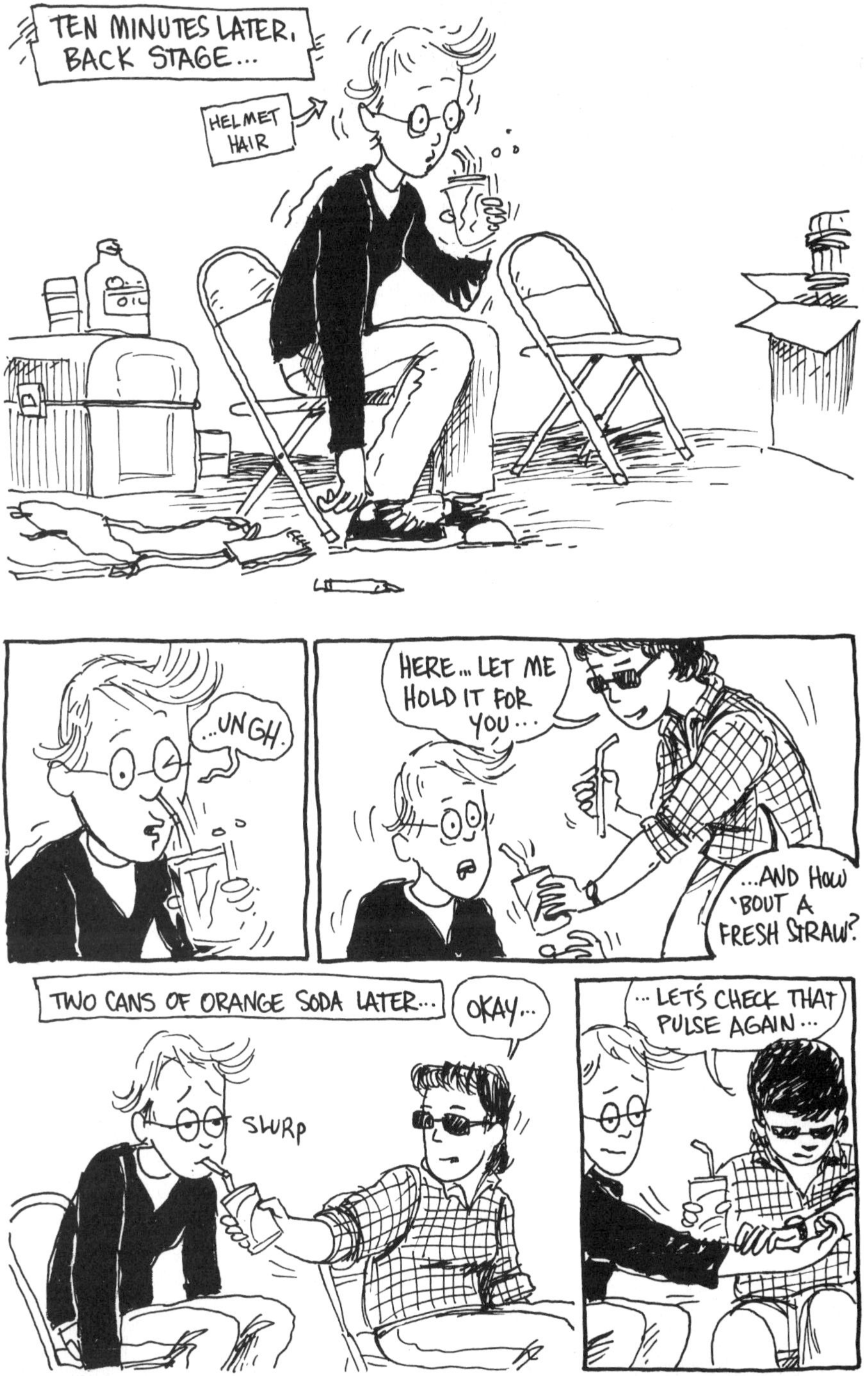
TEN MINUTES LATER, BACK STAGE...
HELMET HAIR
OIL
...UNGH.
HERE... LET ME HOLD IT FOR YOU...
...AND HOW 'BOUT A FRESH STRAW?
TWO CANS OF ORANGE SODA LATER...
OKAY...
SLURP
... LET'S CHECK THAT PULSE AGAIN ...

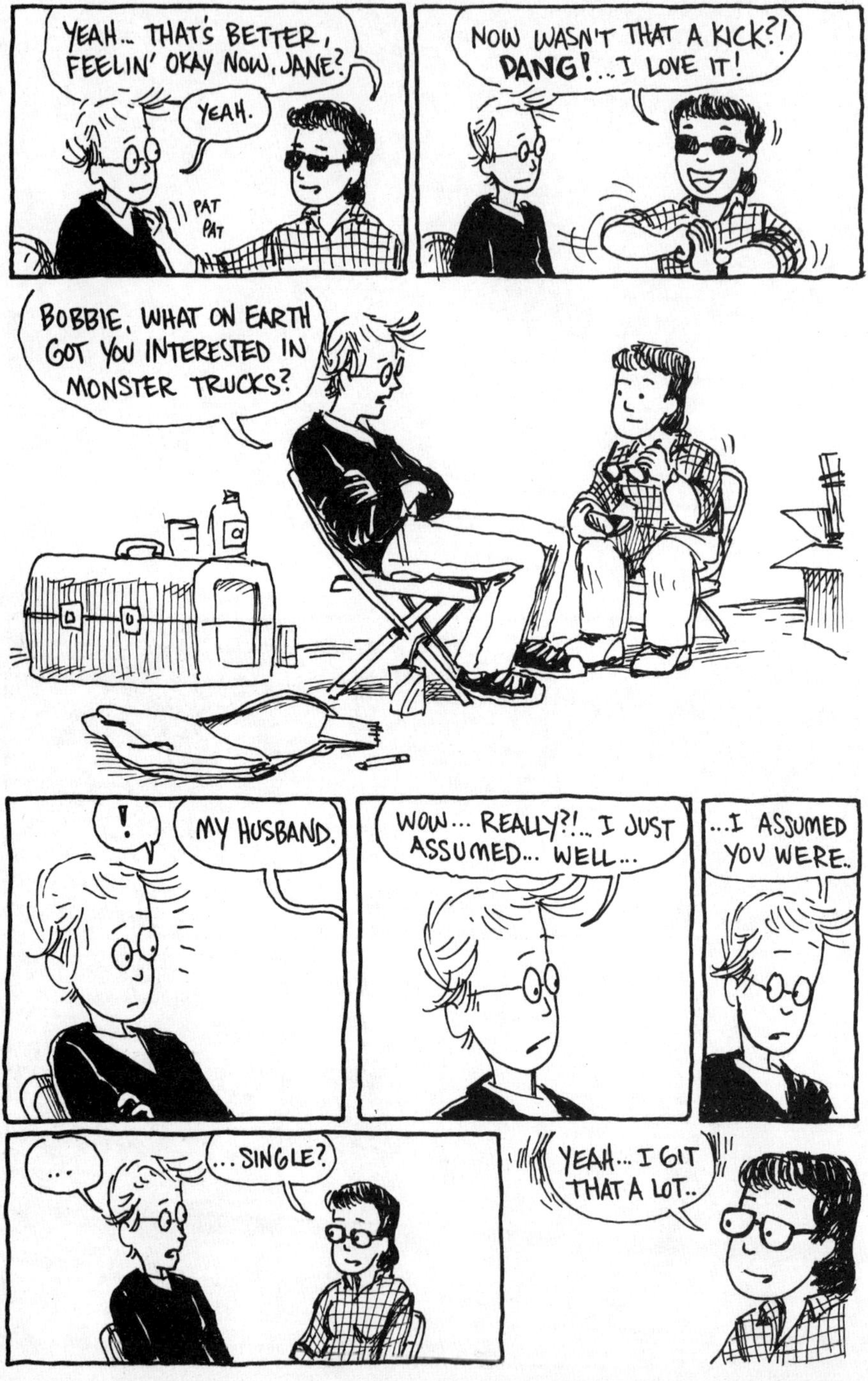
YEAH.. THAT'S BETTER, FEELIN' OKAY NOW, JANE?
YEAH.
PAT PAT
NOW WASN'T THAT A KICK?! DANG!...I LOVE IT!
BOBBIE, WHAT ON EARTH GOT YOU INTERESTED IN MONSTER TRUCKS?
!
MY HUSBAND.
WOW... REALLY?!... I JUST ASSUMED... WELL...
...I ASSUMED YOU WERE.
...
...SINGLE?
YEAH... I GIT THAT A LOT..

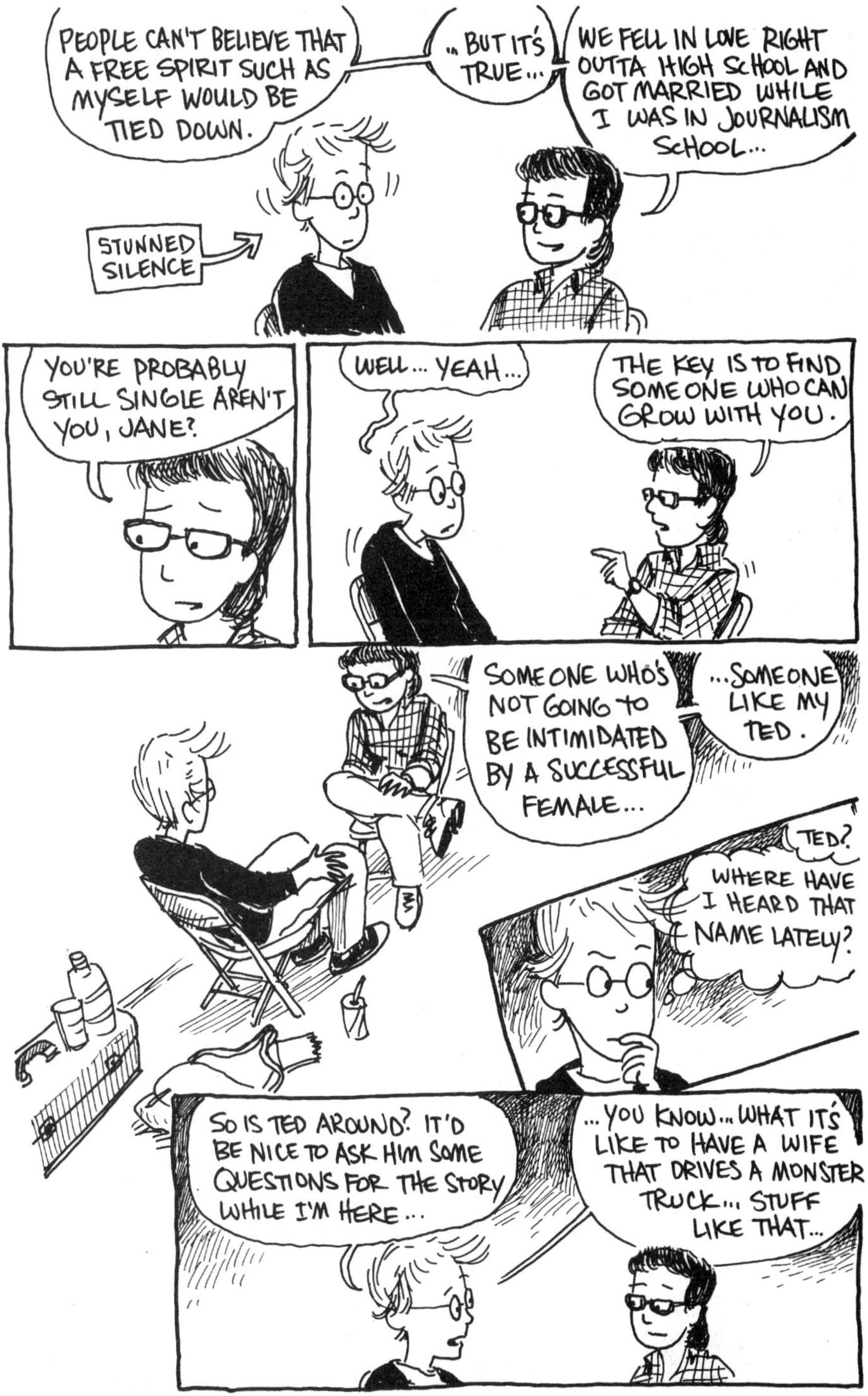
PEOPLE CAN'T BELIEVE THAT A FREE SPIRIT SUCH AS MYSELF WOULD BE TIED DOWN.
... BUT IT'S TRUE...
WE FELL IN LOVE RIGHT OUTTA HIGH SCHOOL AND GOT MARRIED WHILE I WAS IN JOURNALISM SCHOOL...
STUNNED SILENCE
YOU'RE PROBABLY STILL SINGLE AREN'T YOU, JANE?
WELL... YEAH...
THE KEY IS TO FIND SOMEONE WHO CAN GROW WITH YOU.
SOMEONE WHO'S NOT GOING TO BE INTIMIDATED BY A SUCCESSFUL FEMALE...
...SOMEONE LIKE MY TED.
TED?
WHERE HAVE I HEARD THAT NAME LATELY?
SO IS TED AROUND? IT'D BE NICE TO ASK HIM SOME QUESTIONS FOR THE STORY WHILE I'M HERE...
...YOU KNOW... WHAT IT'S LIKE TO HAVE A WIFE THAT DRIVES A MONSTER TRUCK... STUFF LIKE THAT...

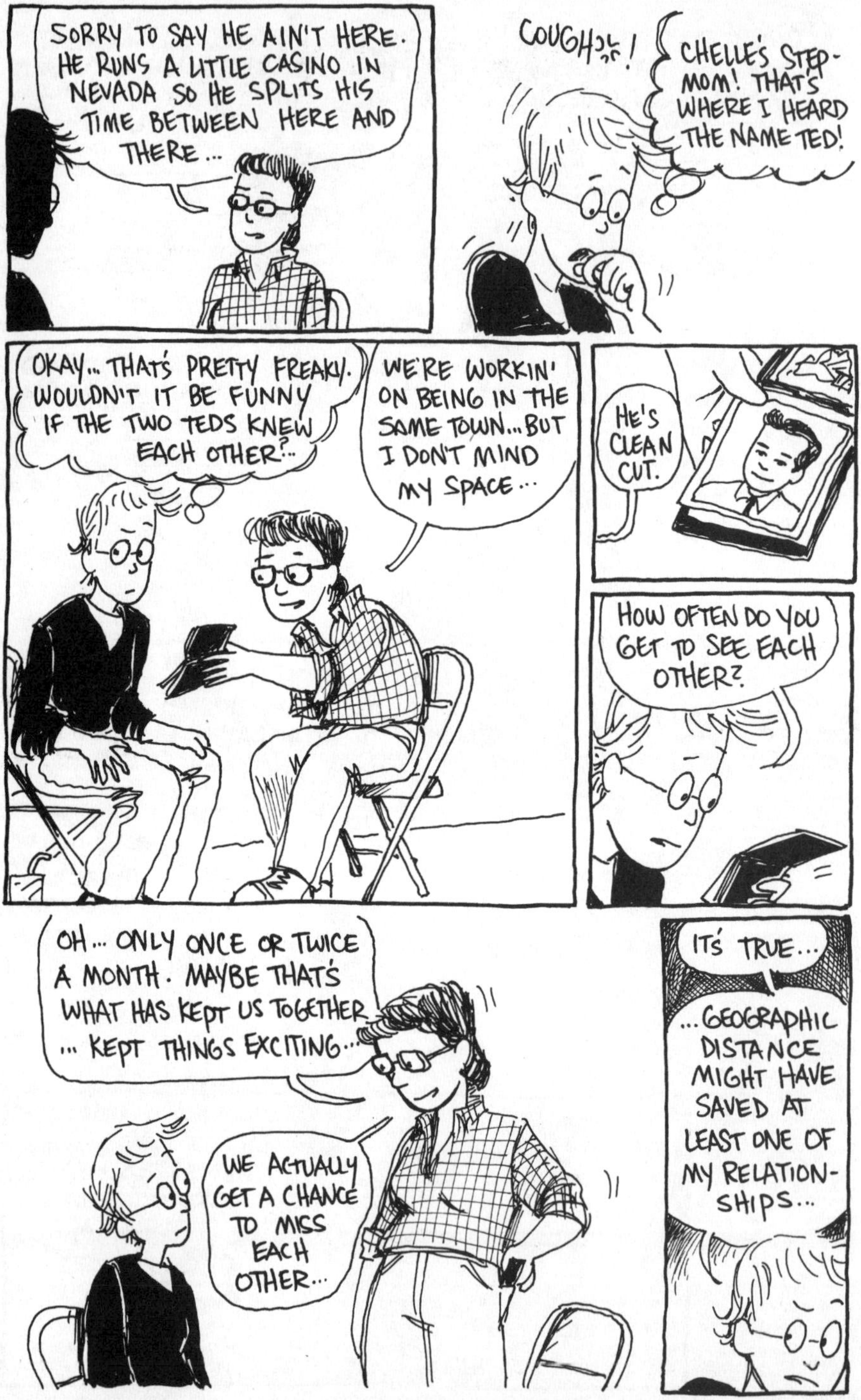
SORRY TO SAY HE AIN'T HERE. HE RUNS A LITTLE CASINO IN NEVADA SO HE SPLITS HIS TIME BETWEEN HERE AND THERE...
COUGH!
CHELLE'S STEP-MOM! THAT'S WHERE I HEARD THE NAME TED!
OKAY... THAT'S PRETTY FREAKY. WOULDN'T IT BE FUNNY IF THE TWO TEDS KNEW EACH OTHER?...
WE'RE WORKIN' ON BEING IN THE SAME TOWN... BUT I DON'T MIND MY SPACE...
HE'S CLEAN CUT.
HOW OFTEN DO YOU GET TO SEE EACH OTHER?
OH... ONLY ONCE OR TWICE A MONTH. MAYBE THAT'S WHAT HAS KEPT US TOGETHER ... KEPT THINGS EXCITING...
WE ACTUALLY GET A CHANCE TO MISS EACH OTHER...
IT'S TRUE...
...GEOGRAPHIC DISTANCE MIGHT HAVE SAVED AT LEAST ONE OF MY RELATION-SHIPS...

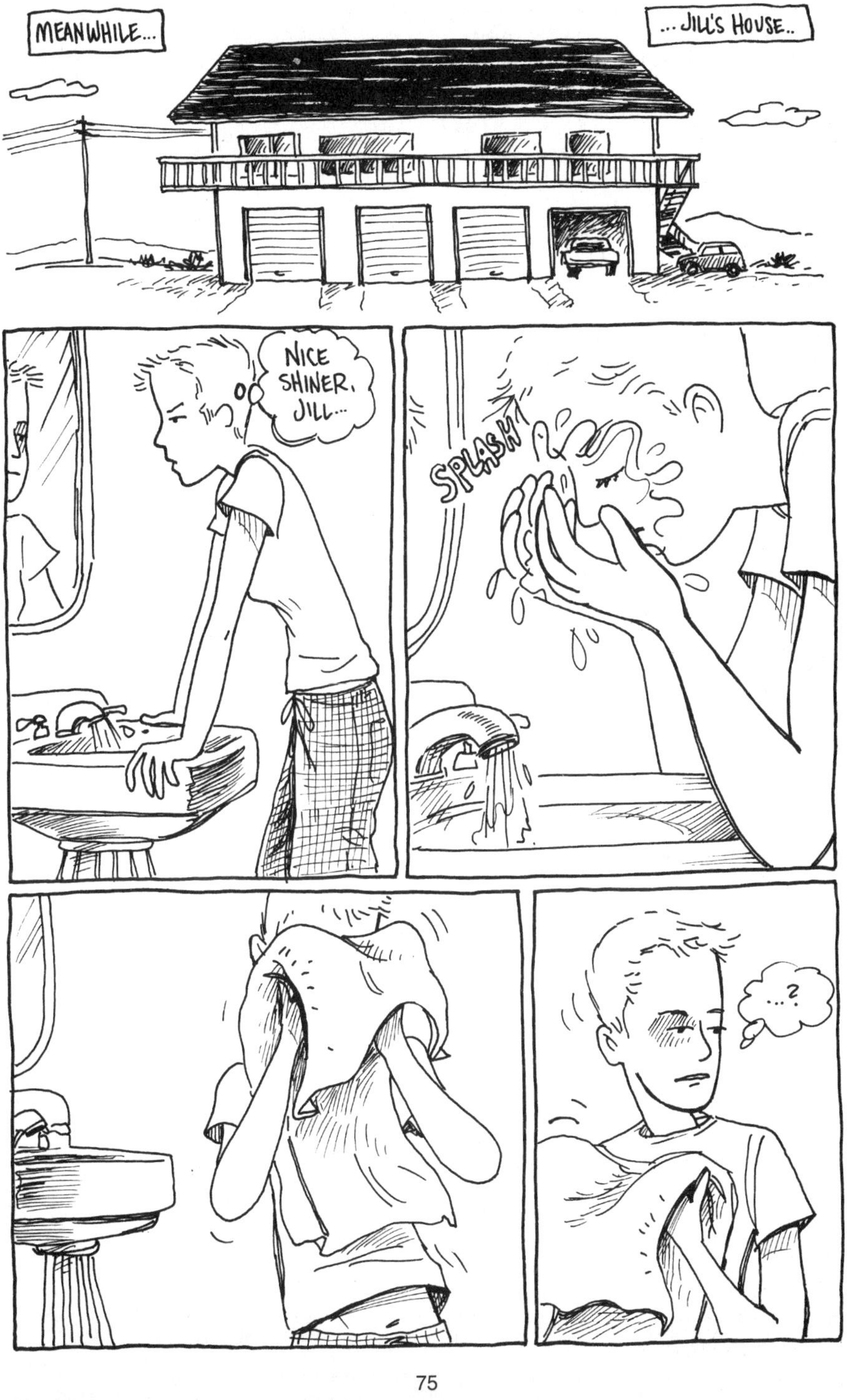
MEANWHILE...
...JILL'S HOUSE..
NICE SHINER, JILL...
SPLASH
...?

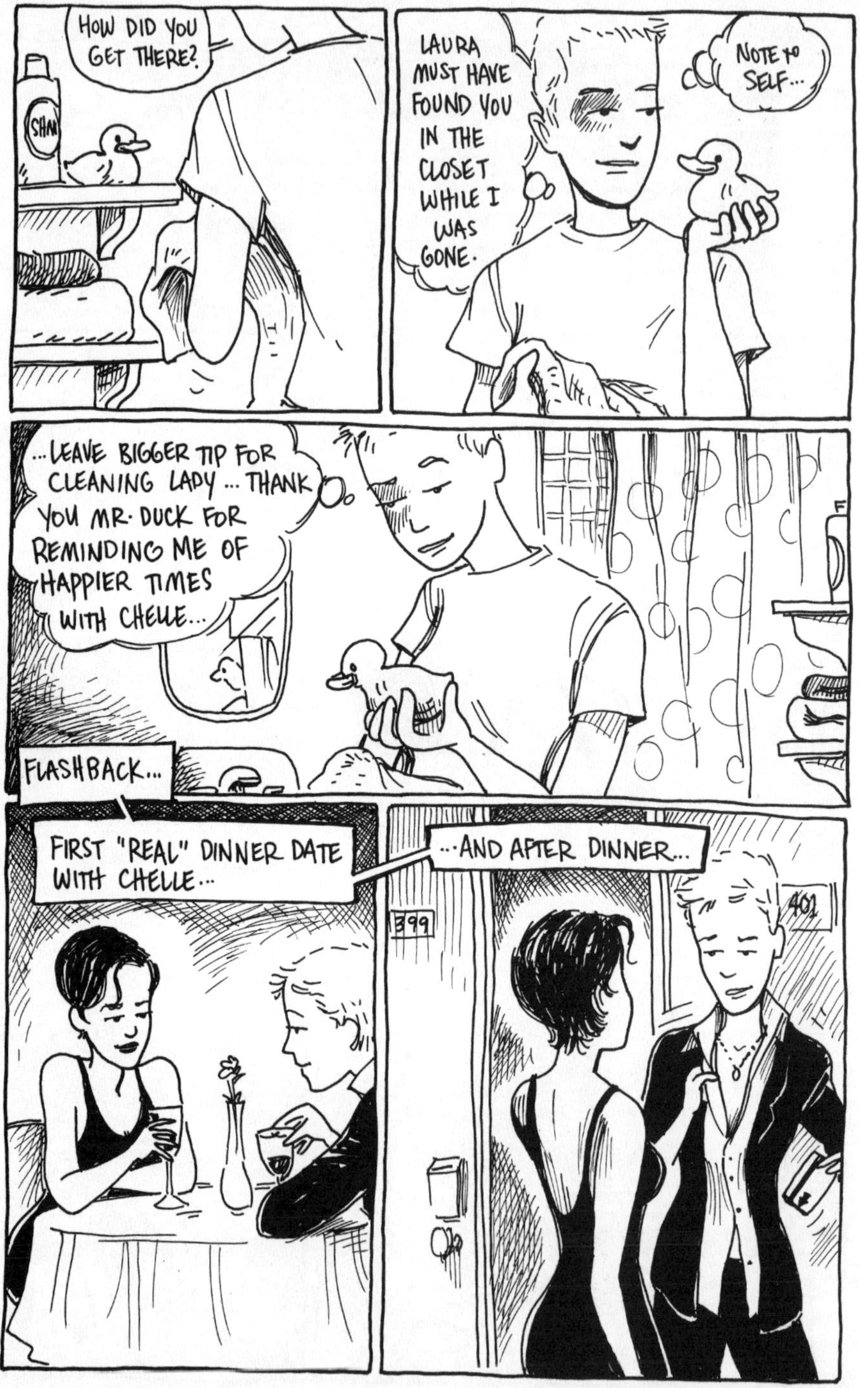
HOW DID YOU GET THERE?
SHAM
LAURA MUST HAVE FOUND YOU IN THE CLOSET WHILE I WAS GONE.
NOTE TO SELF...
...LEAVE BIGGER TIP FOR CLEANING LADY ... THANK YOU MR. DUCK FOR REMINDING ME OF HAPPIER TIMES WITH CHELLE...
FLASHBACK...
FIRST "REAL" DINNER DATE WITH CHELLE...
...AND AFTER DINNER...
399
401

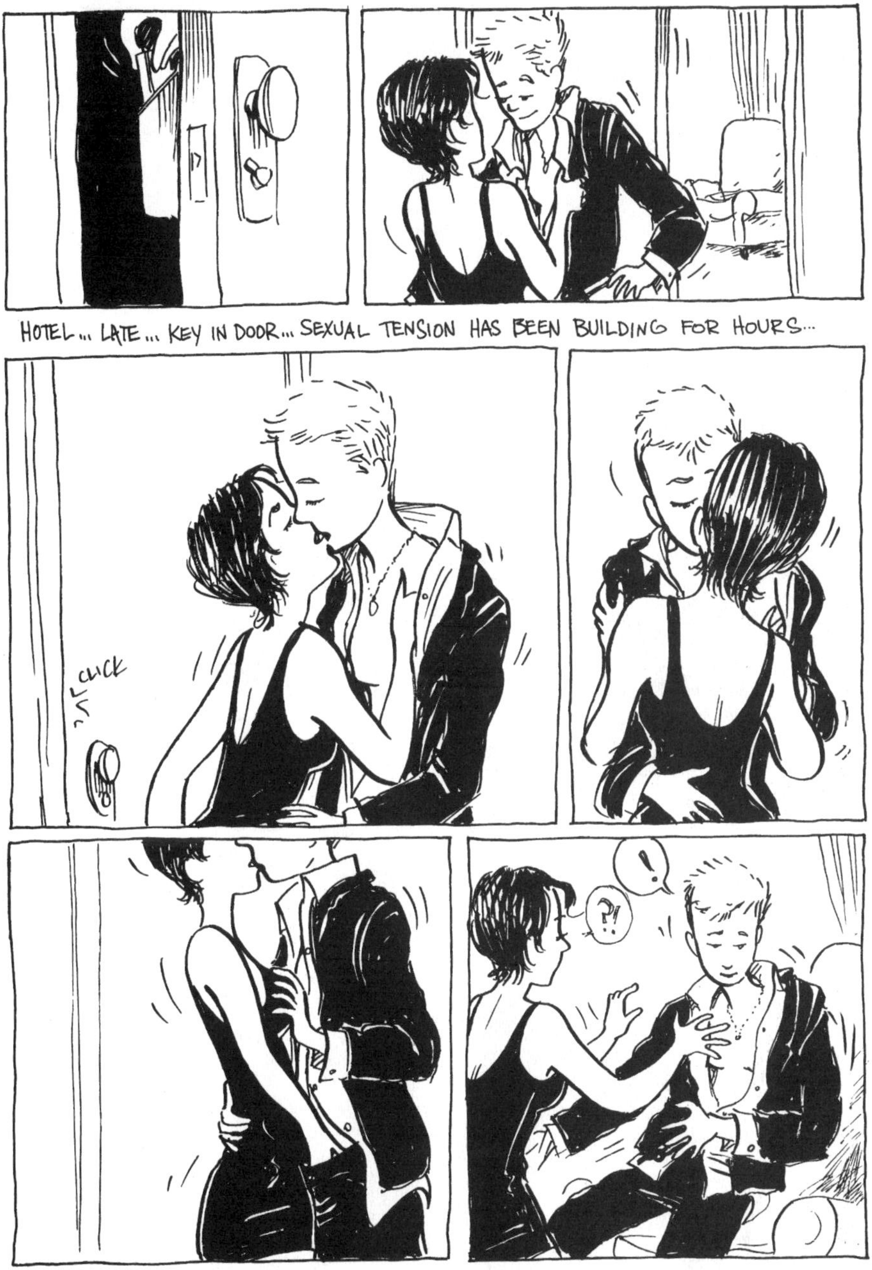
HOTEL... LATE... KEY IN DOOR... SEXUAL TENSION HAS BEEN BUILDING FOR HOURS...
CLICK
?!
!

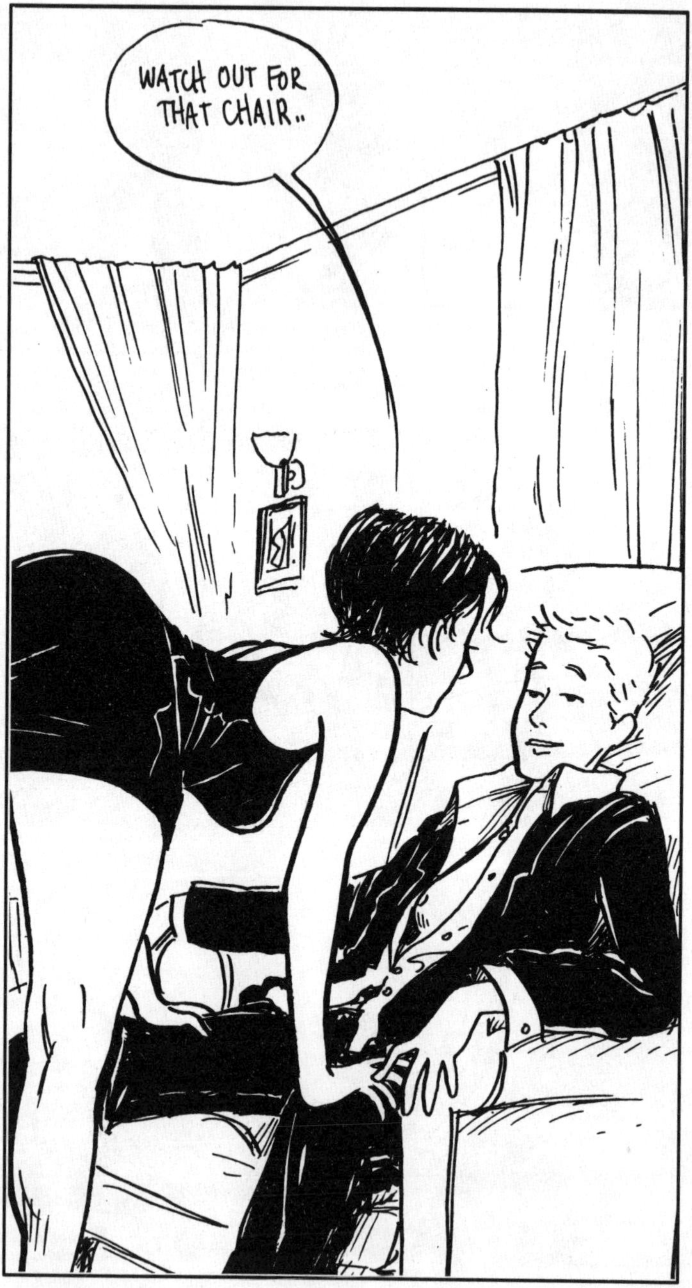
WATCH OUT FOR THAT CHAIR..

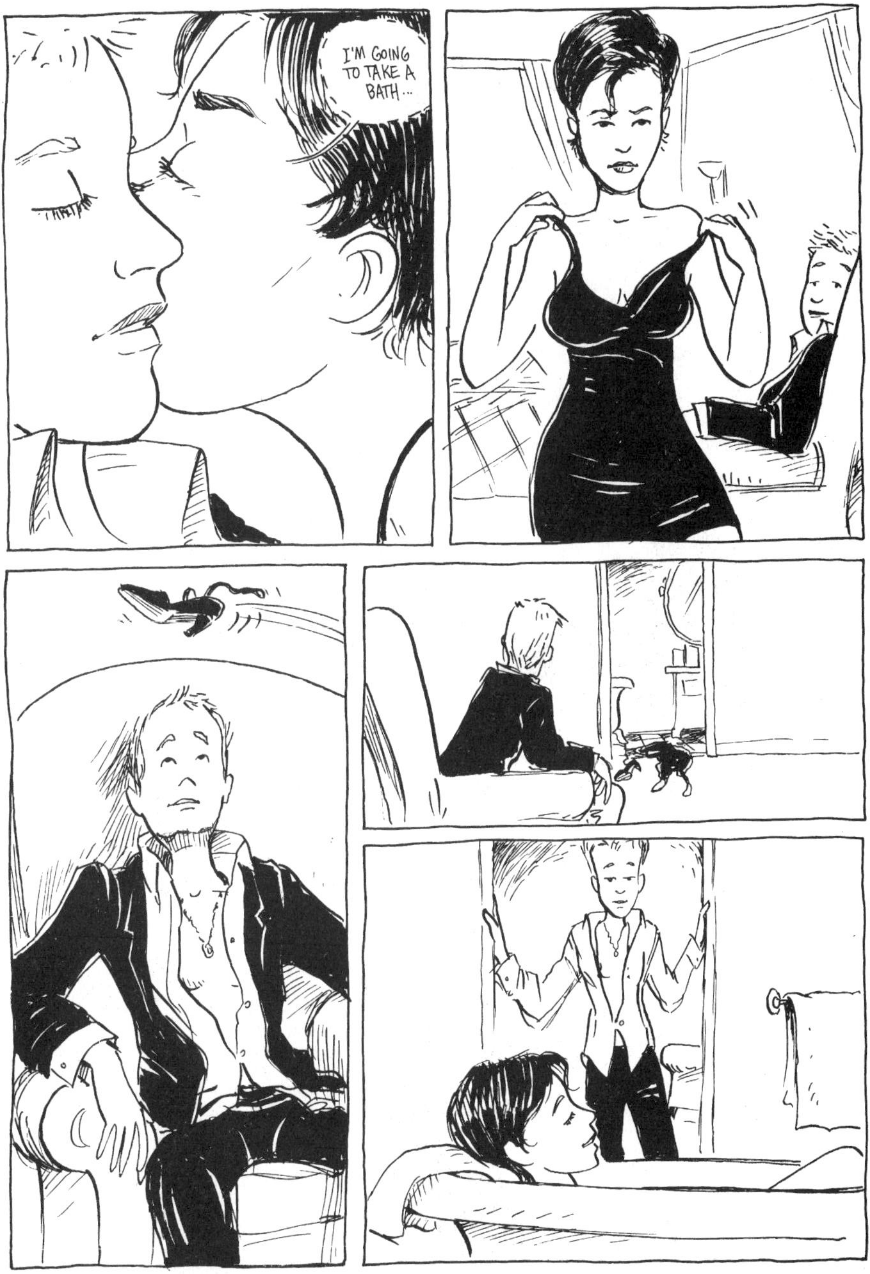
I'M GOING TO TAKE A BATH...

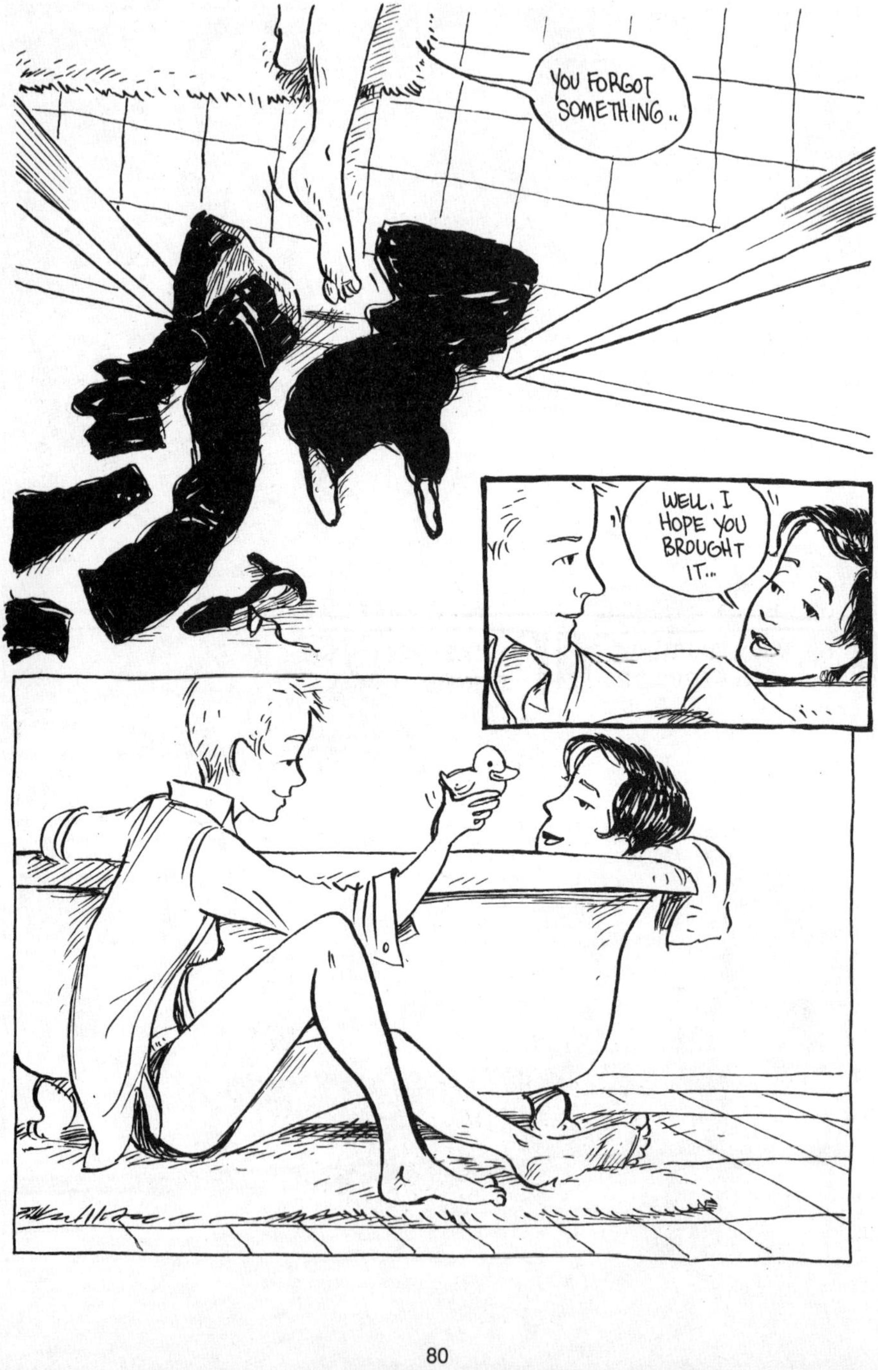
YOU FORGOT SOMETHING..
WELL, I HOPE YOU BROUGHT IT...

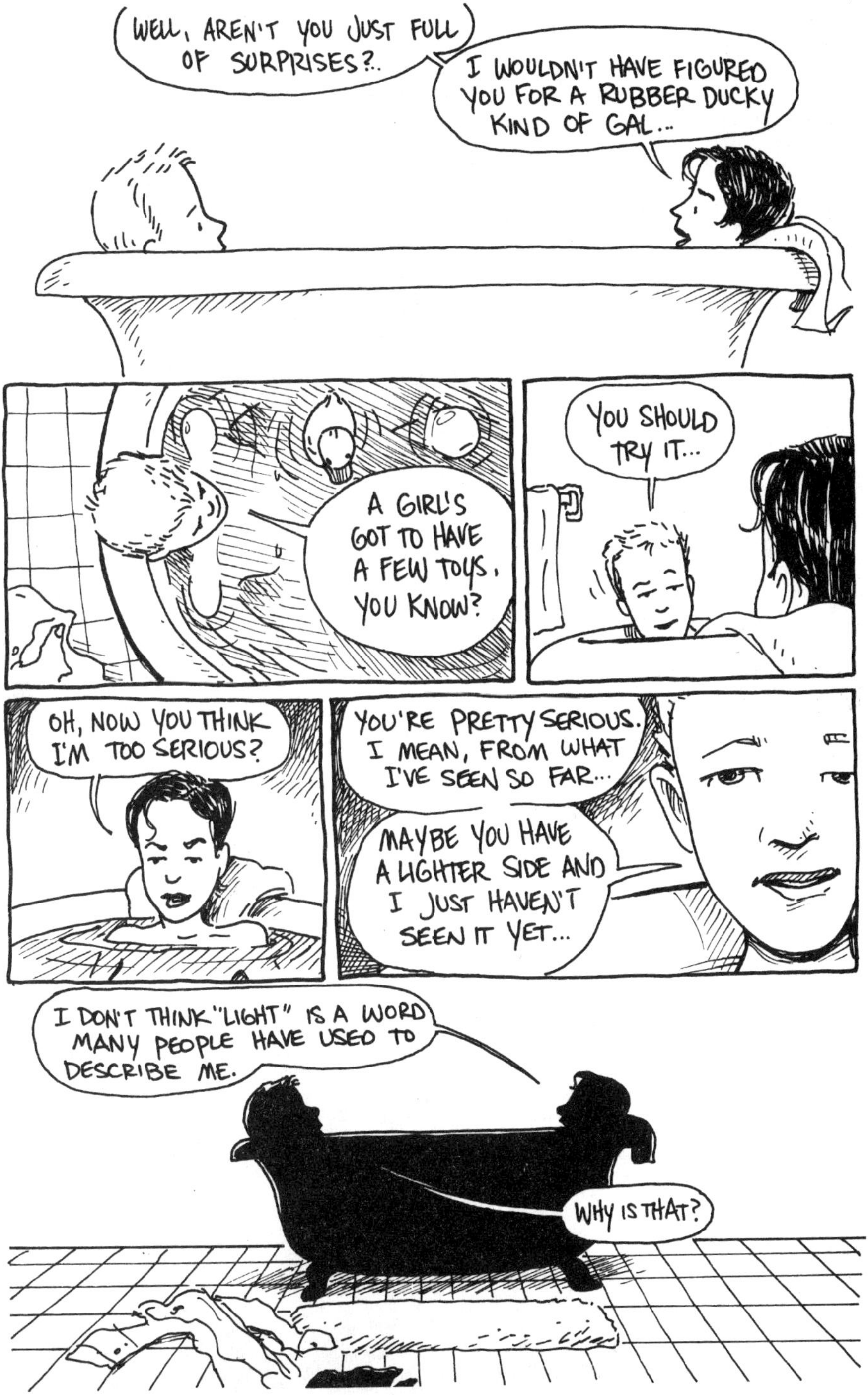
WELL, AREN'T YOU JUST FULL OF SURPRISES?..
I WOULDN'T HAVE FIGURED YOU FOR A RUBBER DUCKY KIND OF GAL...
A GIRL'S GOT TO HAVE A FEW TOYS, YOU KNOW?
YOU SHOULD TRY IT...
OH, NOW YOU THINK I'M TOO SERIOUS?
YOU'RE PRETTY SERIOUS. I MEAN, FROM WHAT I'VE SEEN SO FAR...
MAYBE YOU HAVE A LIGHTER SIDE AND I JUST HAVEN'T SEEN IT YET...
I DON'T THINK "LIGHT" IS A WORD MANY PEOPLE HAVE USED TO DESCRIBE ME.
WHY IS THAT?

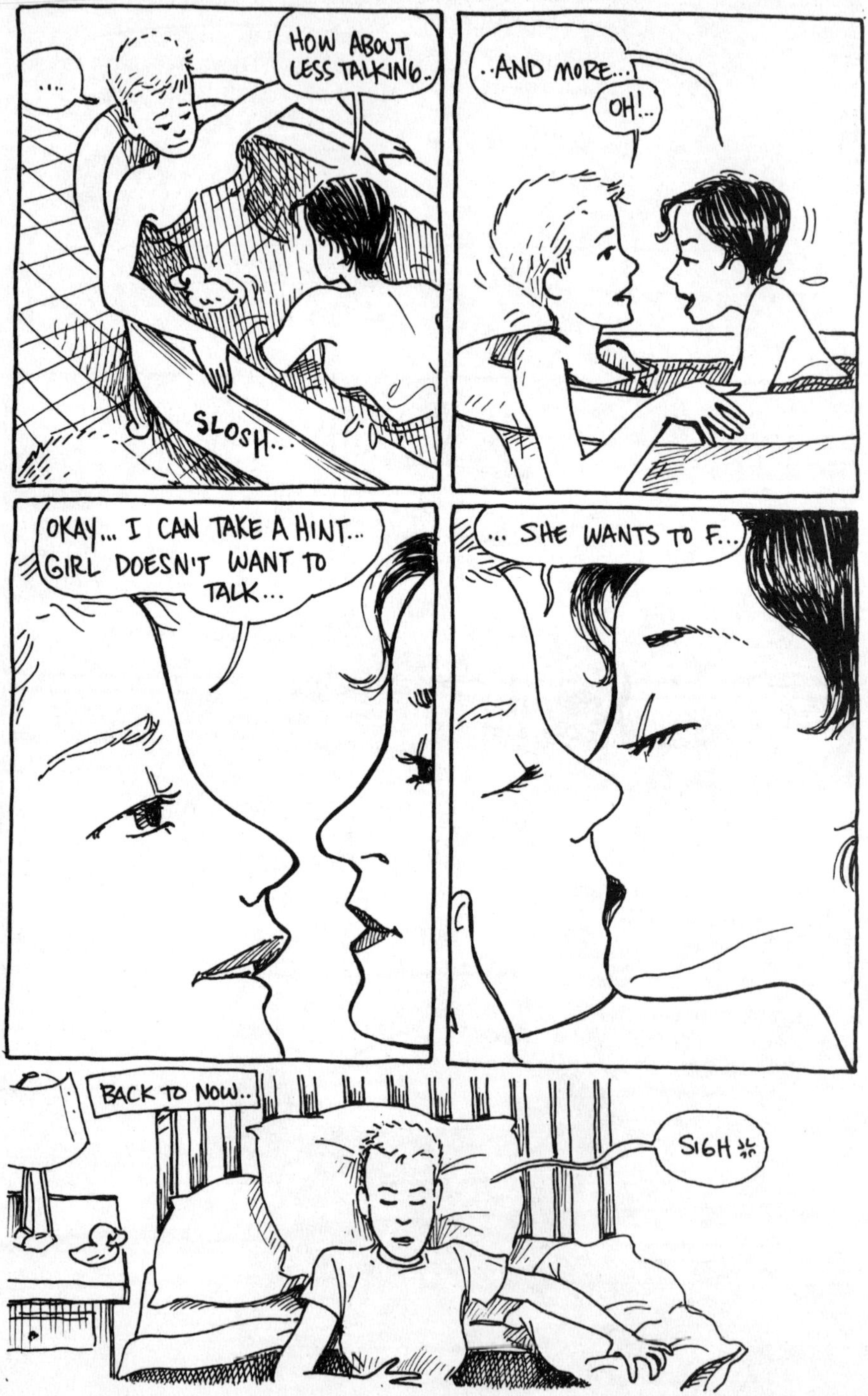
...
HOW ABOUT LESS TALKING..
SLOSH..
..AND MORE..
OH!..
OKAY... I CAN TAKE A HINT... GIRL DOESN'T WANT TO TALK...
... SHE WANTS TO F...
BACK TO NOW..
SIGH

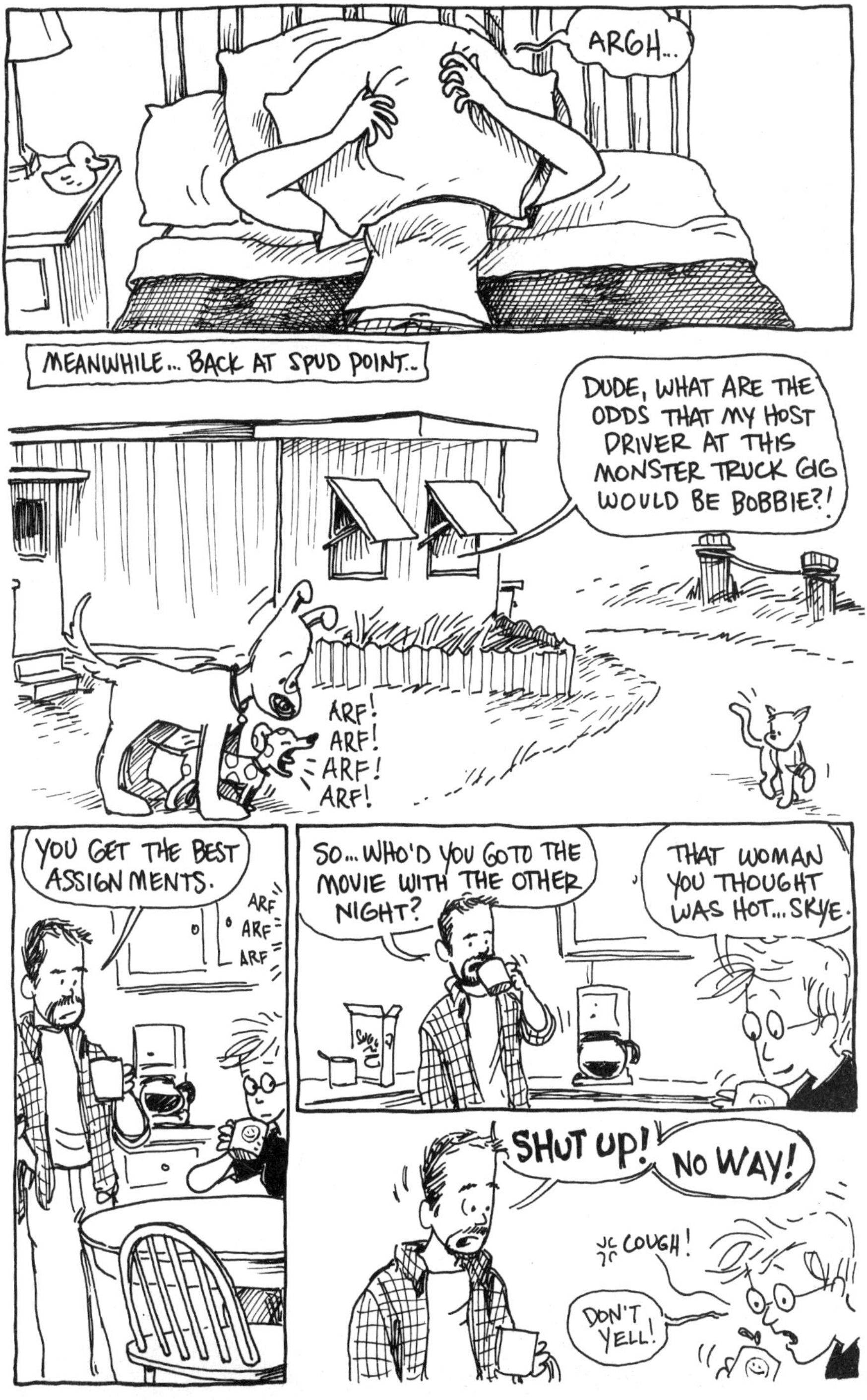
ARGH...
MEANWHILE... BACK AT SPUD POINT..
DUDE, WHAT ARE THE ODDS THAT MY HOST DRIVER AT THIS MONSTER TRUCK GIG WOULD BE BOBBIE?!
ARF! ARF! ARF! ARF!
YOU GET THE BEST ASSIGNMENTS.
ARF ARF ARF
SO... WHO'D YOU GO TO THE MOVIE WITH THE OTHER NIGHT?
THAT WOMAN YOU THOUGHT WAS HOT... SKYE.
SHUT UP!
NO WAY!
COUGH!
DON'T YELL!

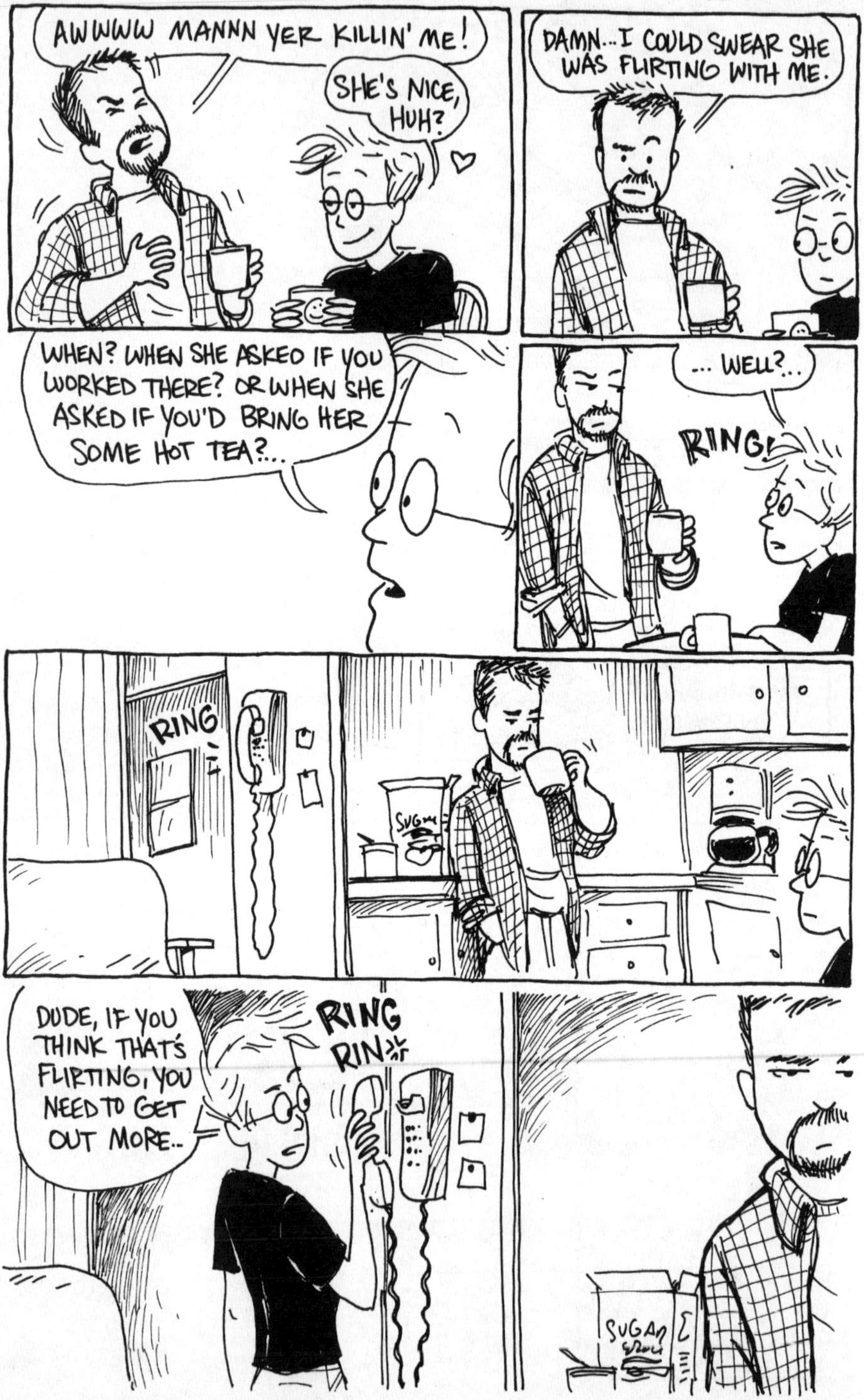
AWWWW MANNN YER KILLIN' ME!
SHE'S NICE, HUH?
DAMN... I COULD SWEAR SHE WAS FLIRTING WITH ME.
WHEN? WHEN SHE ASKED IF YOU WORKED THERE? OR WHEN SHE ASKED IF YOU'D BRING HER SOME HOT TEA?...
... WELL?...
RING!
RING
DUDE, IF YOU THINK THAT'S FLIRTING, YOU NEED TO GET OUT MORE..
RING
RIN

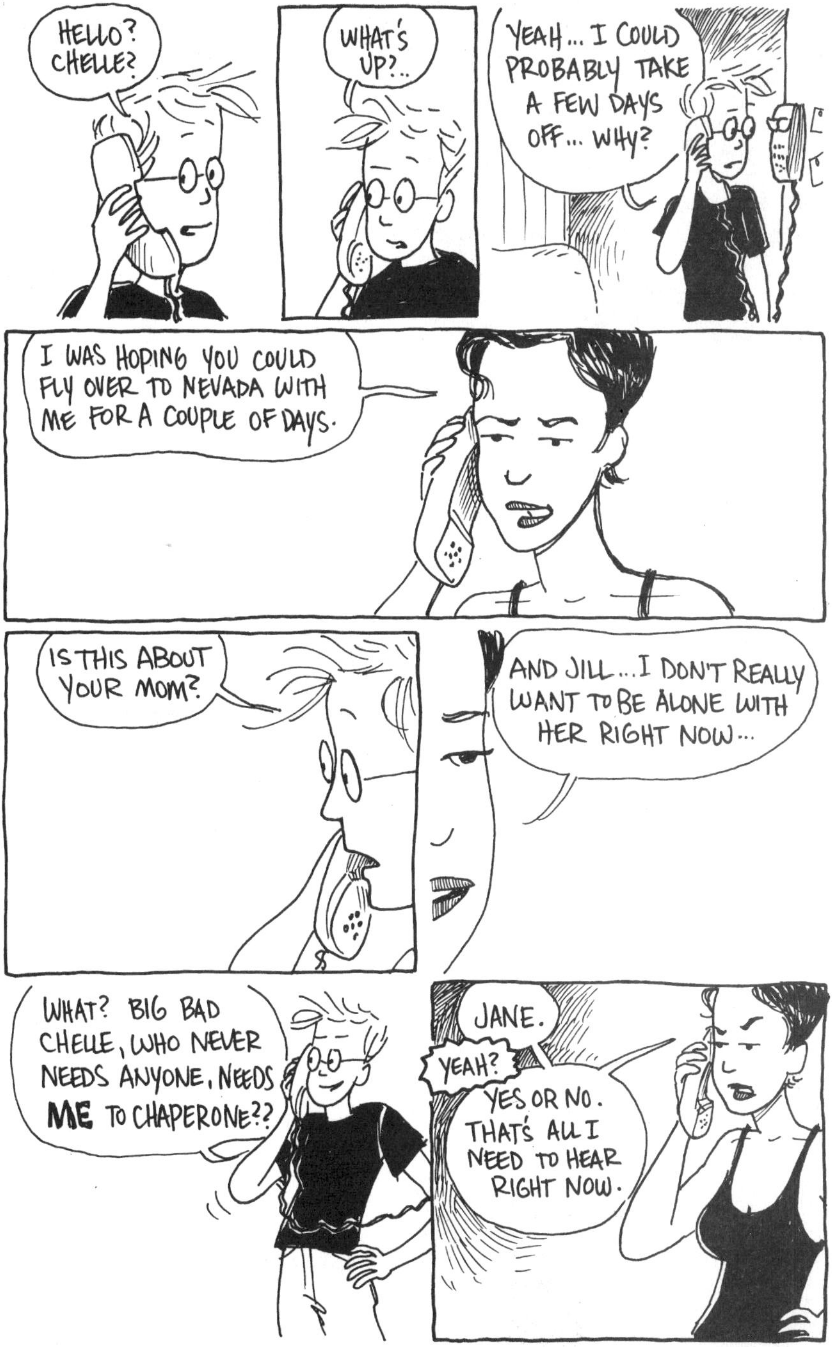
HELLO? CHELLE?
WHAT'S UP?...
YEAH... I COULD PROBABLY TAKE A FEW DAYS OFF... WHY?
I WAS HOPING YOU COULD FLY OVER TO NEVADA WITH ME FOR A COUPLE OF DAYS.
IS THIS ABOUT YOUR MOM?
AND JILL... I DON'T REALLY WANT TO BE ALONE WITH HER RIGHT NOW...
WHAT? BIG BAD CHELLE, WHO NEVER NEEDS ANYONE, NEEDS **ME** TO CHAPERONE??
JANE.
YEAH?
YES OR NO. THAT'S ALL I NEED TO HEAR RIGHT NOW.

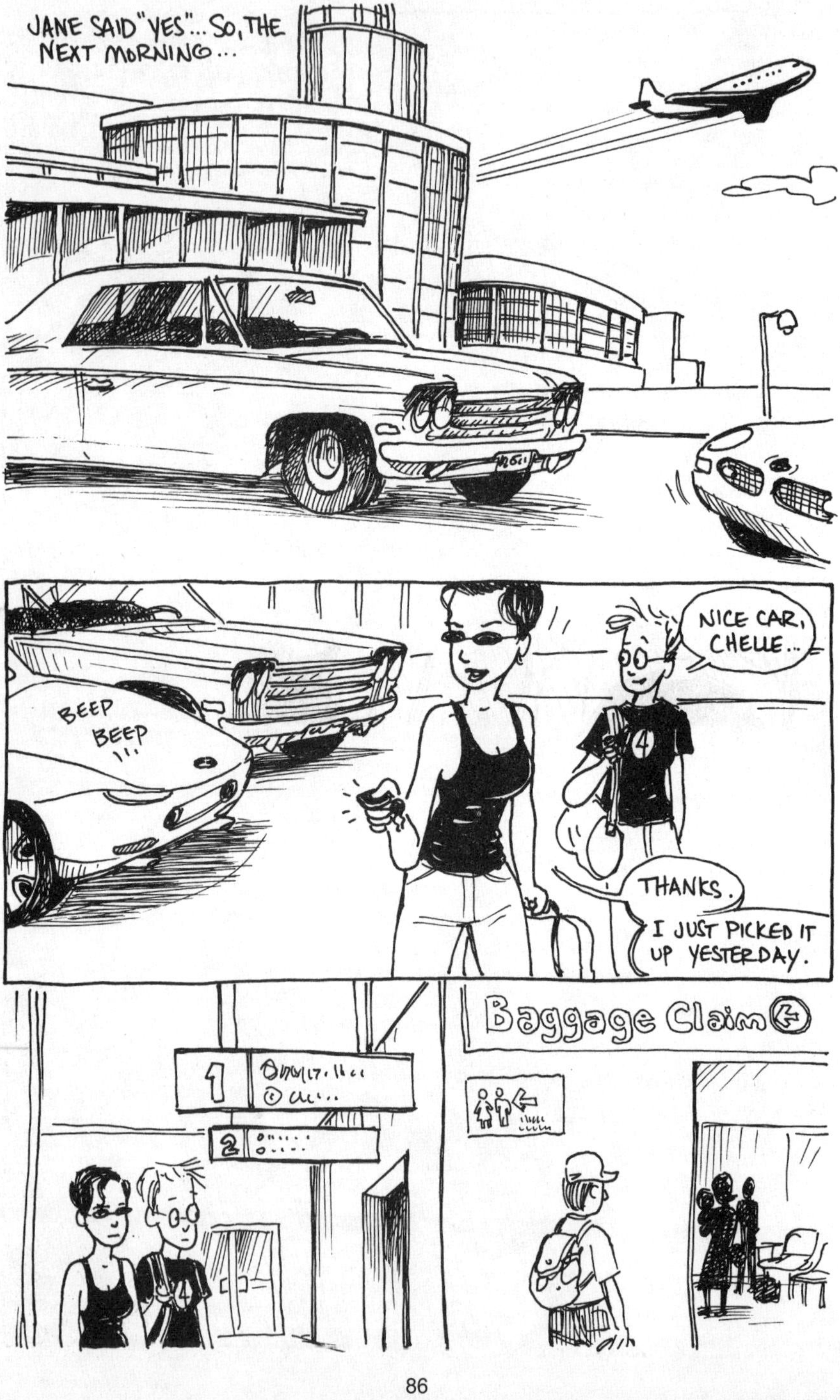
JANE SAID "YES"... SO, THE NEXT MORNING...
BEEP BEEP
NICE CAR, CHELLE...
THANKS.
I JUST PICKED IT UP YESTERDAY.
Baggage Claim

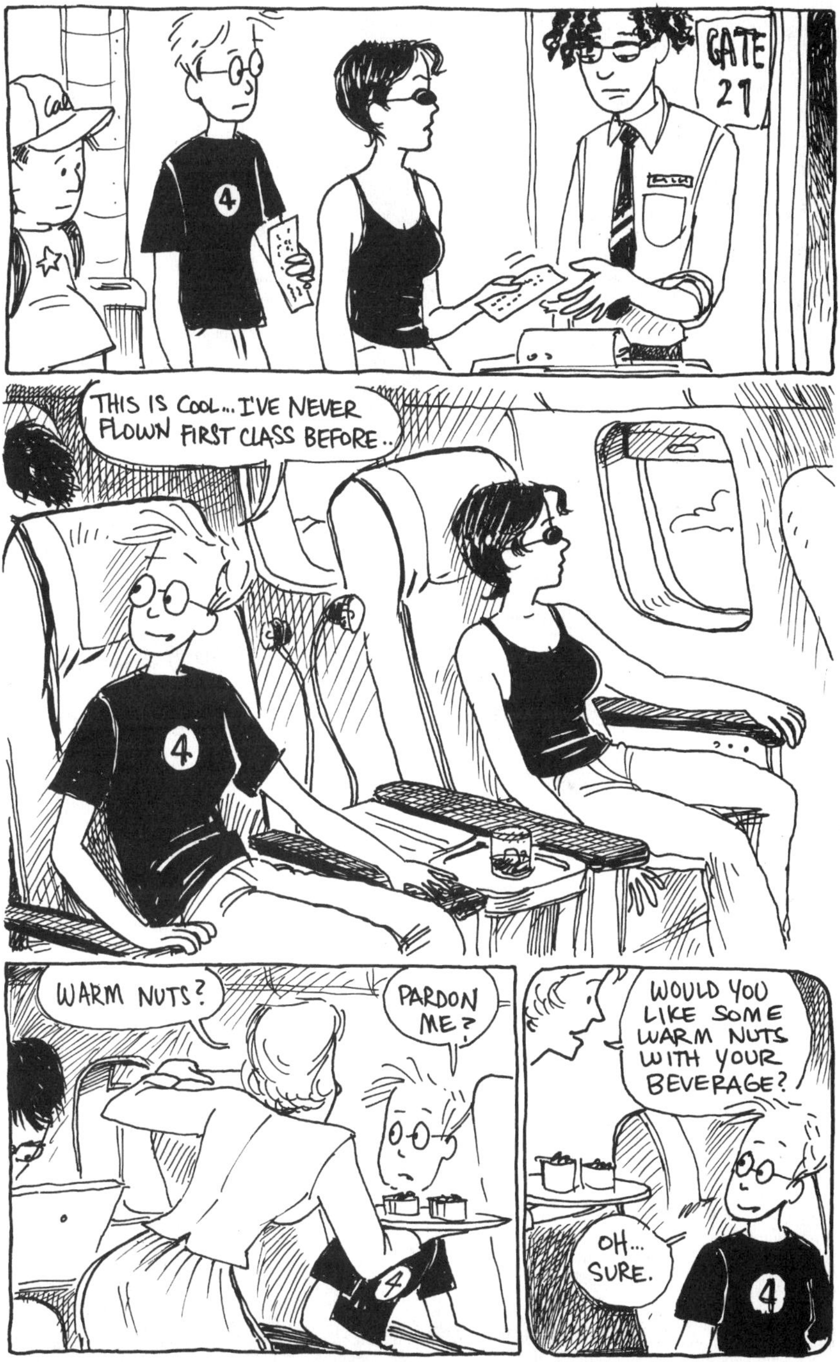
GATE 21
THIS IS COOL... I'VE NEVER FLOWN FIRST CLASS BEFORE..
WARM NUTS?
PARDON ME?
WOULD YOU LIKE SOME WARM NUTS WITH YOUR BEVERAGE?
OH... SURE.

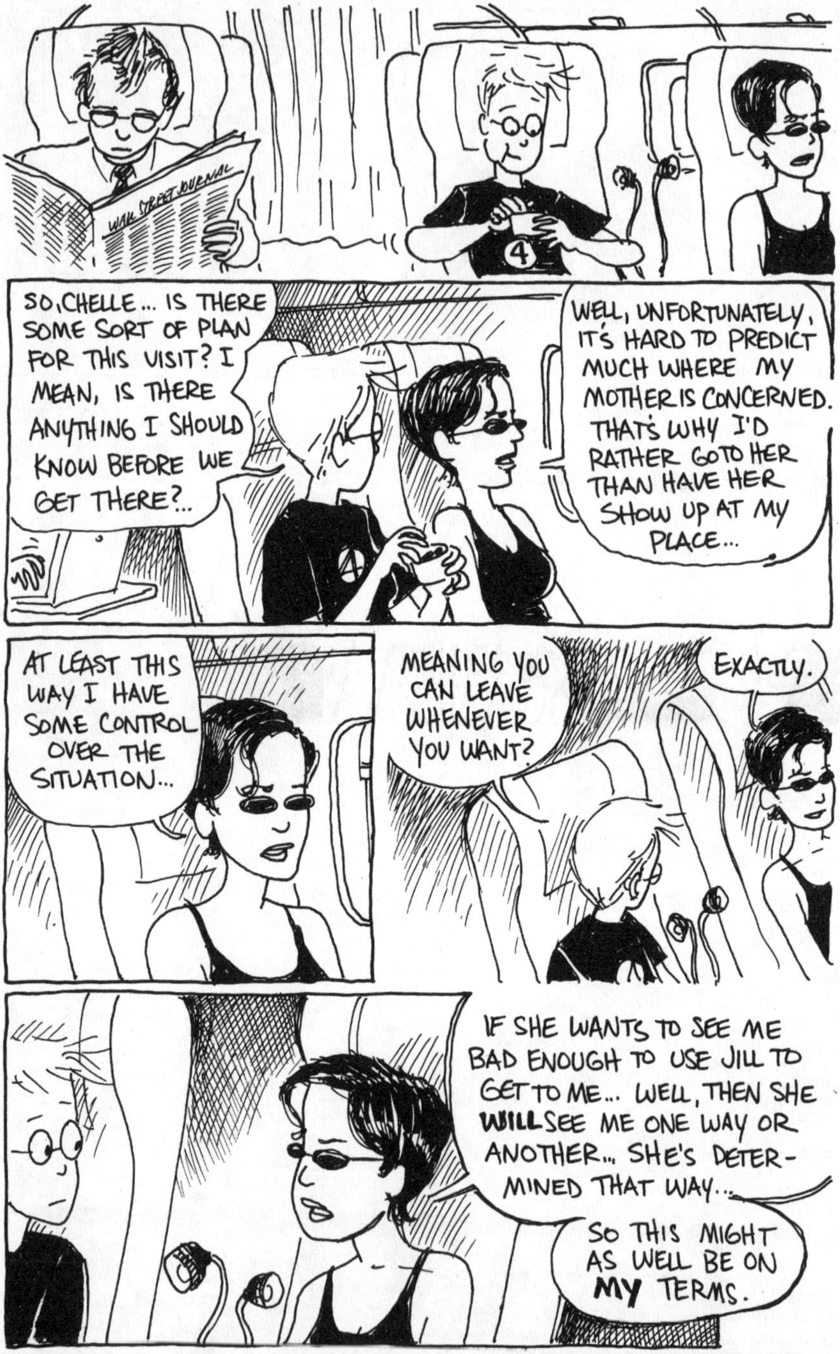
WALL STREET JOURNAL
SO, CHELLE... IS THERE SOME SORT OF PLAN FOR THIS VISIT? I MEAN, IS THERE ANYTHING I SHOULD KNOW BEFORE WE GET THERE?...
WELL, UNFORTUNATELY, IT'S HARD TO PREDICT MUCH WHERE MY MOTHER IS CONCERNED. THAT'S WHY I'D RATHER GO TO HER THAN HAVE HER SHOW UP AT MY PLACE...
AT LEAST THIS WAY I HAVE SOME CONTROL OVER THE SITUATION...
MEANING YOU CAN LEAVE WHENEVER YOU WANT?
EXACTLY.
IF SHE WANTS TO SEE ME BAD ENOUGH TO USE JILL TO GET TO ME... WELL, THEN SHE **WILL** SEE ME ONE WAY OR ANOTHER... SHE'S DETERMINED THAT WAY...
SO THIS MIGHT AS WELL BE ON **MY** TERMS.

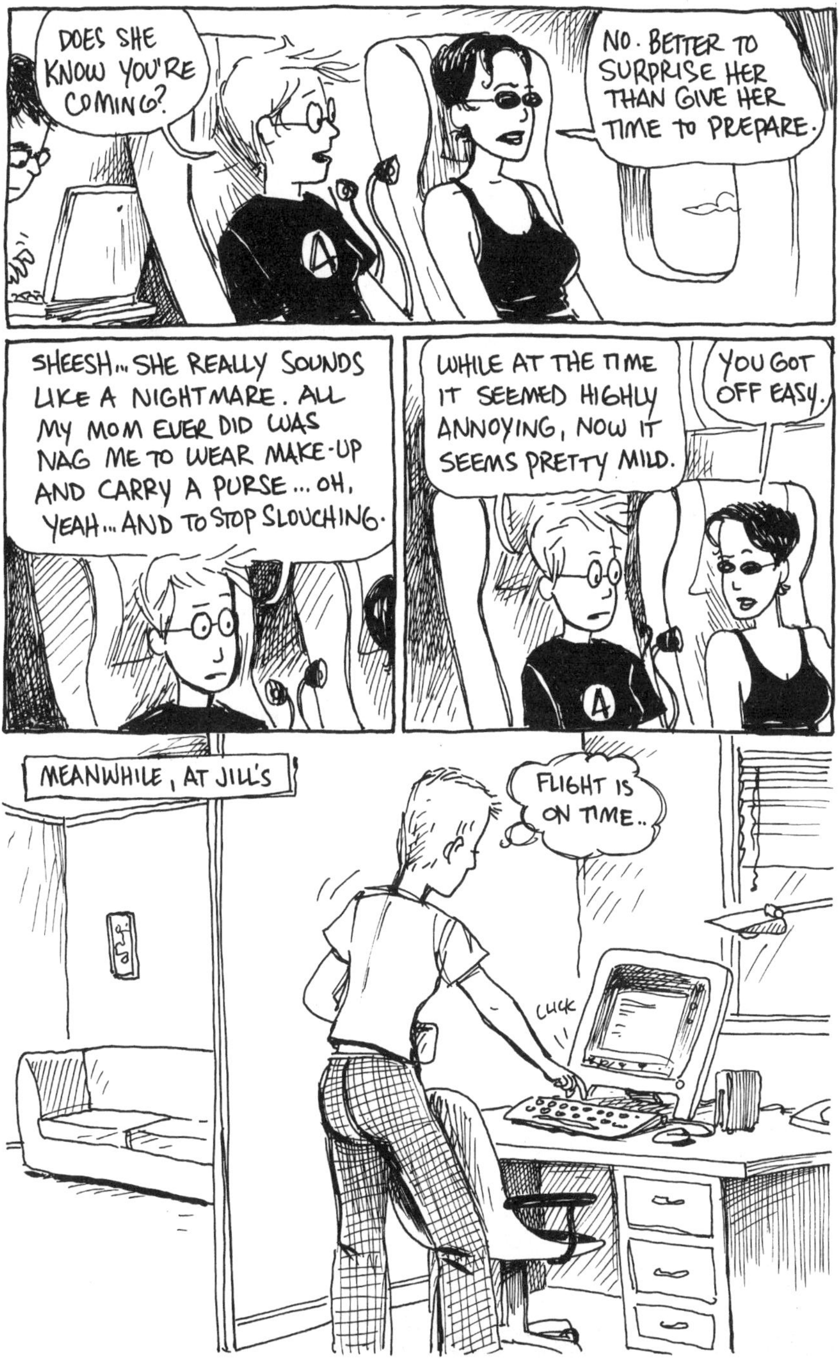
DOES SHE KNOW YOU'RE COMING?
NO. BETTER TO SURPRISE HER THAN GIVE HER TIME TO PREPARE.
SHEESH... SHE REALLY SOUNDS LIKE A NIGHTMARE. ALL MY MOM EVER DID WAS NAG ME TO WEAR MAKE-UP AND CARRY A PURSE... OH, YEAH... AND TO STOP SLOUCHING.
WHILE AT THE TIME IT SEEMED HIGHLY ANNOYING, NOW IT SEEMS PRETTY MILD.
YOU GOT OFF EASY.
MEANWHILE, AT JILL'S
FLIGHT IS ON TIME..
CLICK

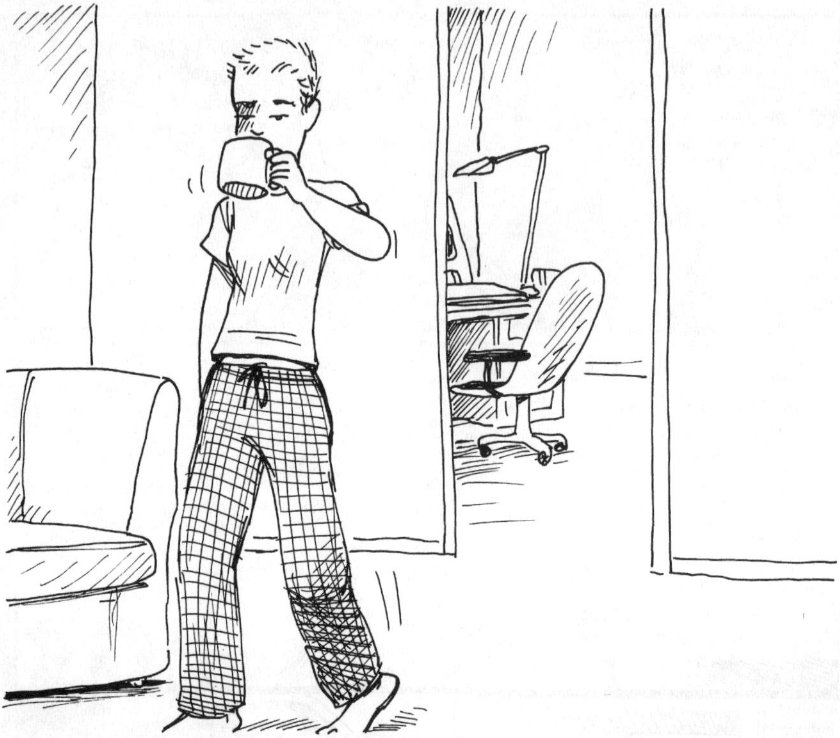

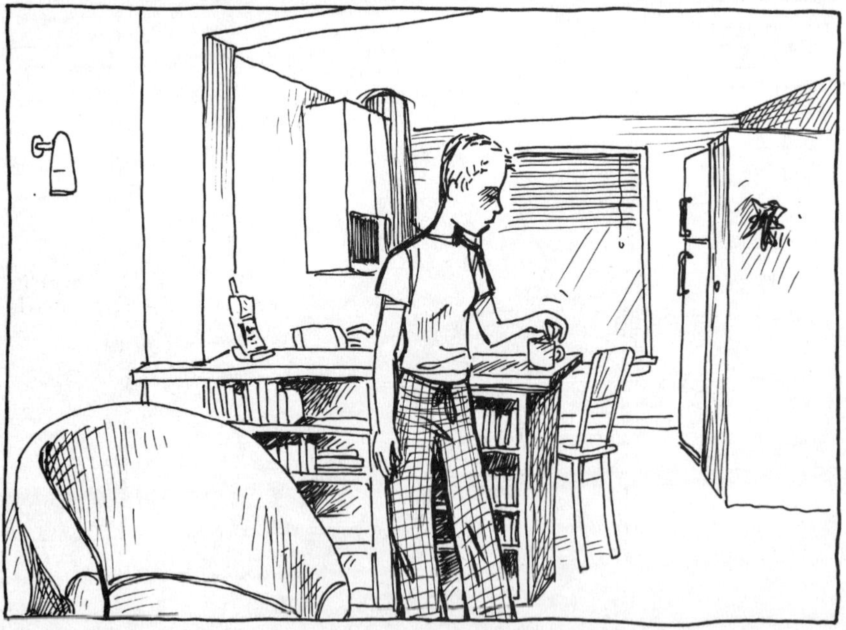

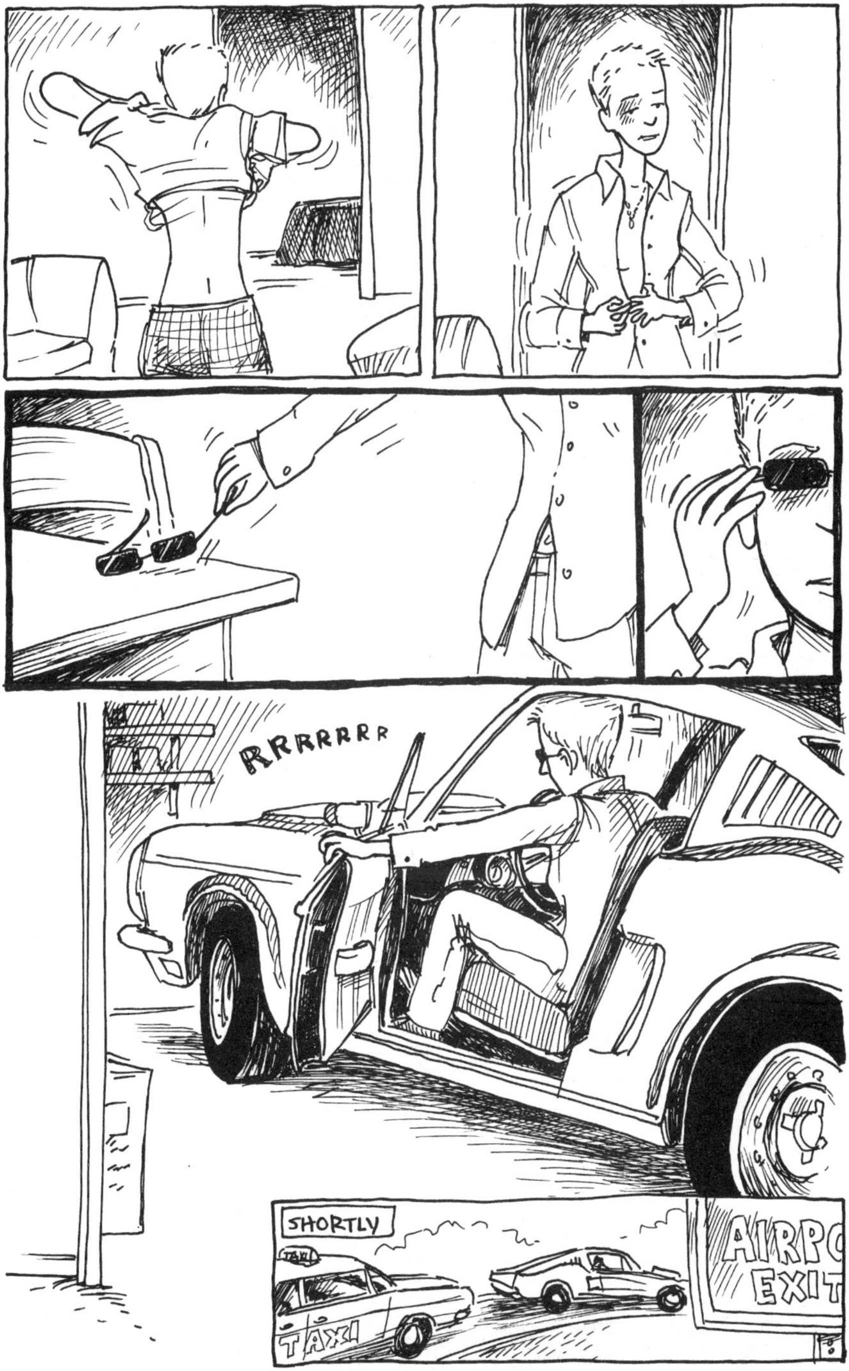
RRRRRRRR
SHORTLY
TAXI
TAXI
AIRPO
EXIT

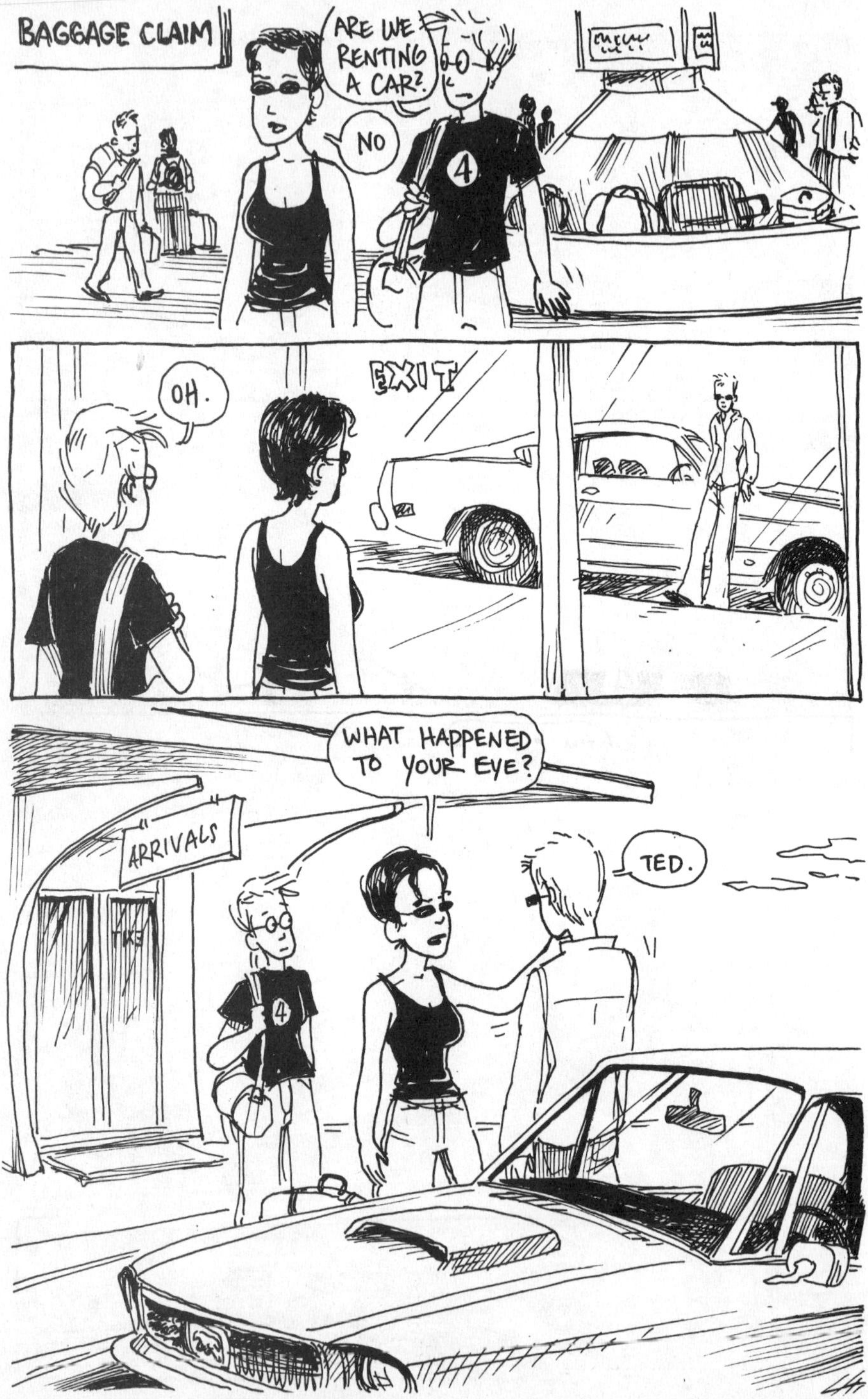
BAGGAGE CLAIM
ARE WE RENTING A CAR?
NO
OH.
EXIT
WHAT HAPPENED TO YOUR EYE?
ARRIVALS
TED.

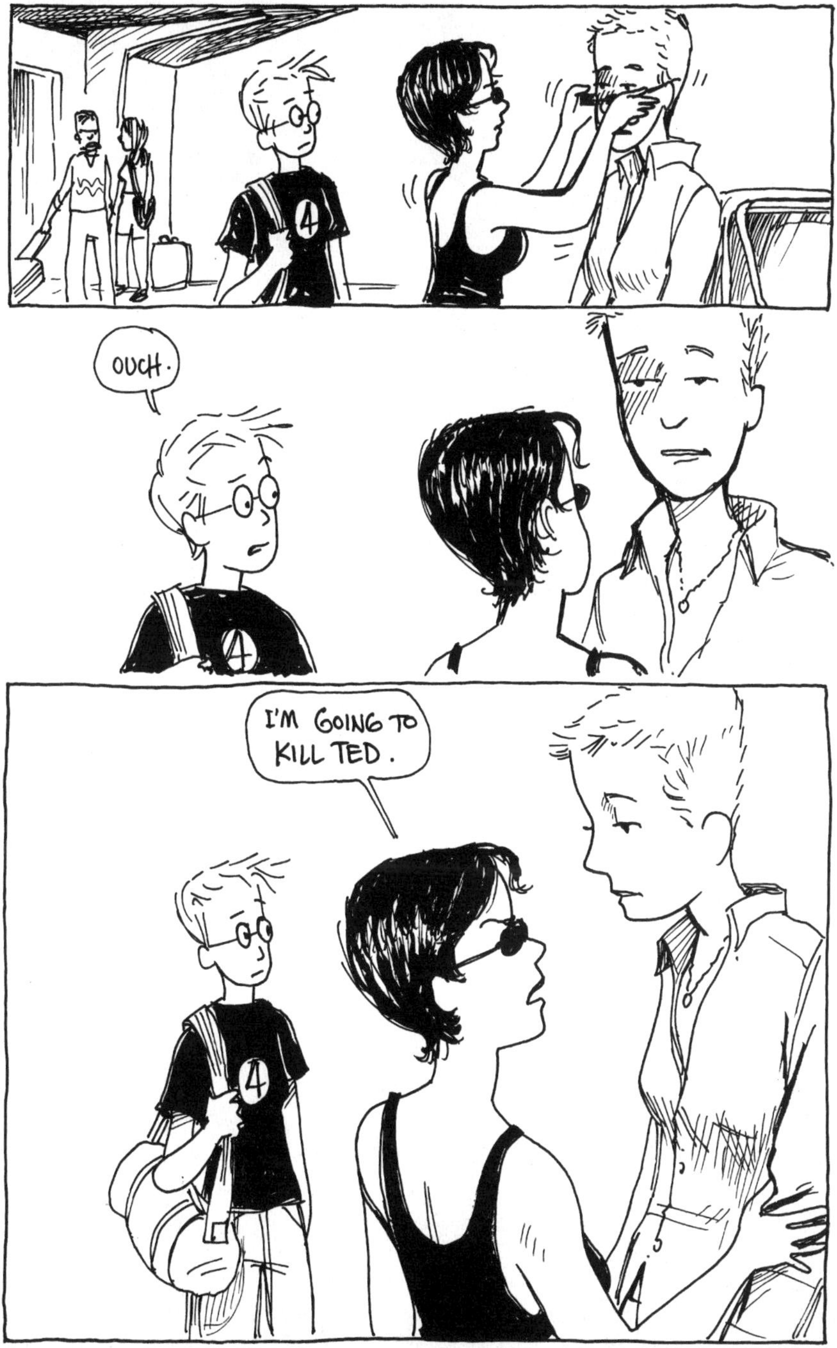
OUCH.
I'M GOING TO KILL TED.

Chapter Three

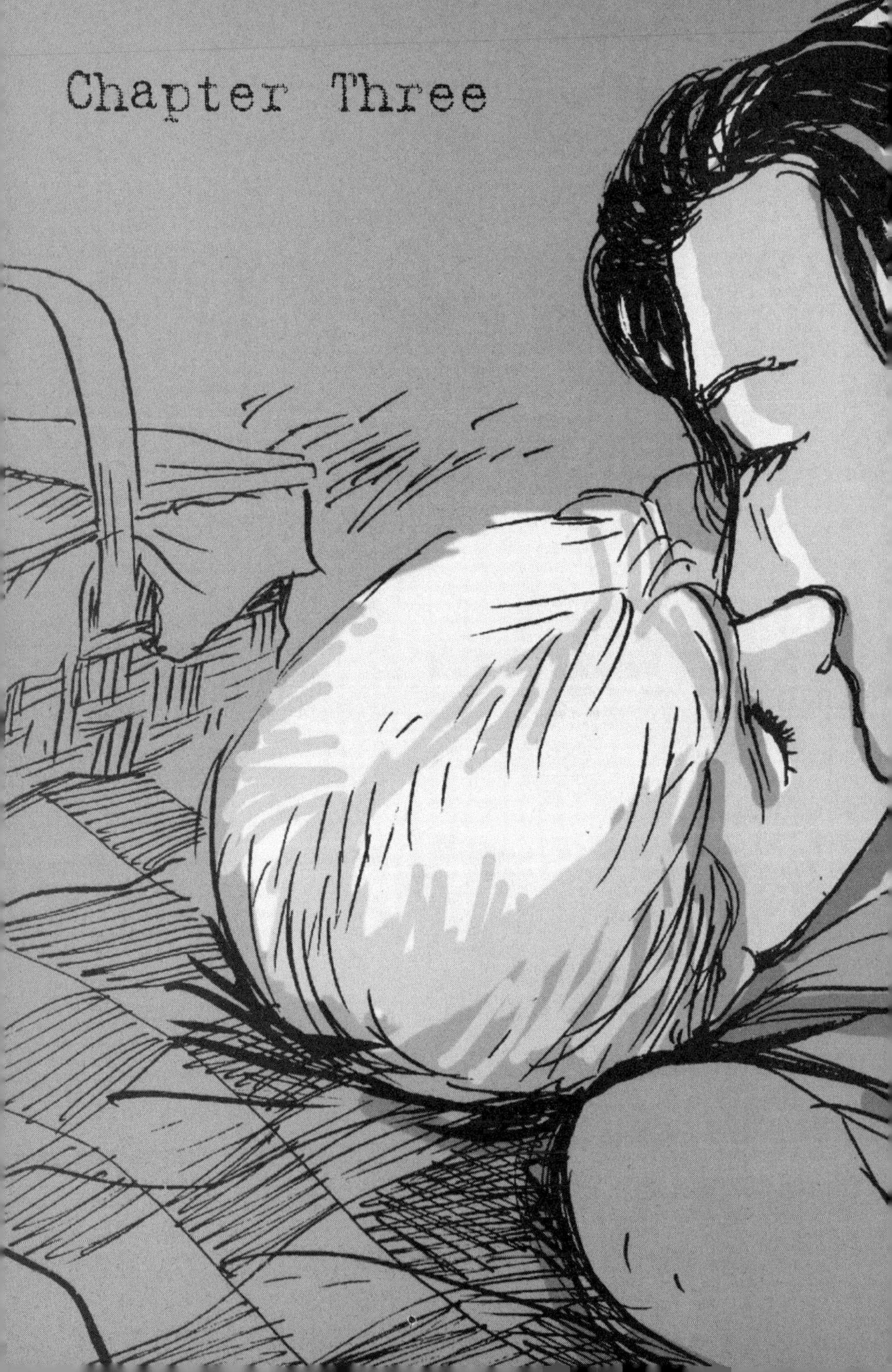

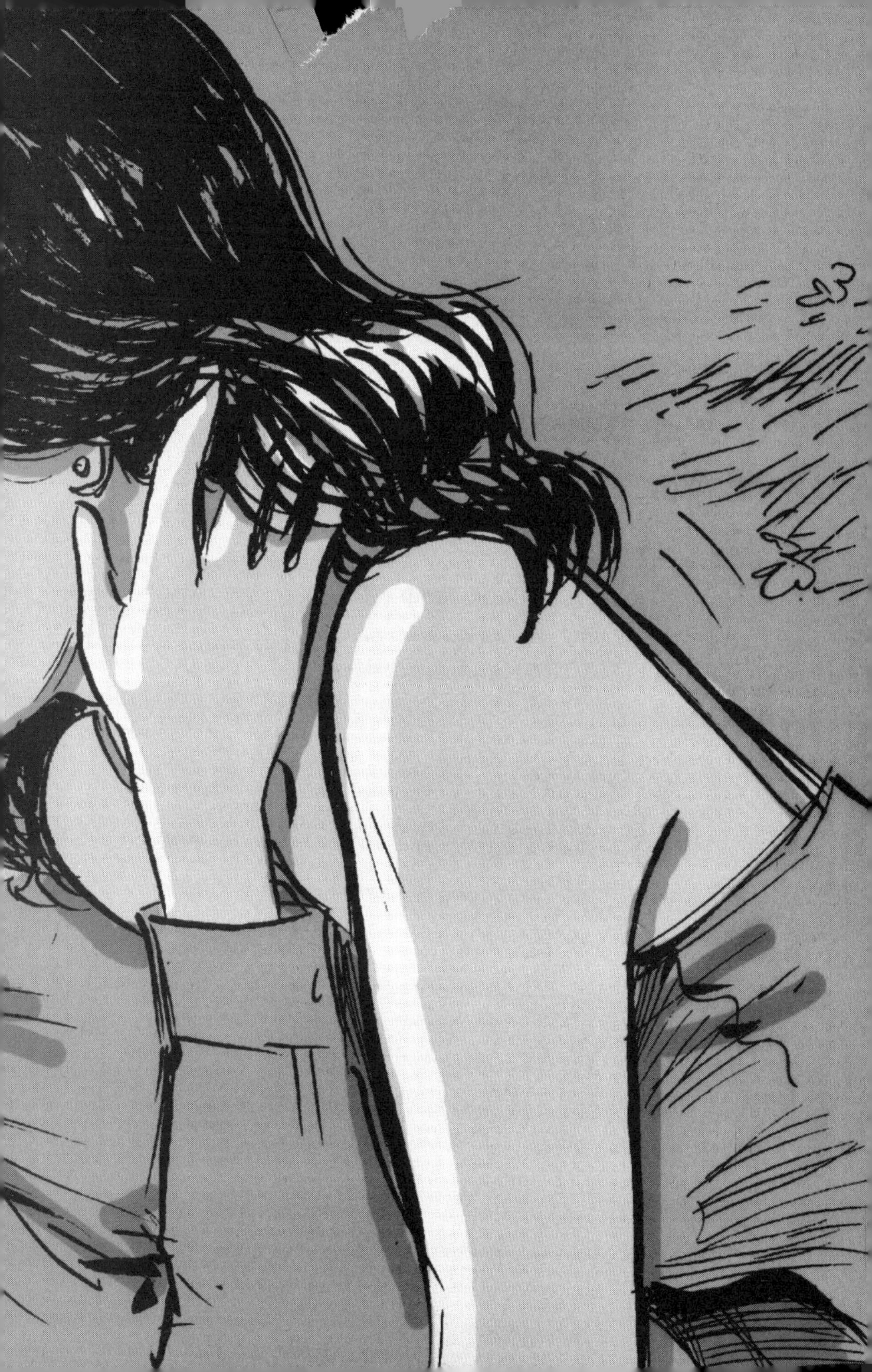

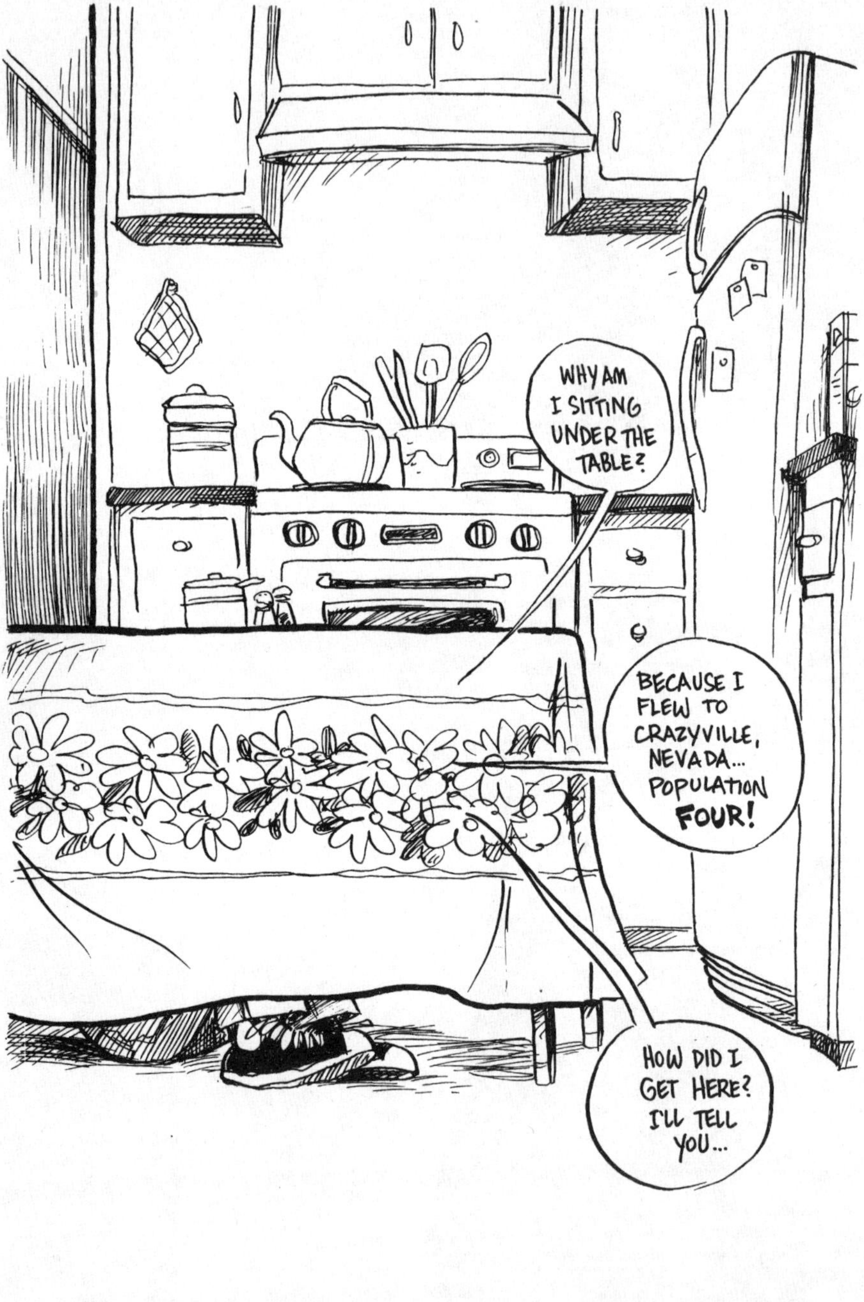
WHY AM I SITTING UNDER THE TABLE?
BECAUSE I FLEW TO CRAZYVILLE, NEVADA... POPULATION FOUR!
HOW DID I GET HERE? I'LL TELL YOU...

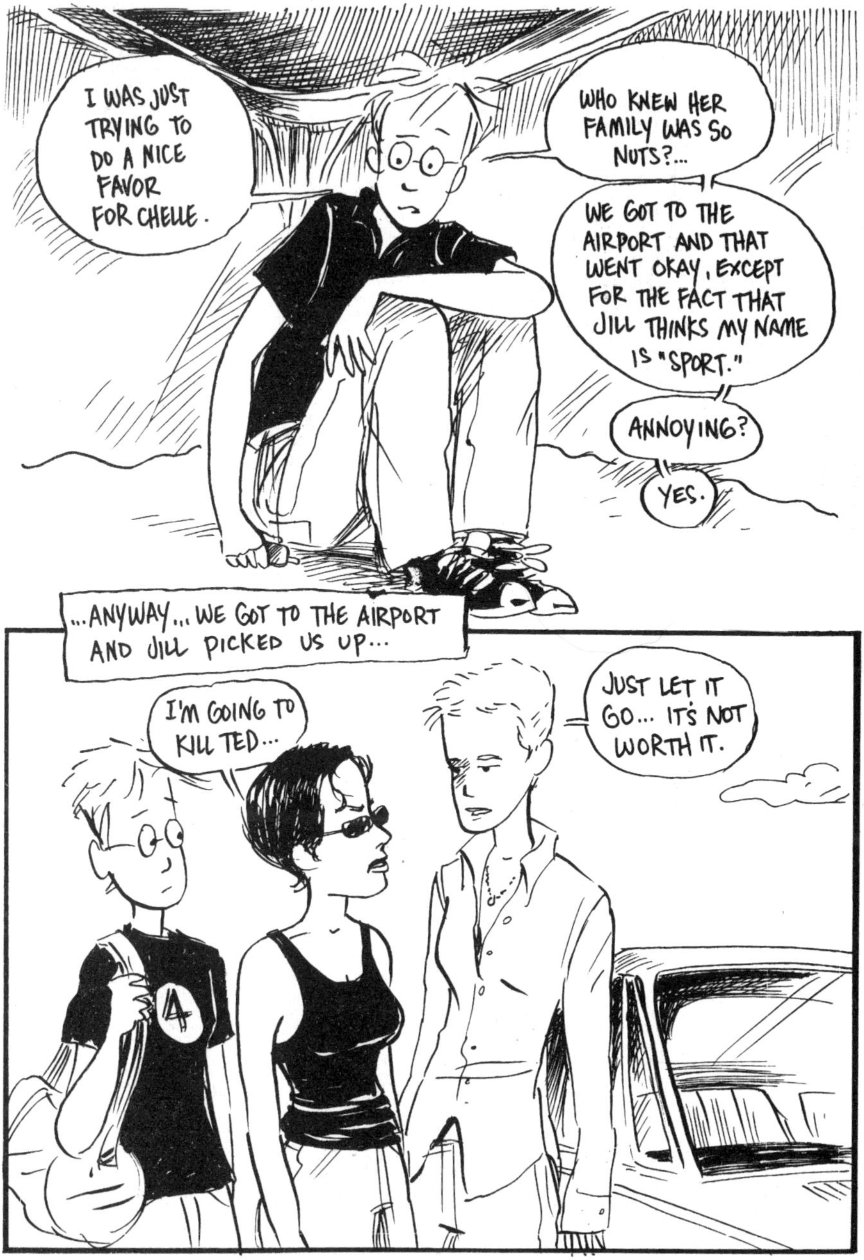
I WAS JUST TRYING TO DO A NICE FAVOR FOR CHELLE.
WHO KNEW HER FAMILY WAS SO NUTS?...
WE GOT TO THE AIRPORT AND THAT WENT OKAY, EXCEPT FOR THE FACT THAT JILL THINKS MY NAME IS "SPORT."
ANNOYING?
YES.
...ANYWAY... WE GOT TO THE AIRPORT AND JILL PICKED US UP...
I'M GOING TO KILL TED...
JUST LET IT GO... IT'S NOT WORTH IT.

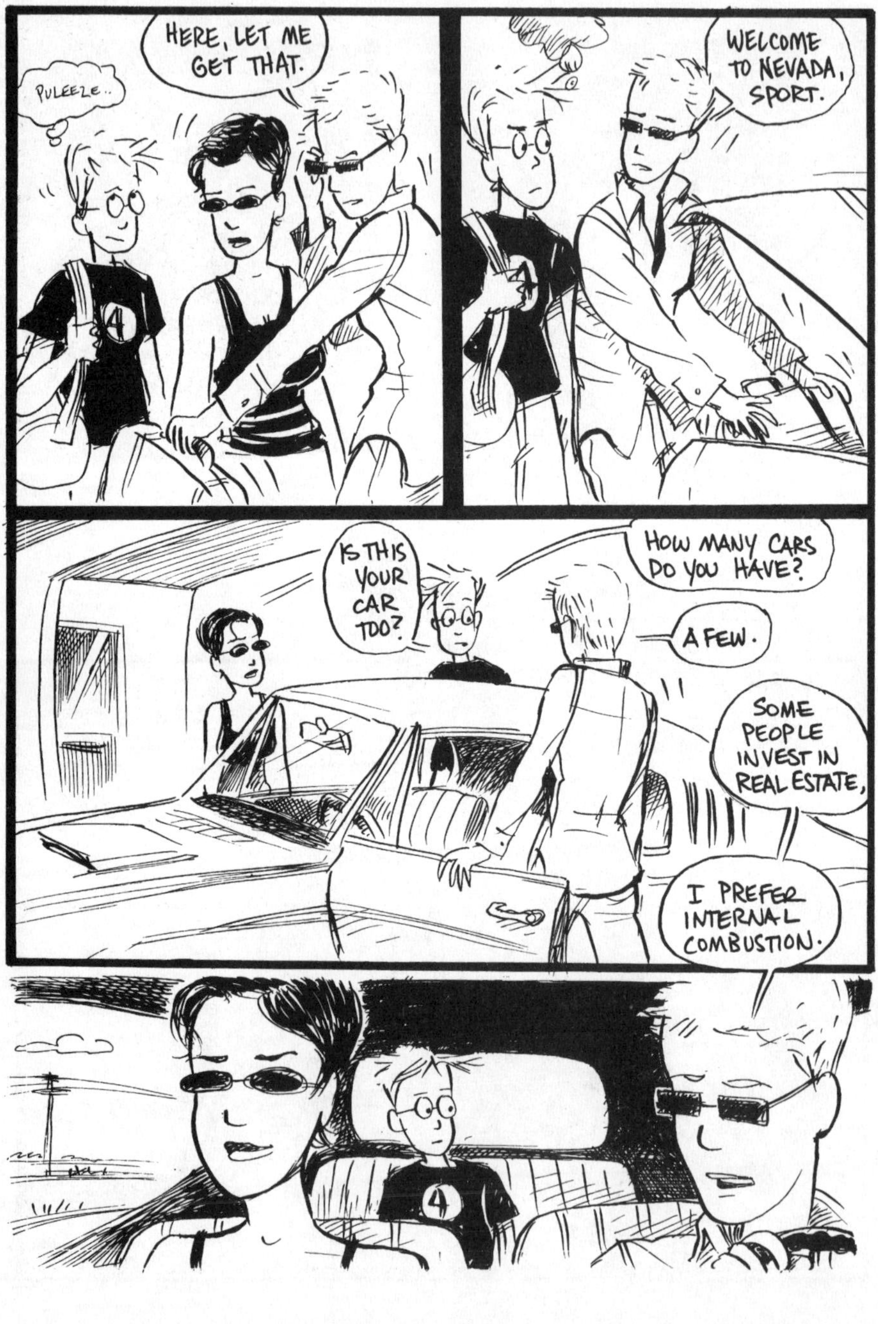
PULEEZE..
HERE, LET ME GET THAT.
WELCOME TO NEVADA, SPORT.
IS THIS YOUR CAR TOO?
HOW MANY CARS DO YOU HAVE?
A FEW.
SOME PEOPLE INVEST IN REAL ESTATE,
I PREFER INTERNAL COMBUSTION.

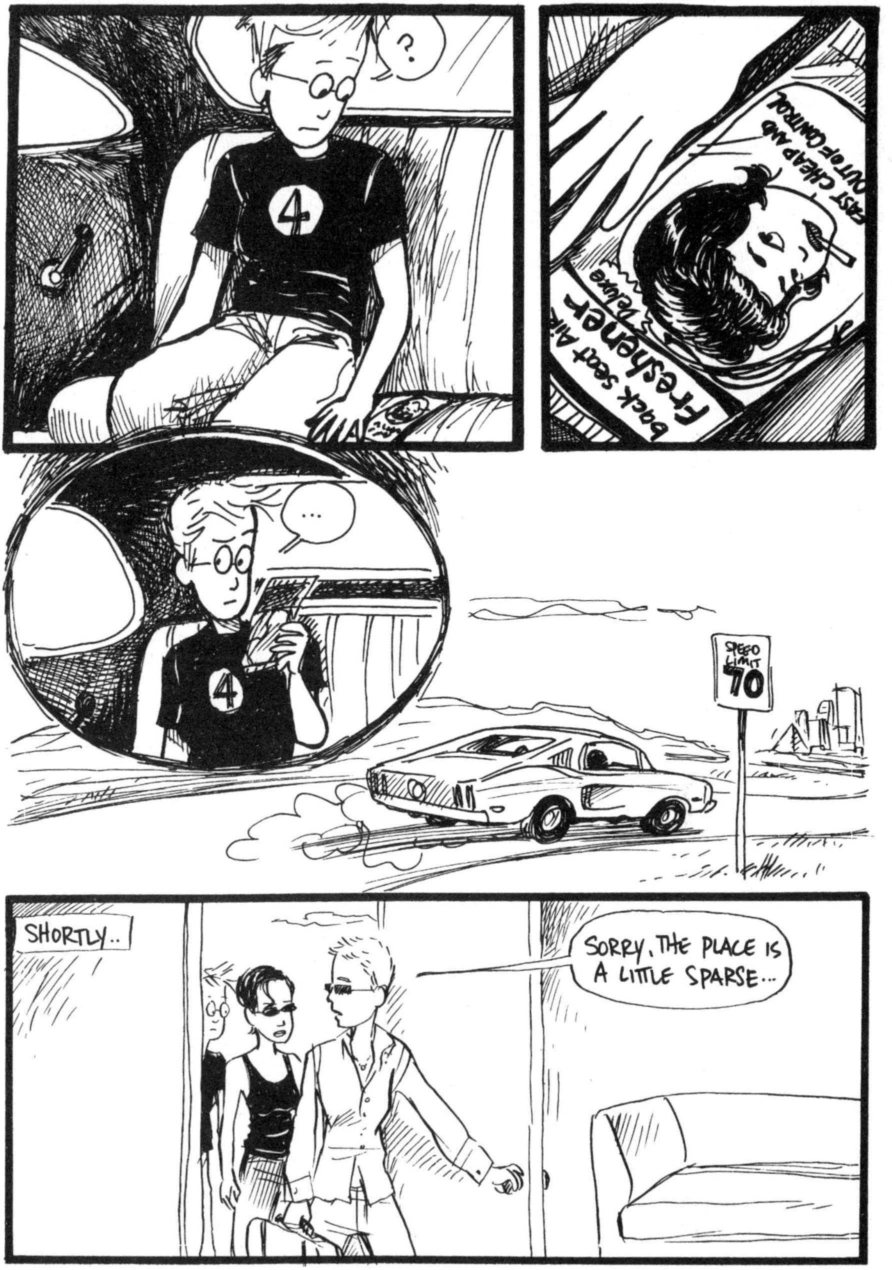
?
back seat
Freshener
Deluxe
FAST CHEAP AND OUT OF CONTROL
...
SPEED LIMIT 70
SHORTLY..
SORRY, THE PLACE IS A LITTLE SPARSE...

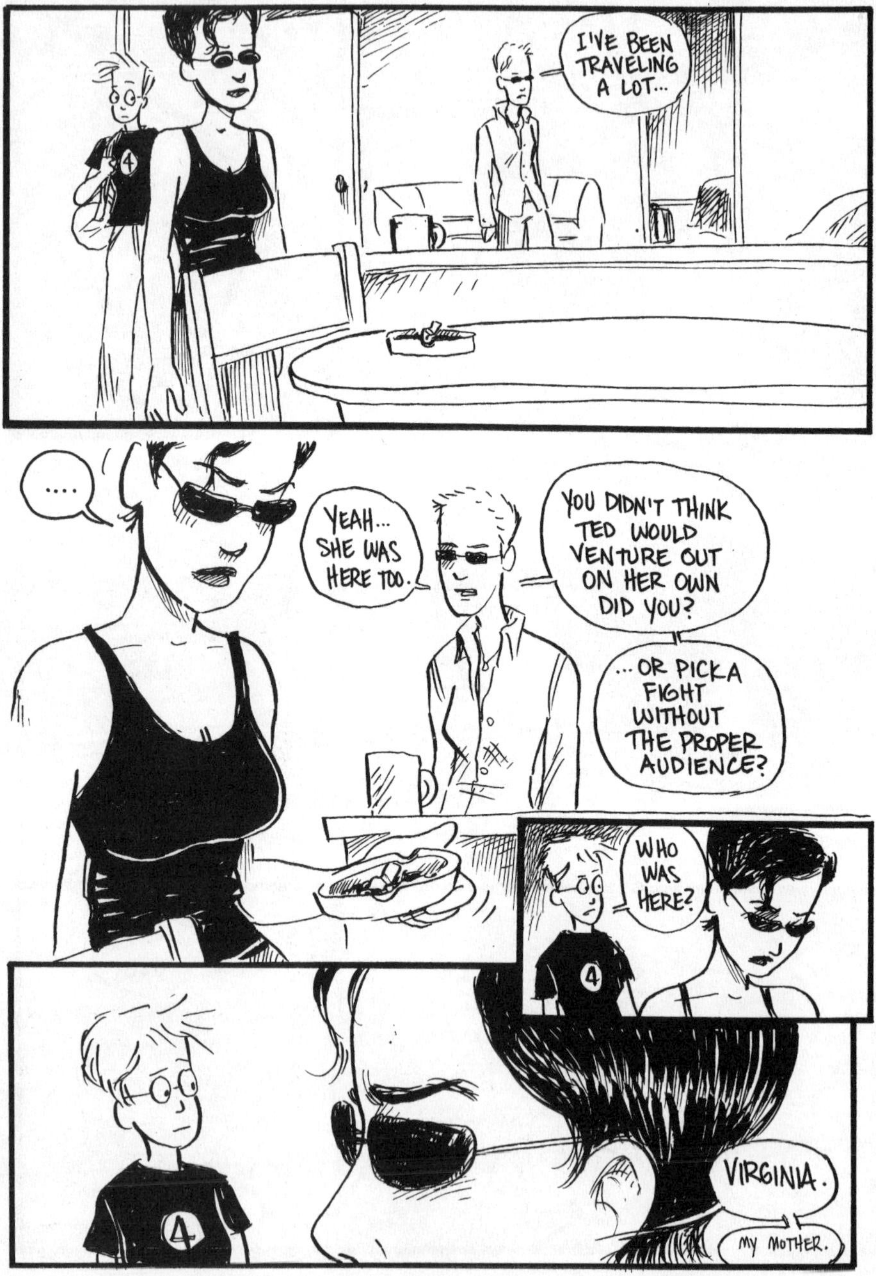
I'VE BEEN TRAVELING A LOT...
....
YEAH... SHE WAS HERE TOO.
YOU DIDN'T THINK TED WOULD VENTURE OUT ON HER OWN DID YOU?
...OR PICK A FIGHT WITHOUT THE PROPER AUDIENCE?
WHO WAS HERE?
VIRGINIA.
MY MOTHER.

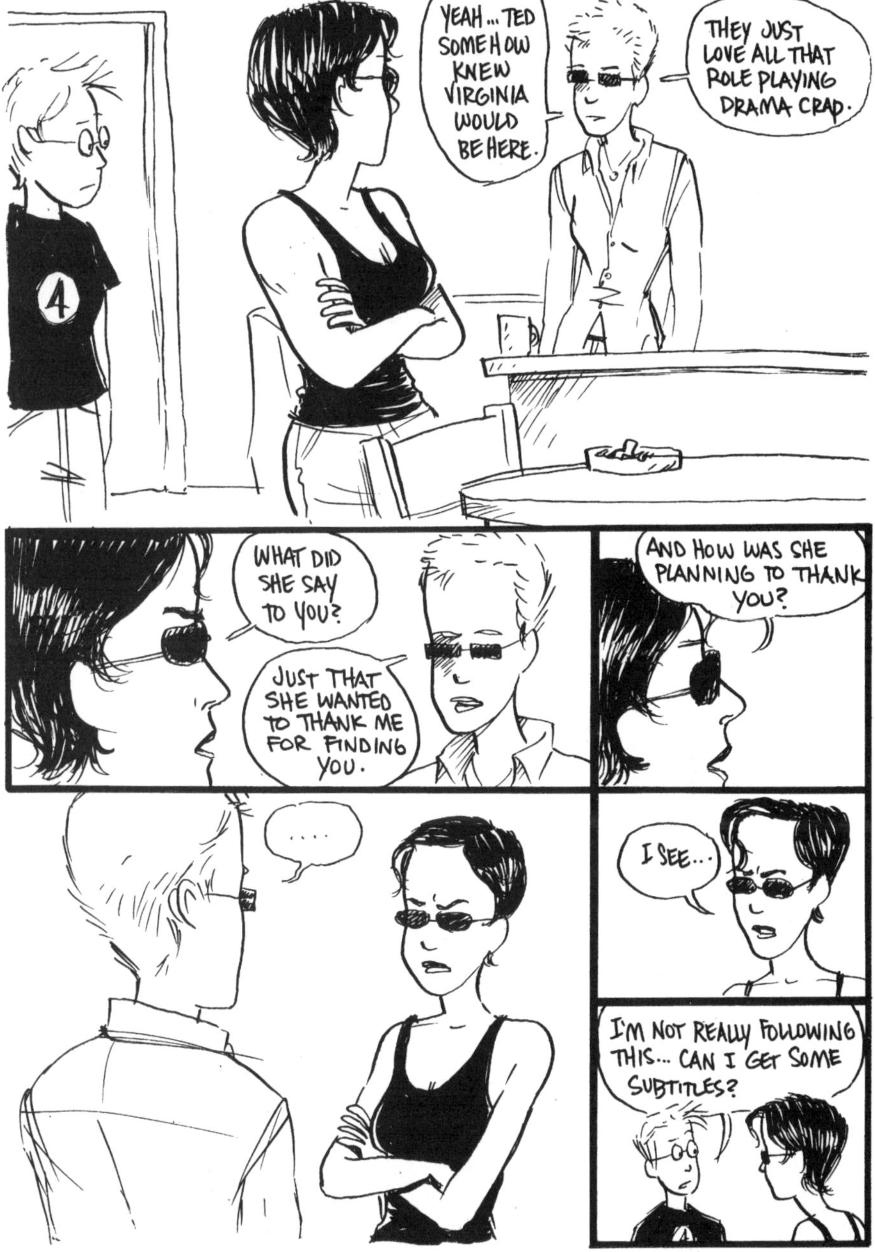
YEAH... TED SOMEHOW KNEW VIRGINIA WOULD BE HERE.
THEY JUST LOVE ALL THAT ROLE PLAYING DRAMA CRAP.
WHAT DID SHE SAY TO YOU?
JUST THAT SHE WANTED TO THANK ME FOR FINDING YOU.
AND HOW WAS SHE PLANNING TO THANK YOU?
....
I SEE...
I'M NOT REALLY FOLLOWING THIS... CAN I GET SOME SUBTITLES?

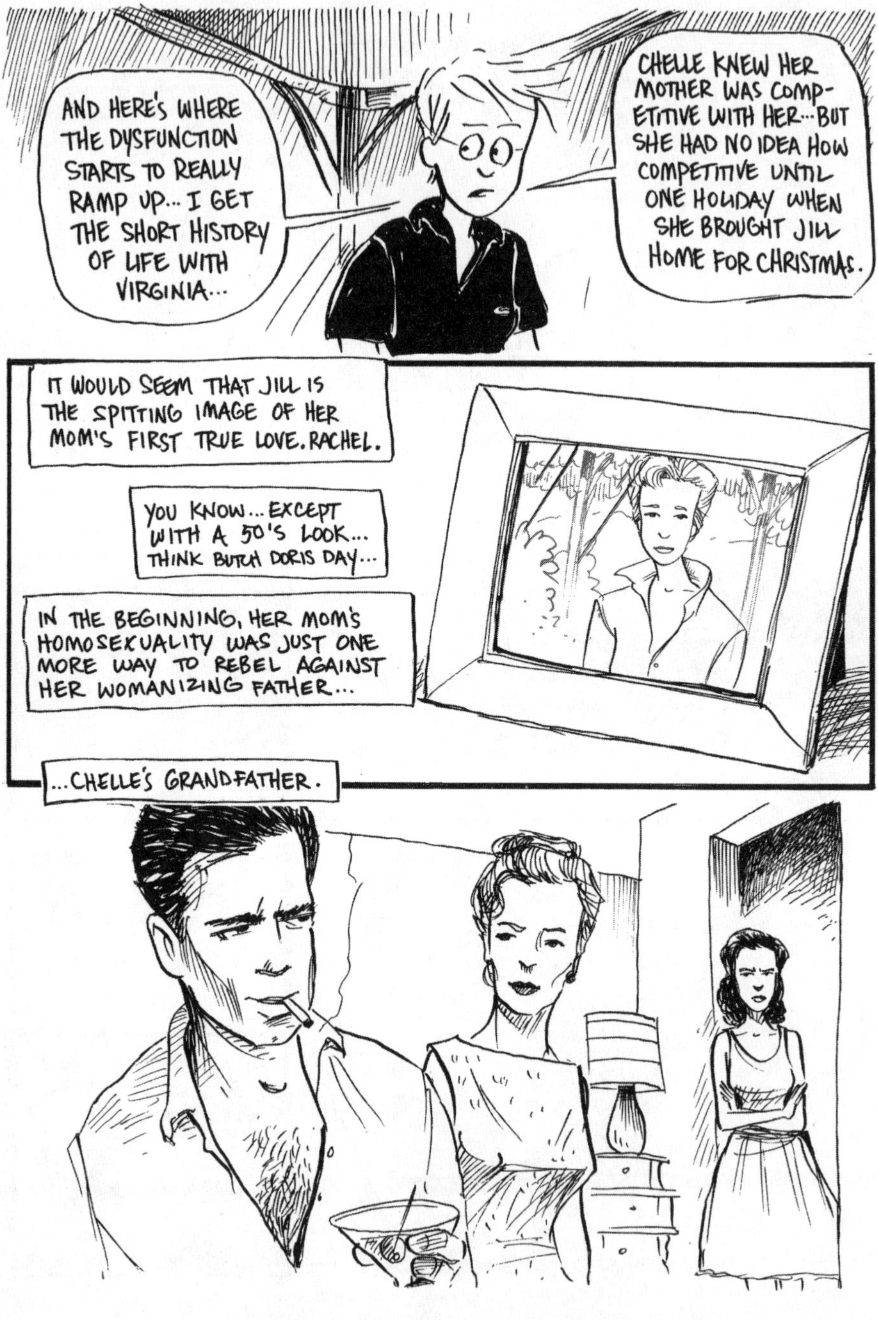
AND HERE'S WHERE THE DYSFUNCTION STARTS TO REALLY RAMP UP... I GET THE SHORT HISTORY OF LIFE WITH VIRGINIA...
CHELLE KNEW HER MOTHER WAS COMPETITIVE WITH HER... BUT SHE HAD NO IDEA HOW COMPETITIVE UNTIL ONE HOLIDAY WHEN SHE BROUGHT JILL HOME FOR CHRISTMAS.
IT WOULD SEEM THAT JILL IS THE SPITTING IMAGE OF HER MOM'S FIRST TRUE LOVE. RACHEL.
YOU KNOW... EXCEPT WITH A 50'S LOOK... THINK BUTCH DORIS DAY...
IN THE BEGINNING, HER MOM'S HOMOSEXUALITY WAS JUST ONE MORE WAY TO REBEL AGAINST HER WOMANIZING FATHER...
...CHELLE'S GRANDFATHER.

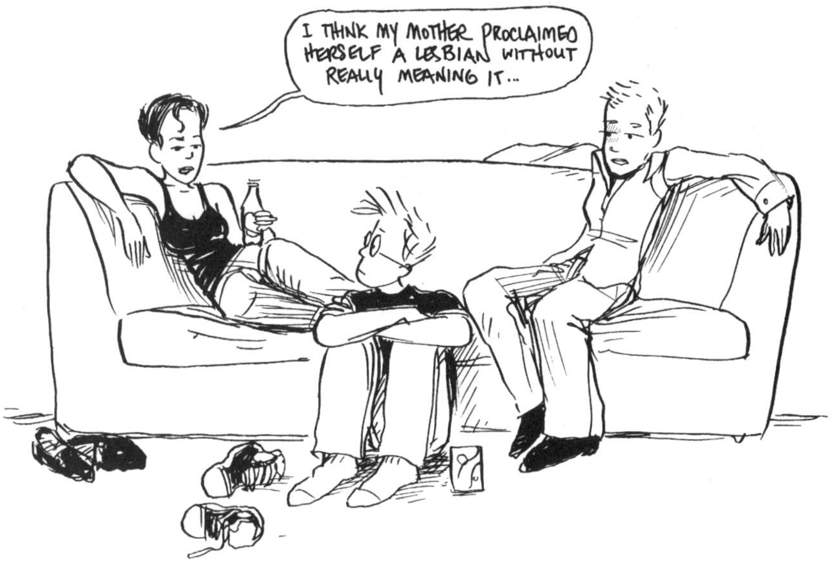
I THINK MY MOTHER PROCLAIMED HERSELF A LESBIAN WITHOUT REALLY MEANING IT...

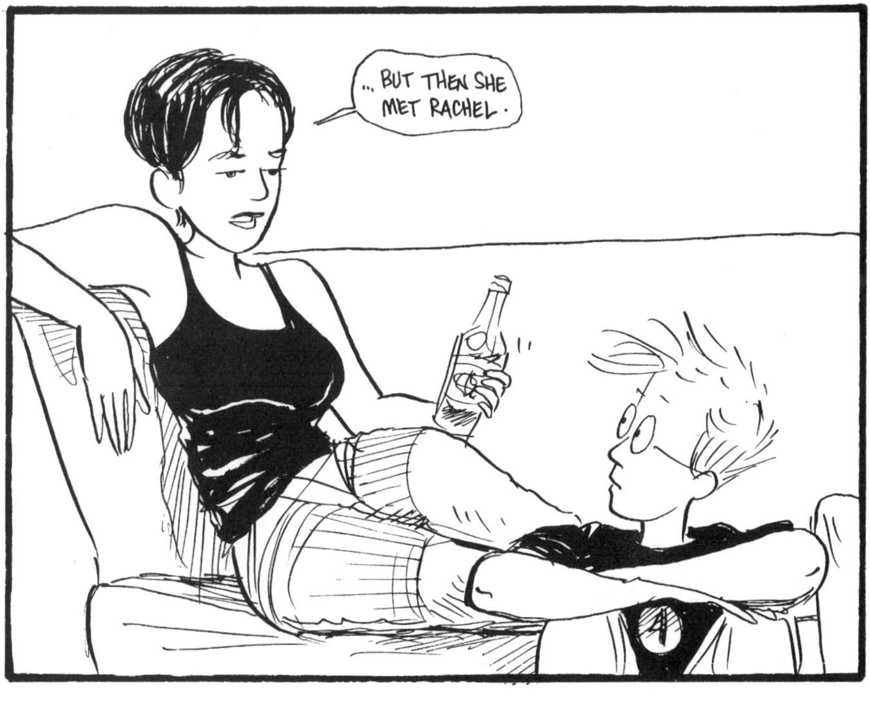
... BUT THEN SHE MET RACHEL.

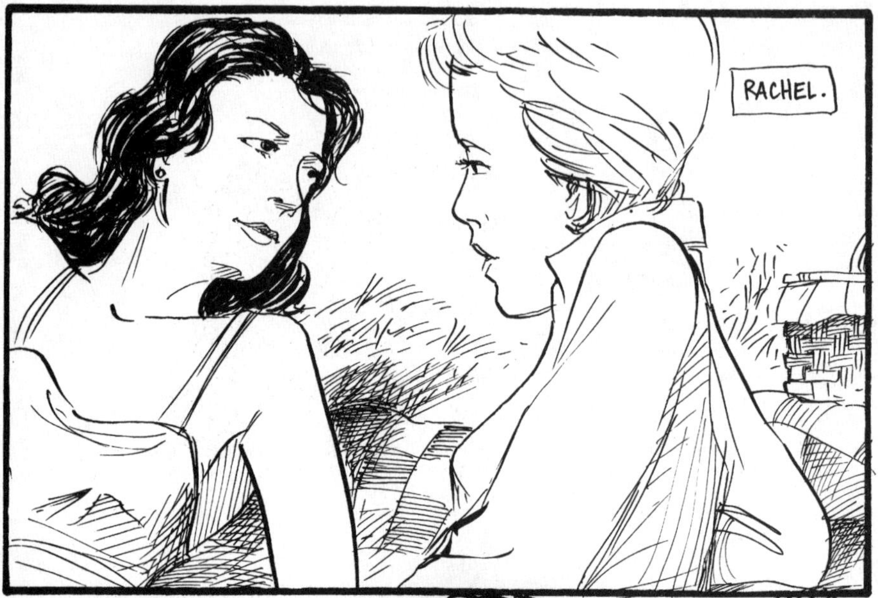
RACHEL.

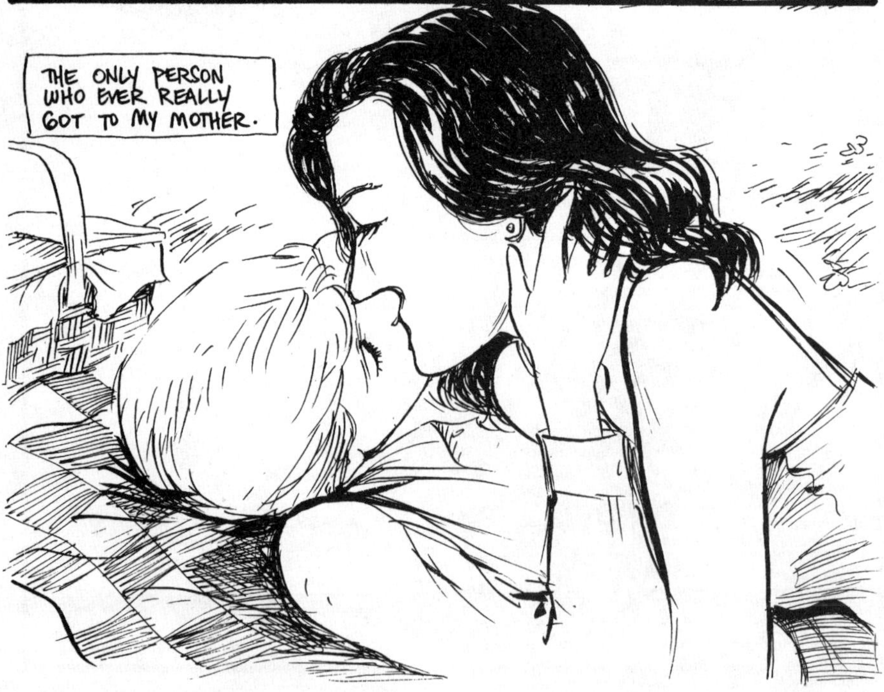
THE ONLY PERSON WHO EVER REALLY GOT TO MY MOTHER.

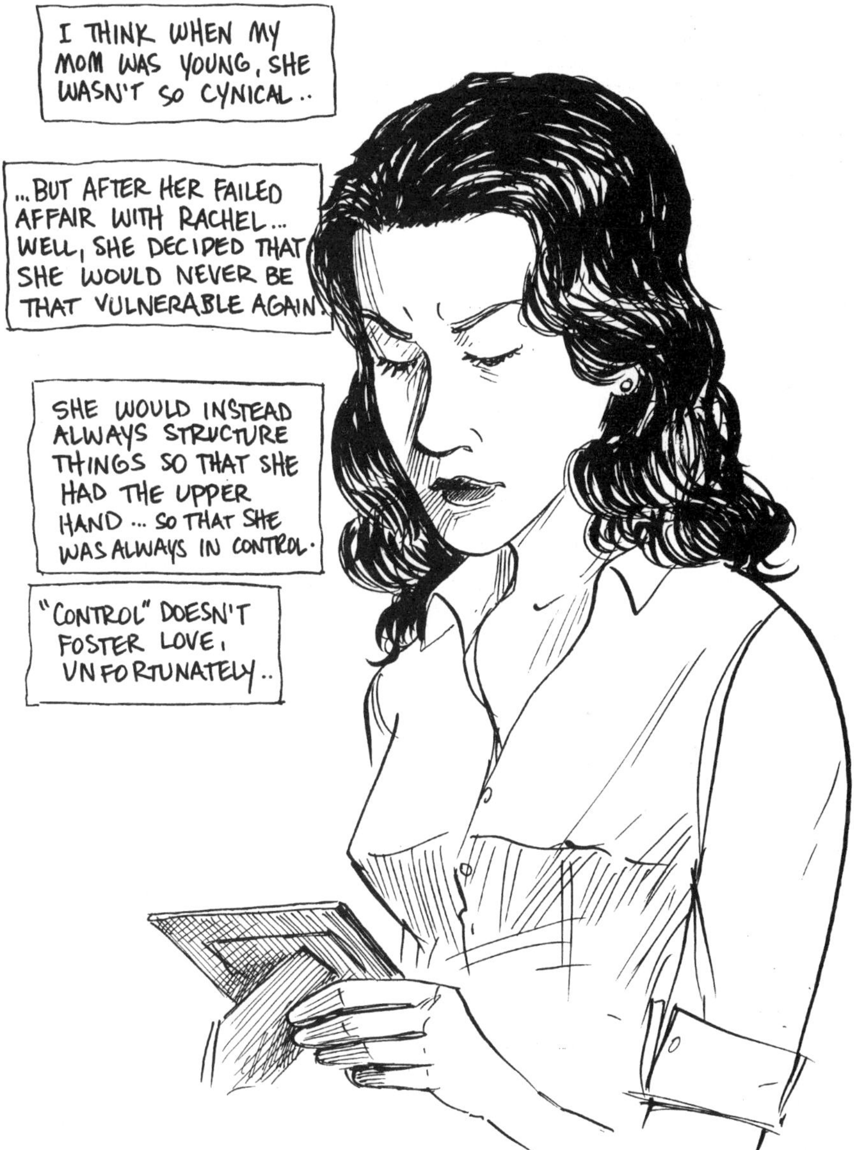
I THINK WHEN MY MOM WAS YOUNG, SHE WASN'T SO CYNICAL..
...BUT AFTER HER FAILED AFFAIR WITH RACHEL... WELL, SHE DECIDED THAT SHE WOULD NEVER BE THAT VULNERABLE AGAIN.
SHE WOULD INSTEAD ALWAYS STRUCTURE THINGS SO THAT SHE HAD THE UPPER HAND ... SO THAT SHE WAS ALWAYS IN CONTROL.
"CONTROL" DOESN'T FOSTER LOVE, UNFORTUNATELY..

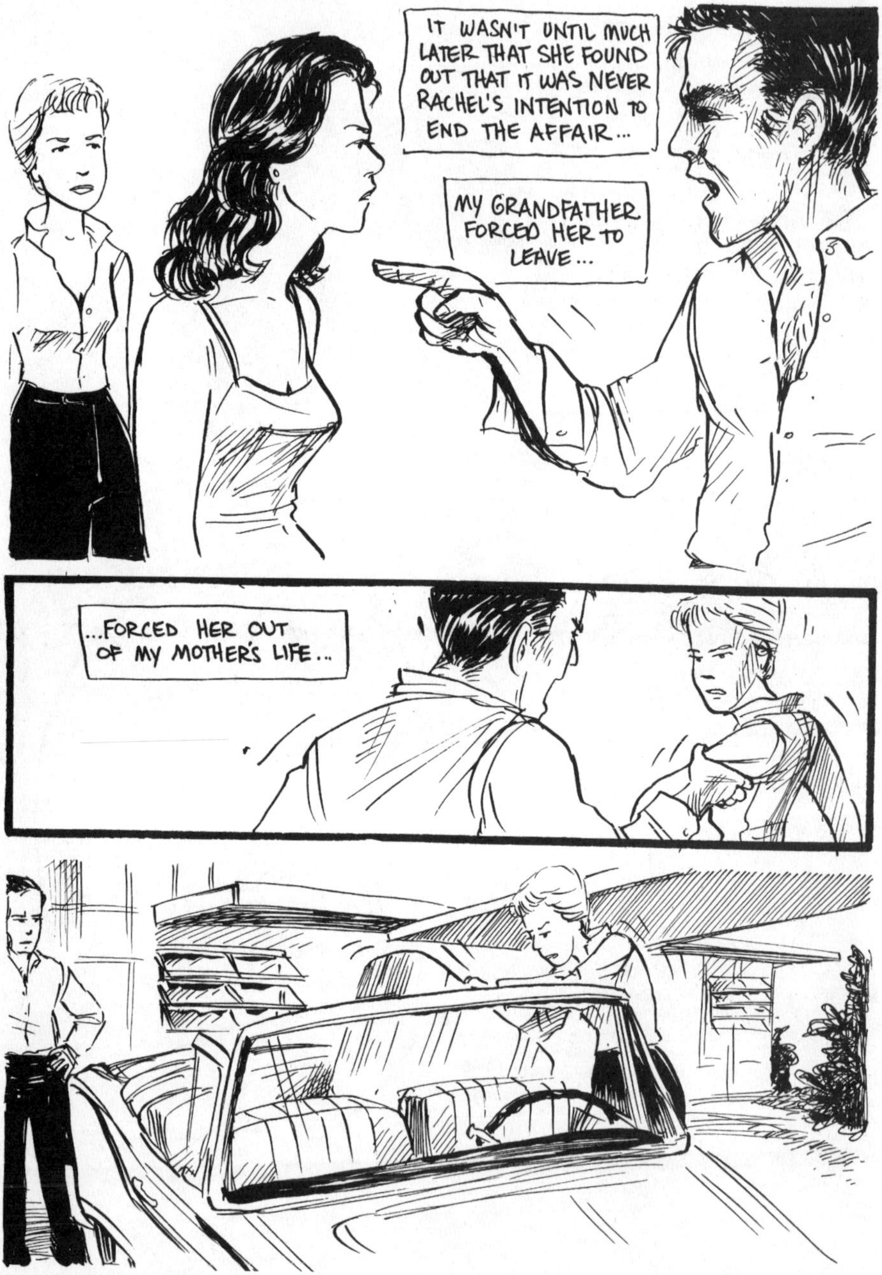
IT WASN'T UNTIL MUCH LATER THAT SHE FOUND OUT THAT IT WAS NEVER RACHEL'S INTENTION TO END THE AFFAIR...
MY GRANDFATHER FORCED HER TO LEAVE...
...FORCED HER OUT OF MY MOTHER'S LIFE...

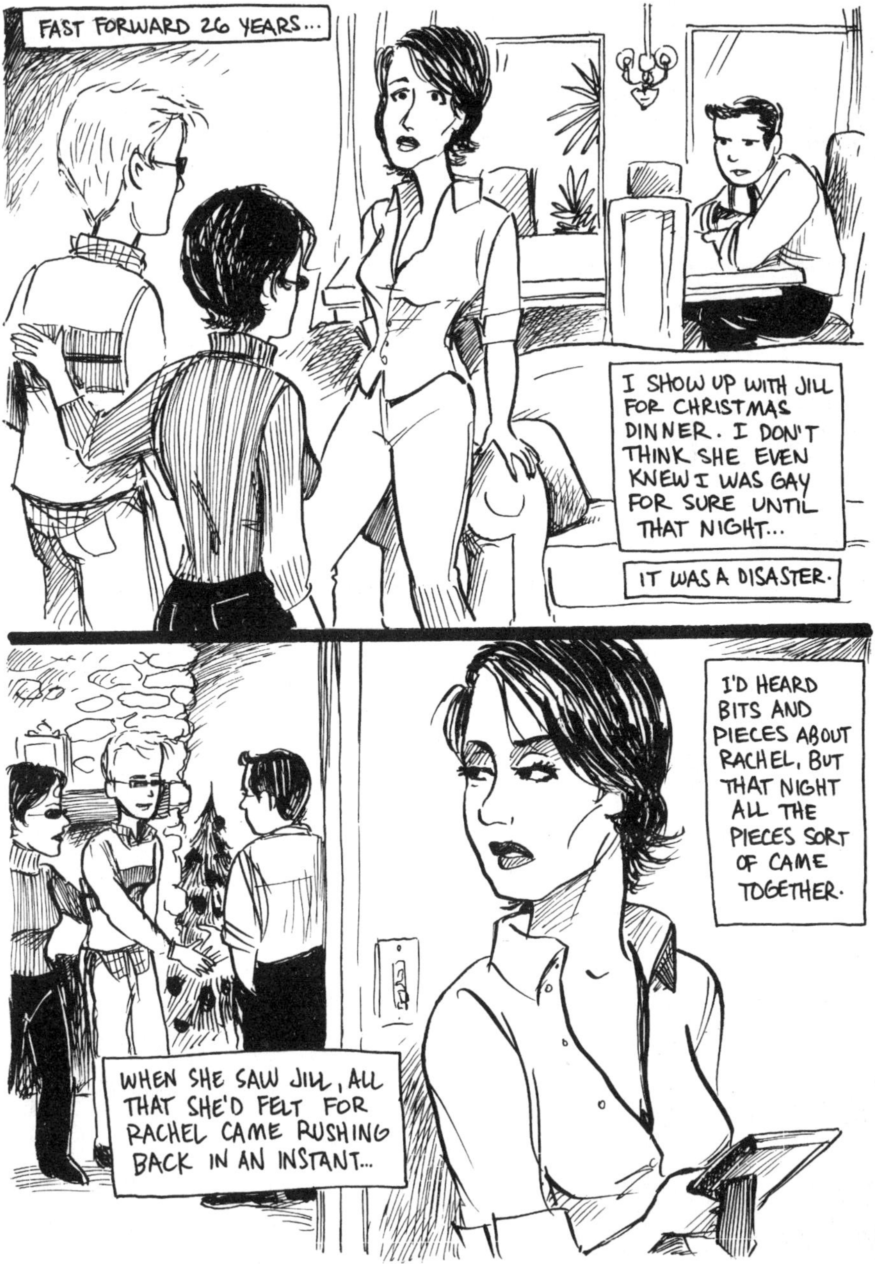
FAST FORWARD 26 YEARS...
I SHOW UP WITH JILL FOR CHRISTMAS DINNER. I DON'T THINK SHE EVEN KNEW I WAS GAY FOR SURE UNTIL THAT NIGHT...
IT WAS A DISASTER.
I'D HEARD BITS AND PIECES ABOUT RACHEL, BUT THAT NIGHT ALL THE PIECES SORT OF CAME TOGETHER.
WHEN SHE SAW JILL, ALL THAT SHE'D FELT FOR RACHEL CAME RUSHING BACK IN AN INSTANT...

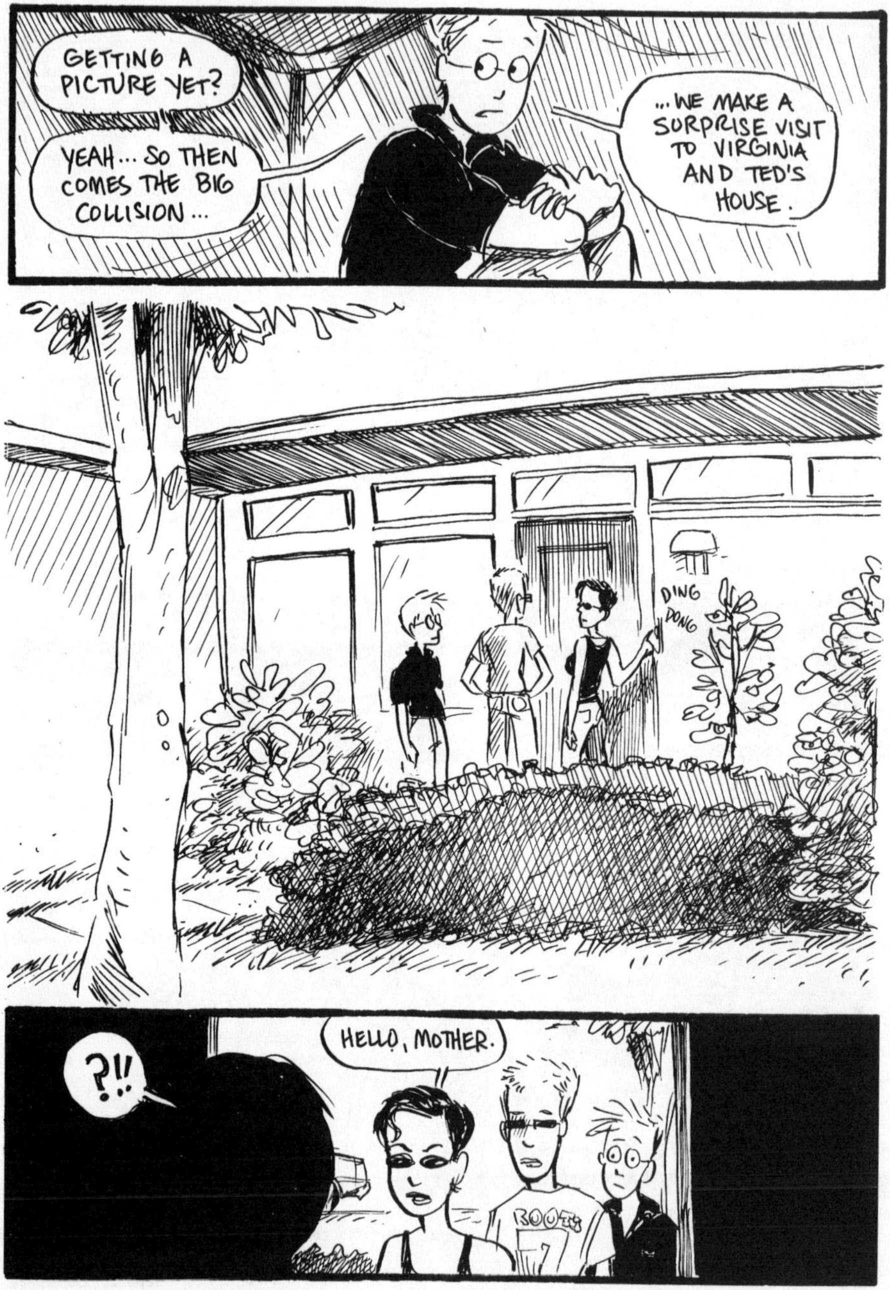
GETTING A PICTURE YET?
YEAH... SO THEN COMES THE BIG COLLISION...
...WE MAKE A SURPRISE VISIT TO VIRGINIA AND TED'S HOUSE.
DING DONG
?!!
HELLO, MOTHER.

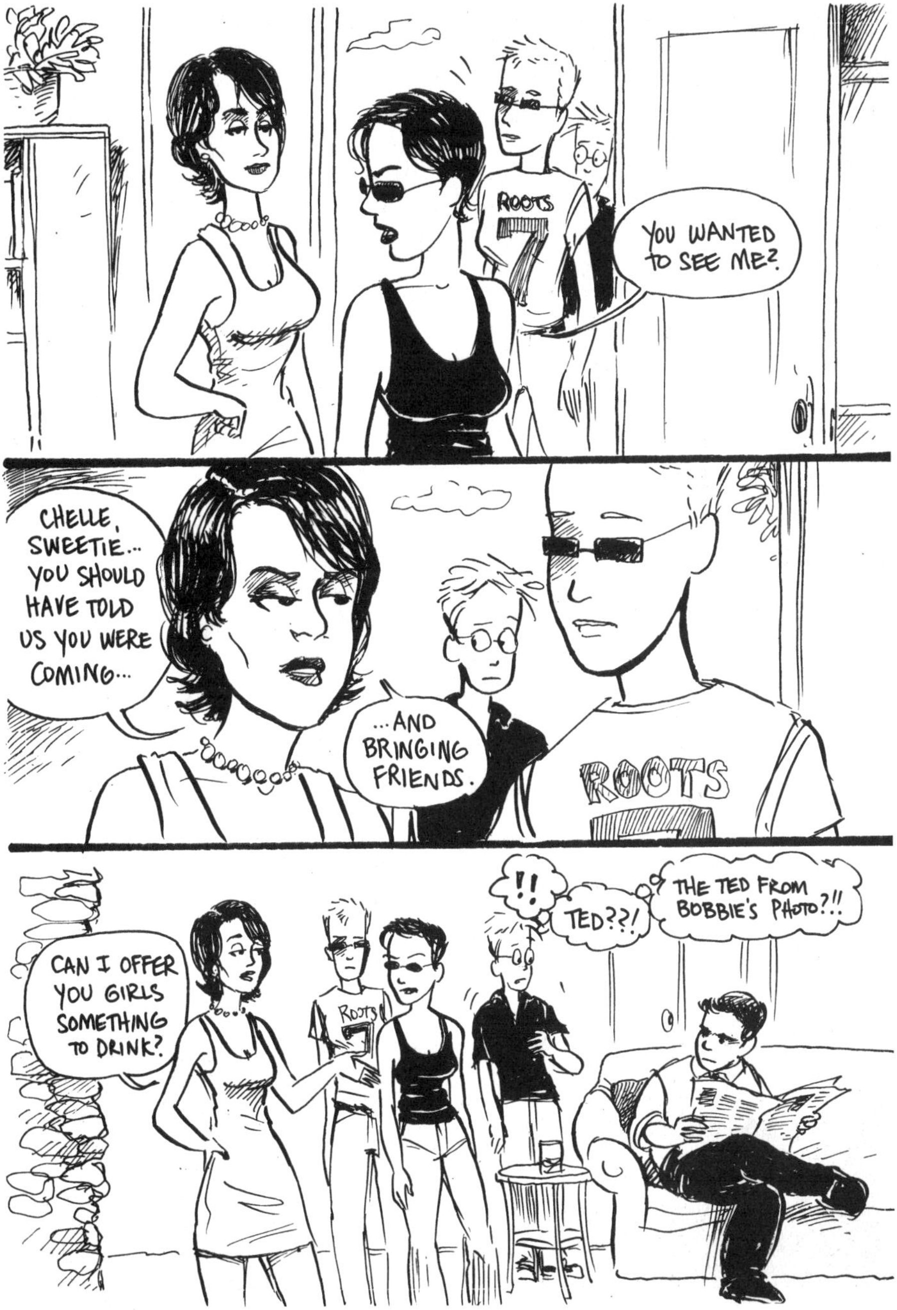
YOU WANTED TO SEE ME?
ROOTS 7
CHELLE, SWEETIE... YOU SHOULD HAVE TOLD US YOU WERE COMING...
...AND BRINGING FRIENDS.
ROOTS
CAN I OFFER YOU GIRLS SOMETHING TO DRINK?
ROOTS 7
!!
TED??!
THE TED FROM BOBBIE'S PHOTO?!!

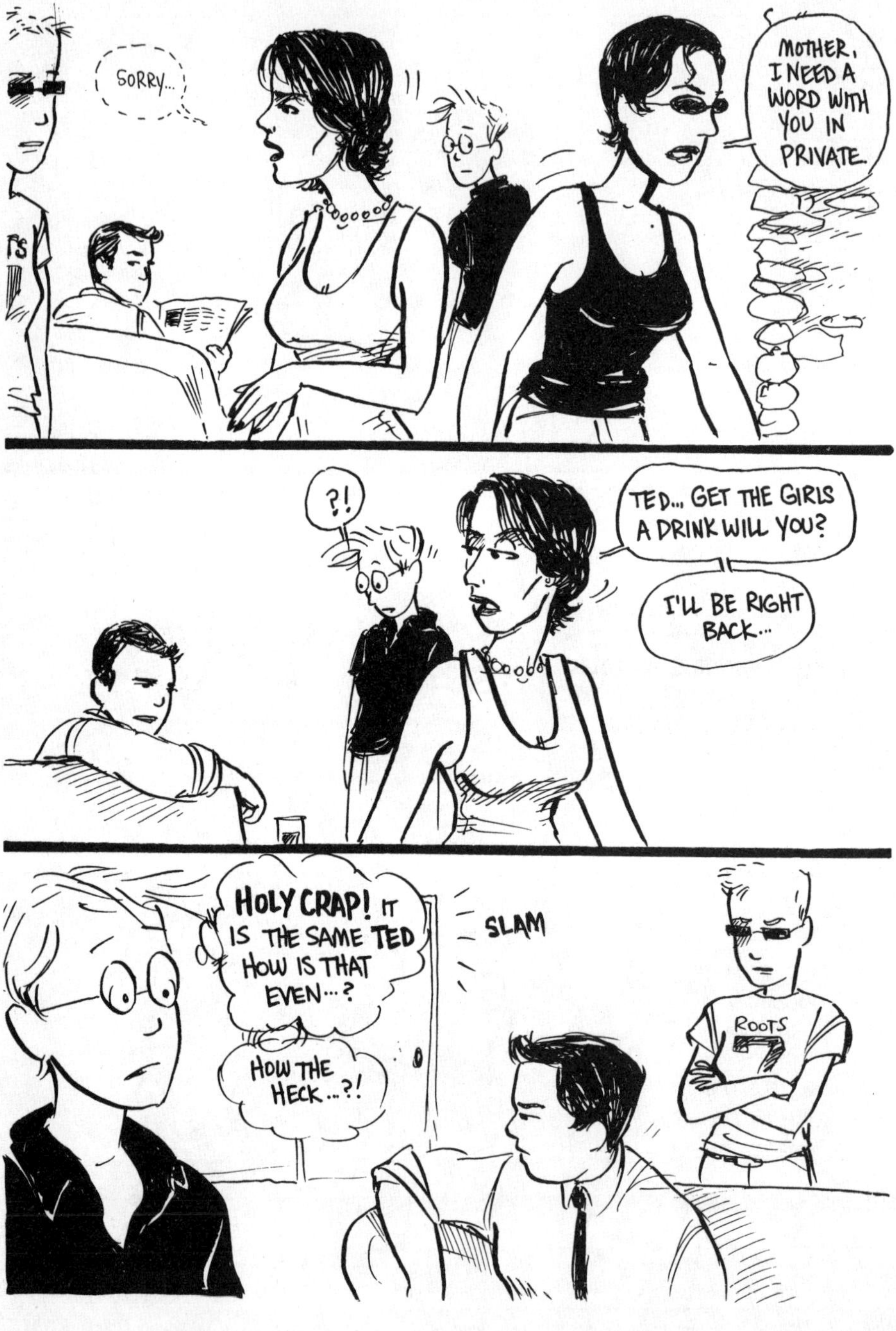
SORRY...
MOTHER, I NEED A WORD WITH YOU IN PRIVATE.
?!
TED... GET THE GIRLS A DRINK WILL YOU?
I'LL BE RIGHT BACK...
HOLY CRAP! IT IS THE SAME TED HOW IS THAT EVEN...?
HOW THE HECK...?!
SLAM
ROOTS
7

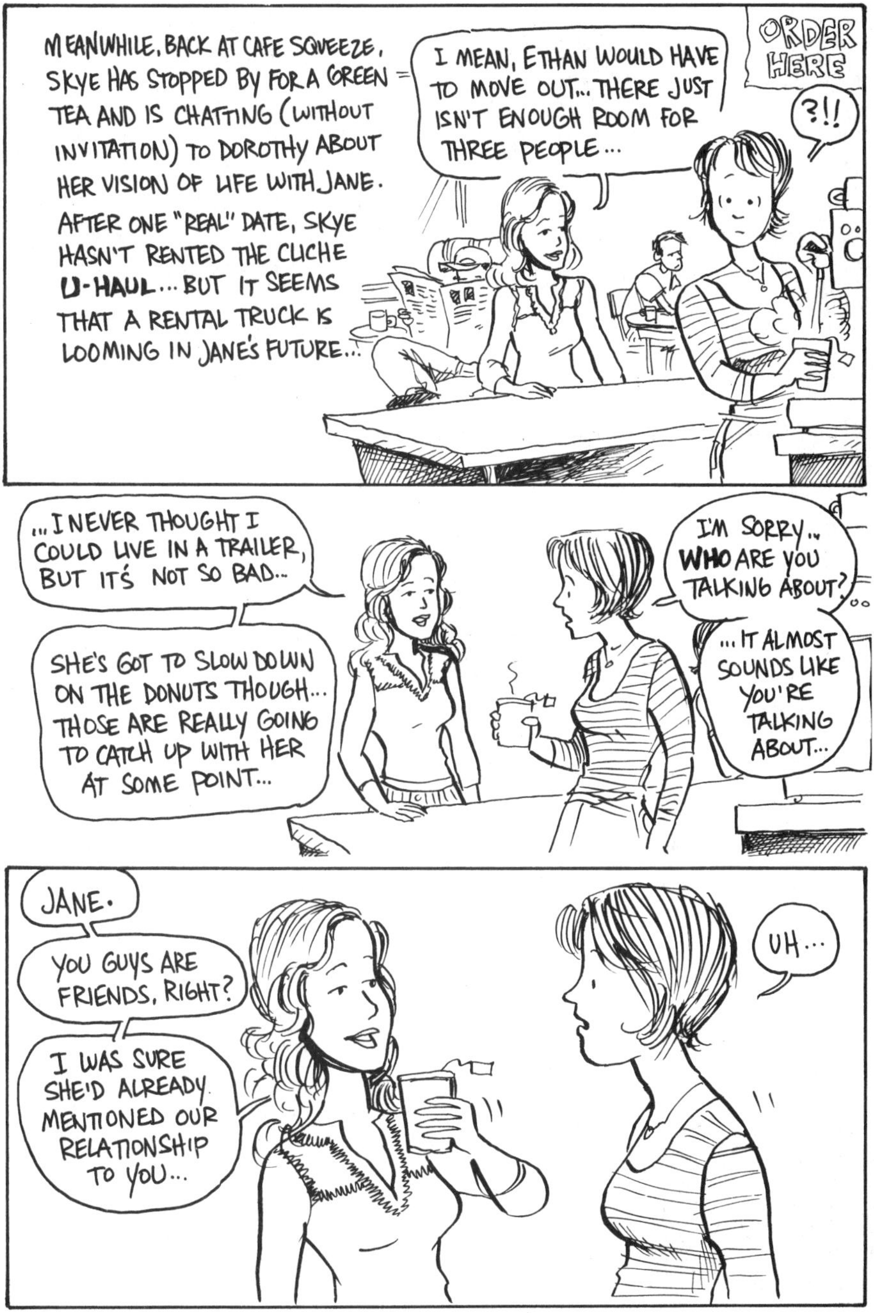
MEANWHILE, BACK AT CAFE SQUEEZE, SKYE HAS STOPPED BY FOR A GREEN TEA AND IS CHATTING (WITHOUT INVITATION) TO DOROTHY ABOUT HER VISION OF LIFE WITH JANE.
AFTER ONE "REAL" DATE, SKYE HASN'T RENTED THE CLICHE U-HAUL... BUT IT SEEMS THAT A RENTAL TRUCK IS LOOMING IN JANE'S FUTURE...
I MEAN, ETHAN WOULD HAVE TO MOVE OUT... THERE JUST ISN'T ENOUGH ROOM FOR THREE PEOPLE...
ORDER HERE
?!!
...I NEVER THOUGHT I COULD LIVE IN A TRAILER, BUT IT'S NOT SO BAD...
SHE'S GOT TO SLOW DOWN ON THE DONUTS THOUGH... THOSE ARE REALLY GOING TO CATCH UP WITH HER AT SOME POINT...
I'M SORRY.. WHO ARE YOU TALKING ABOUT?
...IT ALMOST SOUNDS LIKE YOU'RE TALKING ABOUT...
JANE.
YOU GUYS ARE FRIENDS, RIGHT?
I WAS SURE SHE'D ALREADY MENTIONED OUR RELATIONSHIP TO YOU...
UH...

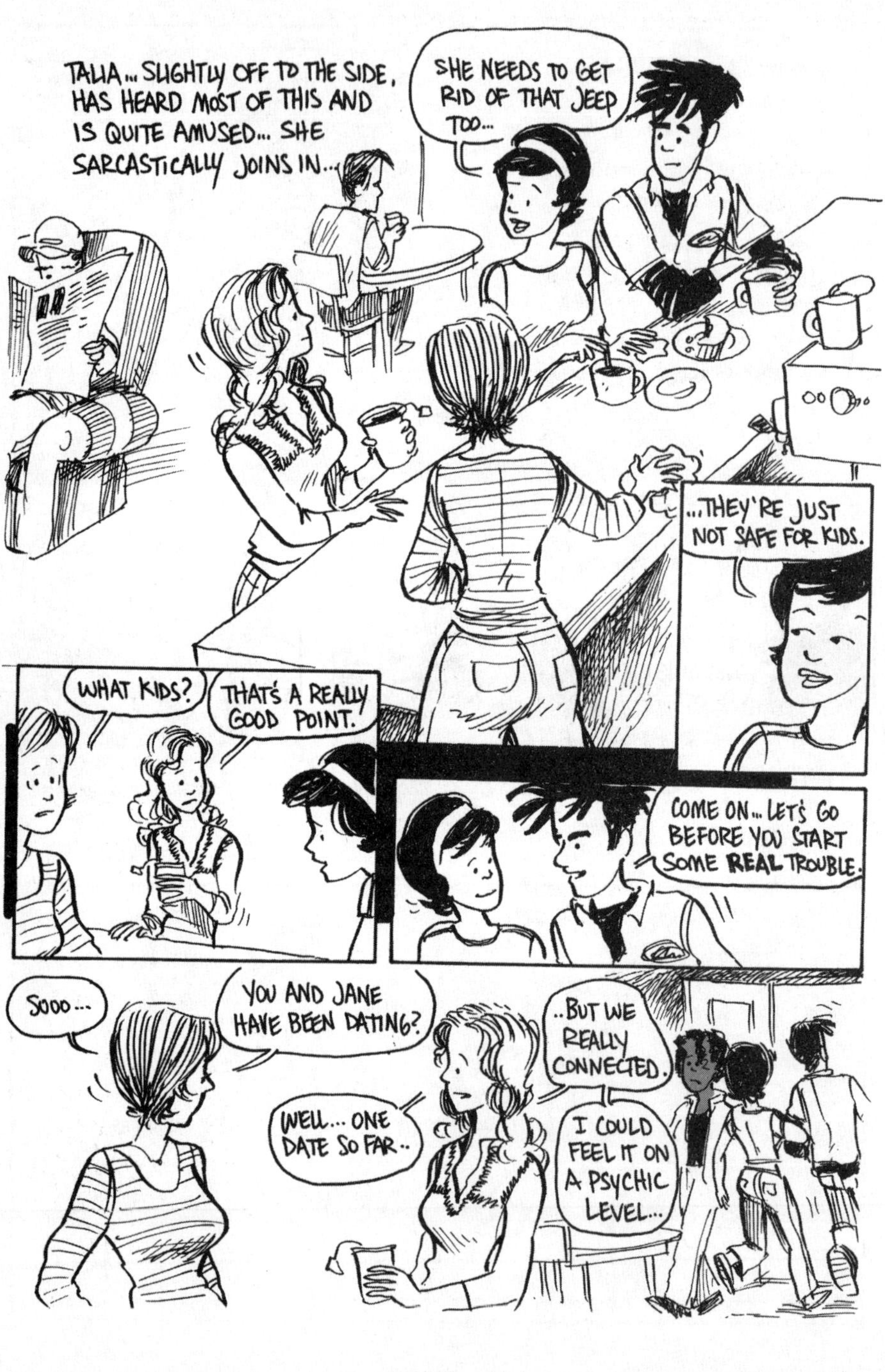
TALIA... SLIGHTLY OFF TO THE SIDE, HAS HEARD MOST OF THIS AND IS QUITE AMUSED... SHE SARCASTICALLY JOINS IN...
SHE NEEDS TO GET RID OF THAT JEEP TOO...
...THEY'RE JUST NOT SAFE FOR KIDS.
WHAT KIDS?
THAT'S A REALLY GOOD POINT.
COME ON... LET'S GO BEFORE YOU START SOME **REAL** TROUBLE.
SOOO...
YOU AND JANE HAVE BEEN DATING?
WELL... ONE DATE SO FAR..
..BUT WE REALLY CONNECTED.
I COULD FEEL IT ON A PSYCHIC LEVEL...

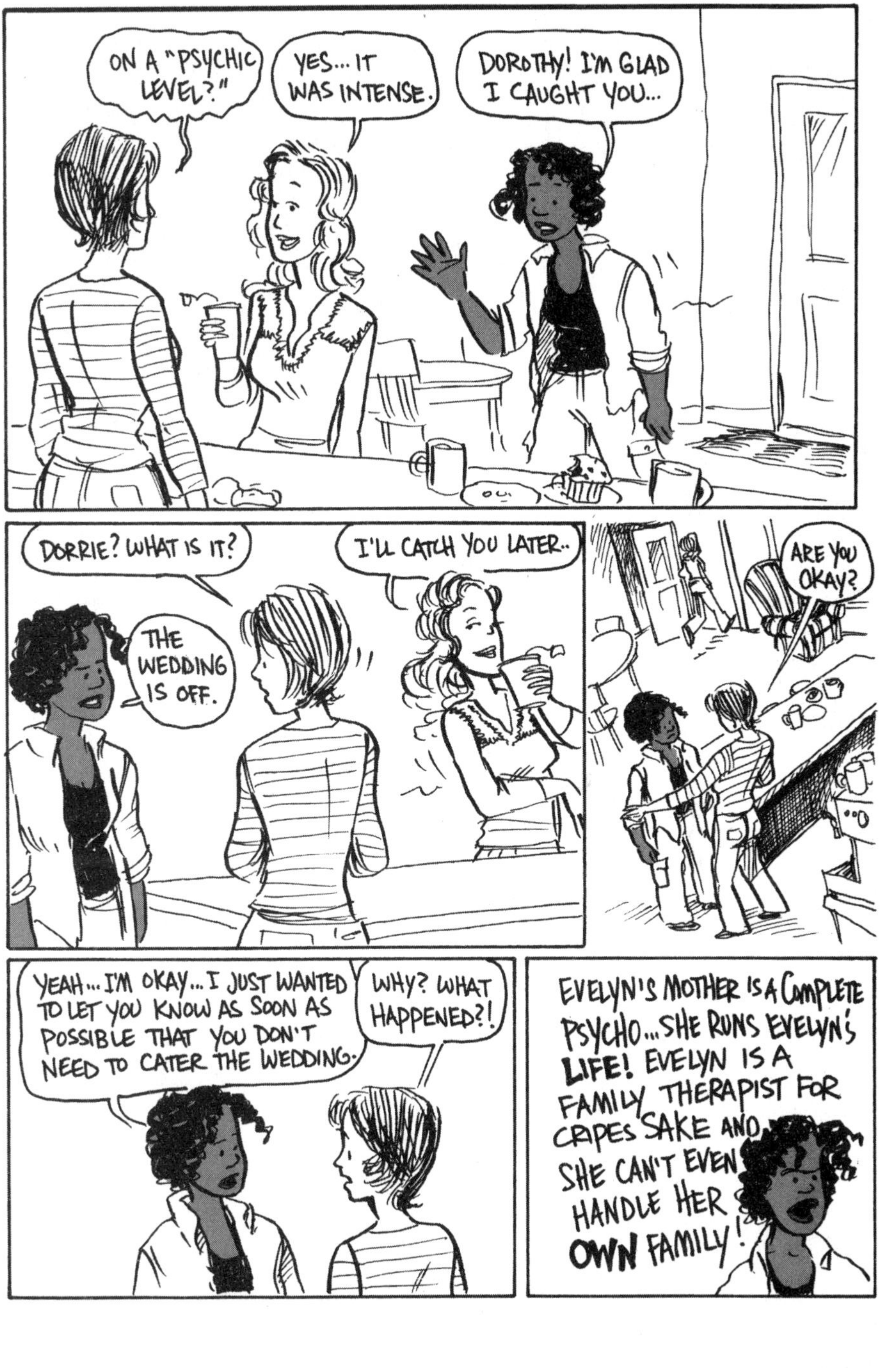
ON A "PSYCHIC LEVEL?"
YES... IT WAS INTENSE.
DOROTHY! I'M GLAD I CAUGHT YOU...
DORRIE? WHAT IS IT?
I'LL CATCH YOU LATER..
THE WEDDING IS OFF.
ARE YOU OKAY?
YEAH... I'M OKAY... I JUST WANTED TO LET YOU KNOW AS SOON AS POSSIBLE THAT YOU DON'T NEED TO CATER THE WEDDING.
WHY? WHAT HAPPENED?!
EVELYN'S MOTHER IS A COMPLETE PSYCHO... SHE RUNS EVELYN'S LIFE! EVELYN IS A FAMILY THERAPIST FOR CRIPES SAKE AND SHE CAN'T EVEN HANDLE HER OWN FAMILY!

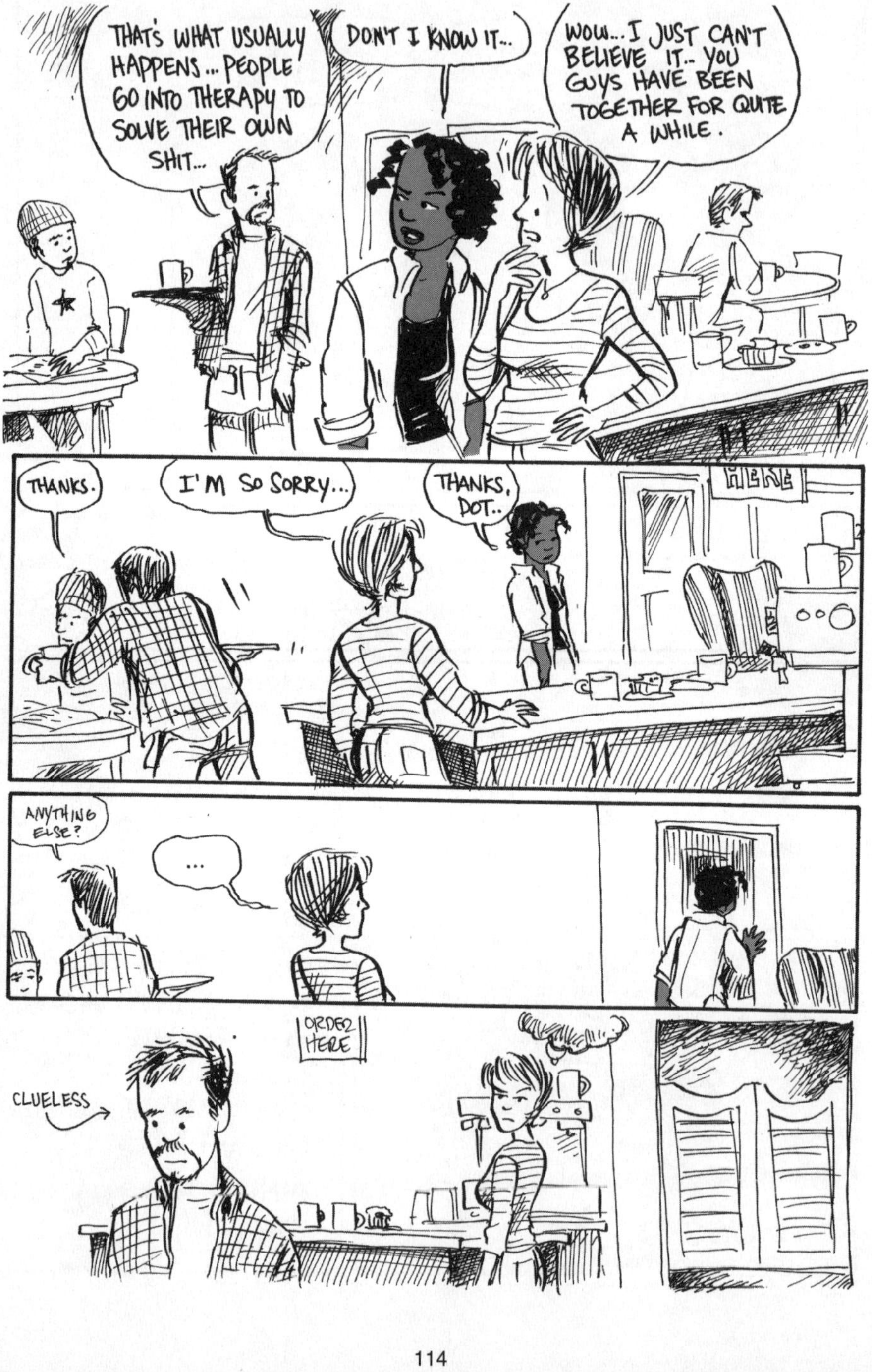

THAT'S WHAT USUALLY HAPPENS... PEOPLE GO INTO THERAPY TO SOLVE THEIR OWN SHIT...
DON'T I KNOW IT..
WOW... I JUST CAN'T BELIEVE IT.. YOU GUYS HAVE BEEN TOGETHER FOR QUITE A WHILE.
THANKS.
I'M SO SORRY...
THANKS, DOT..
ANYTHING ELSE?
...
ORDER HERE
CLUELESS

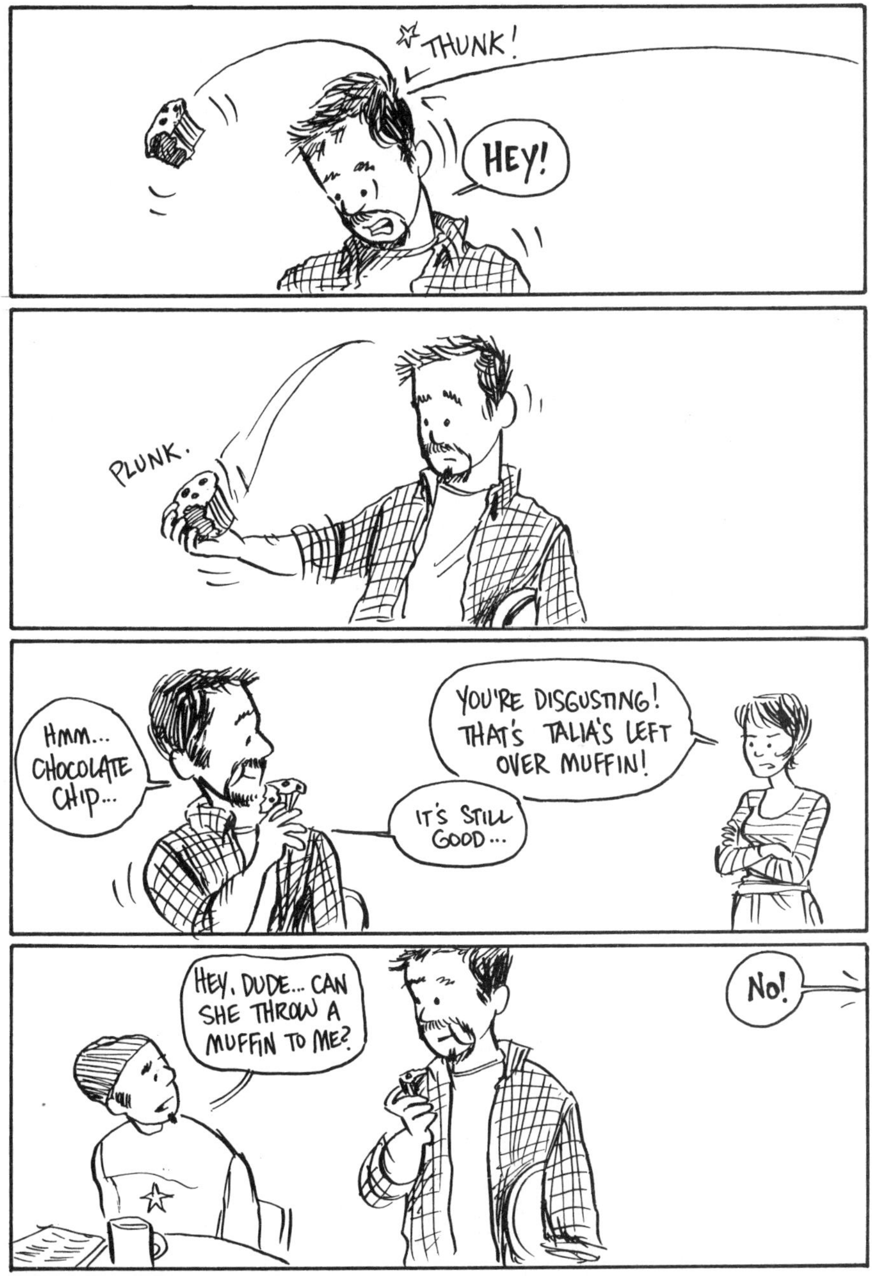
THUNK!
HEY!
PLUNK.
HMM... CHOCOLATE CHIP...
YOU'RE DISGUSTING! THAT'S TALIA'S LEFT OVER MUFFIN!
IT'S STILL GOOD...
HEY, DUDE... CAN SHE THROW A MUFFIN TO ME?
No!

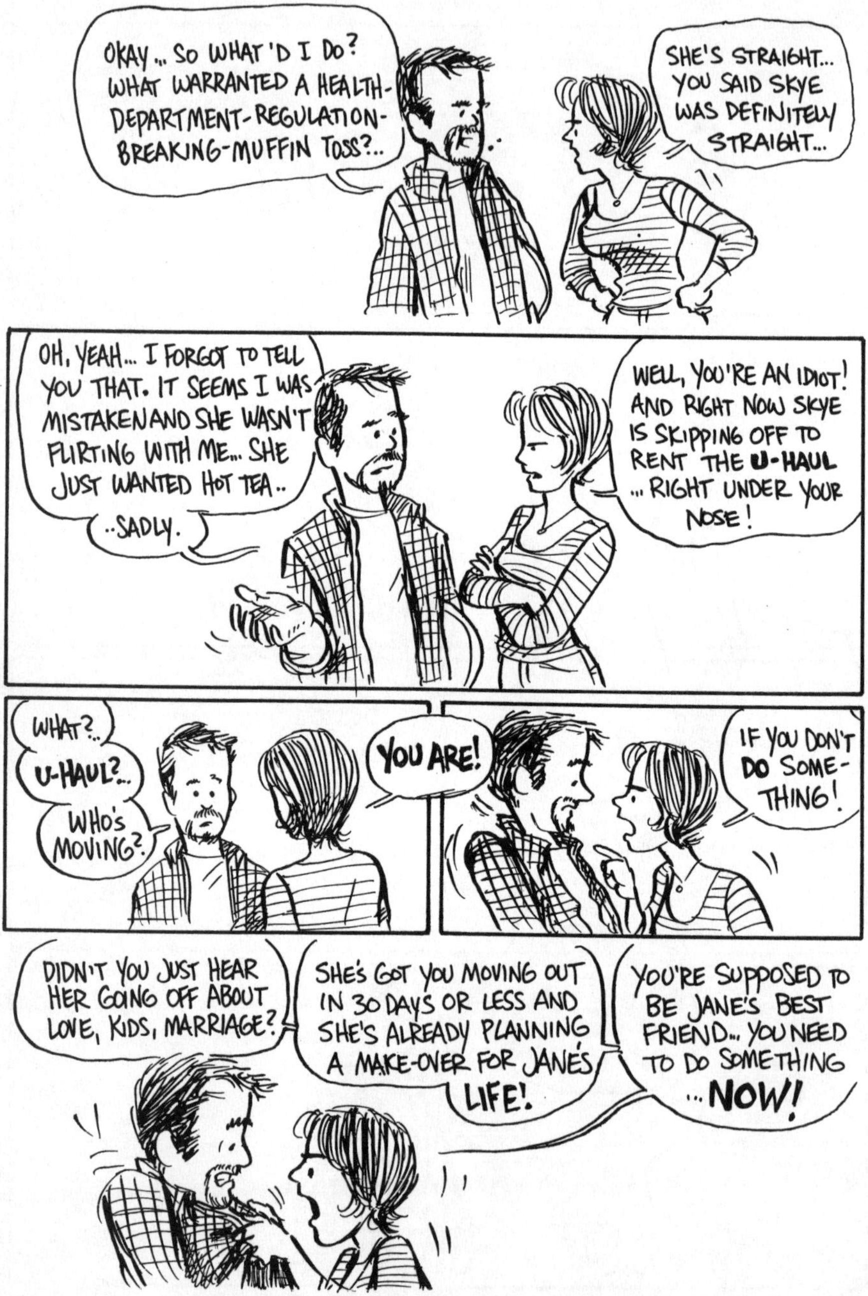
OKAY.. SO WHAT'D I DO? WHAT WARRANTED A HEALTH-DEPARTMENT-REGULATION-BREAKING-MUFFIN TOSS?..
SHE'S STRAIGHT... YOU SAID SKYE WAS DEFINITELY STRAIGHT...
OH, YEAH... I FORGOT TO TELL YOU THAT. IT SEEMS I WAS MISTAKEN AND SHE WASN'T FLIRTING WITH ME... SHE JUST WANTED HOT TEA..
..SADLY.
WELL, YOU'RE AN IDIOT! AND RIGHT NOW SKYE IS SKIPPING OFF TO RENT THE U-HAUL ... RIGHT UNDER YOUR NOSE!
WHAT?..
U-HAUL?..
WHO'S MOVING?
YOU ARE!
IF YOU DON'T DO SOME-THING!
DIDN'T YOU JUST HEAR HER GOING OFF ABOUT LOVE, KIDS, MARRIAGE?
SHE'S GOT YOU MOVING OUT IN 30 DAYS OR LESS AND SHE'S ALREADY PLANNING A MAKE-OVER FOR JANE'S LIFE!
YOU'RE SUPPOSED TO BE JANE'S BEST FRIEND... YOU NEED TO DO SOMETHING ...NOW!

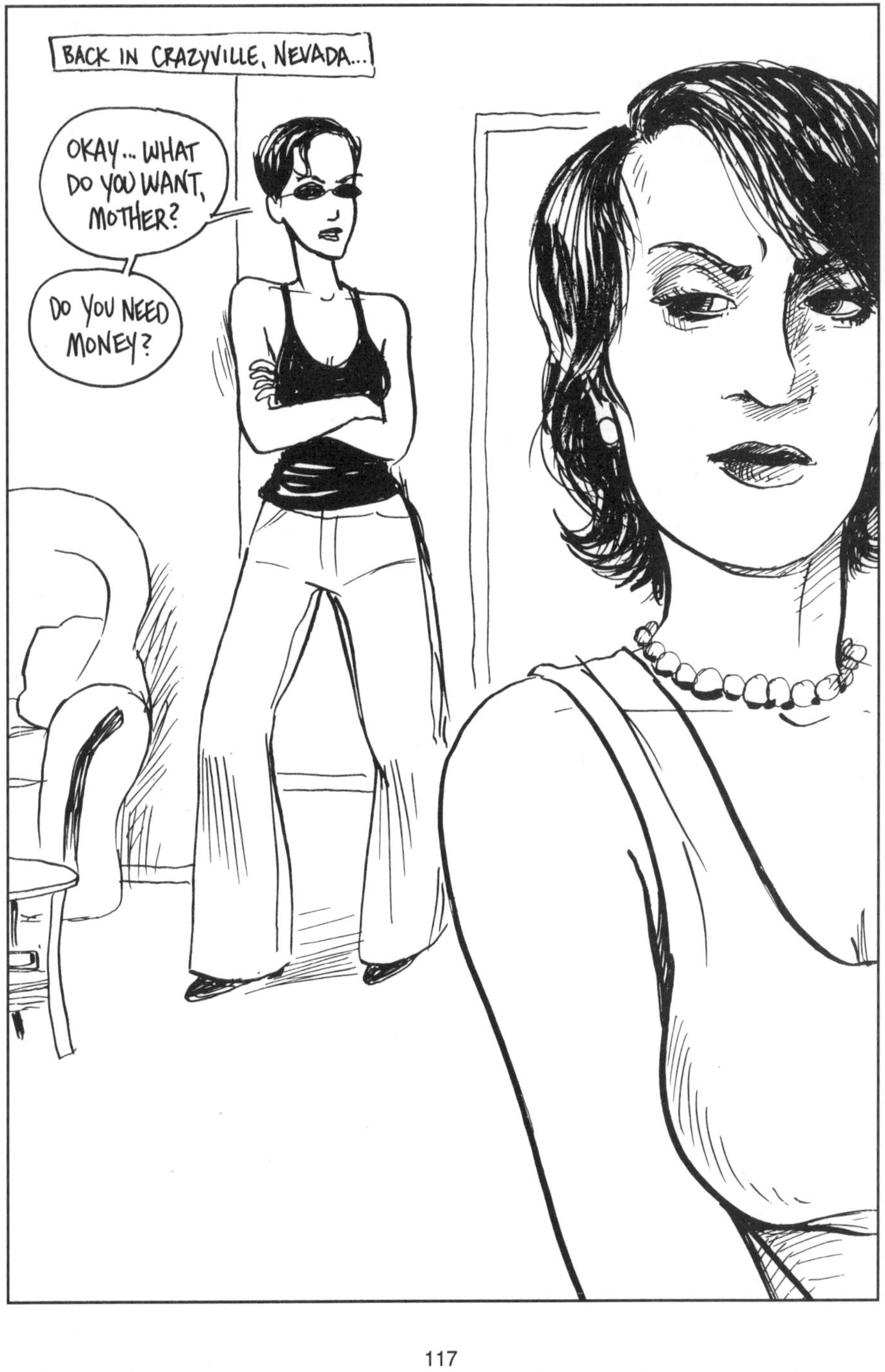
BACK IN CRAZYVILLE, NEVADA...
OKAY... WHAT DO YOU WANT, MOTHER?
DO YOU NEED MONEY?

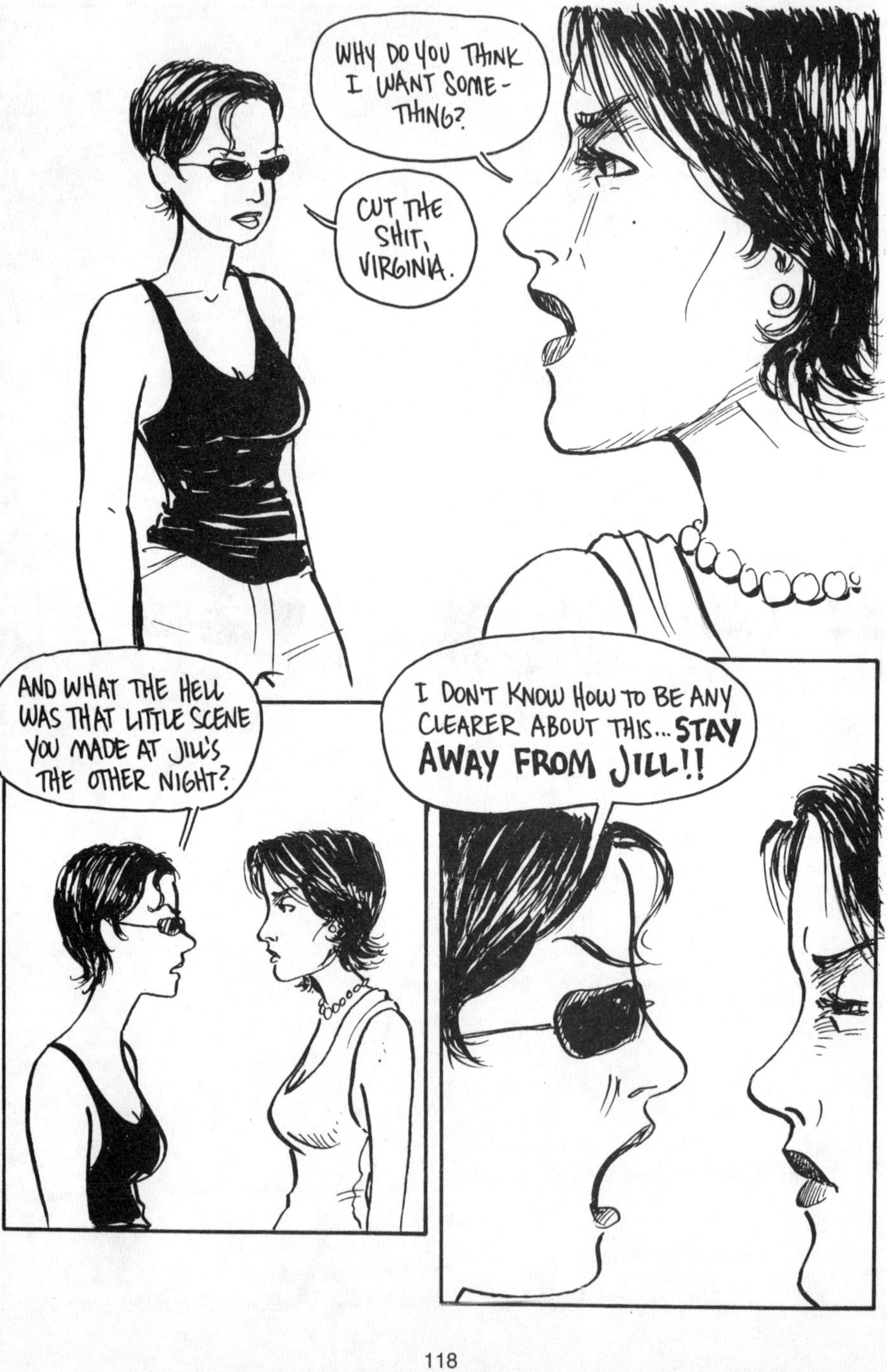
WHY DO YOU THINK I WANT SOME-THING?
CUT THE SHIT, VIRGINIA.
AND WHAT THE HELL WAS THAT LITTLE SCENE YOU MADE AT JILL'S THE OTHER NIGHT?
I DON'T KNOW HOW TO BE ANY CLEARER ABOUT THIS... **STAY AWAY FROM JILL!!**

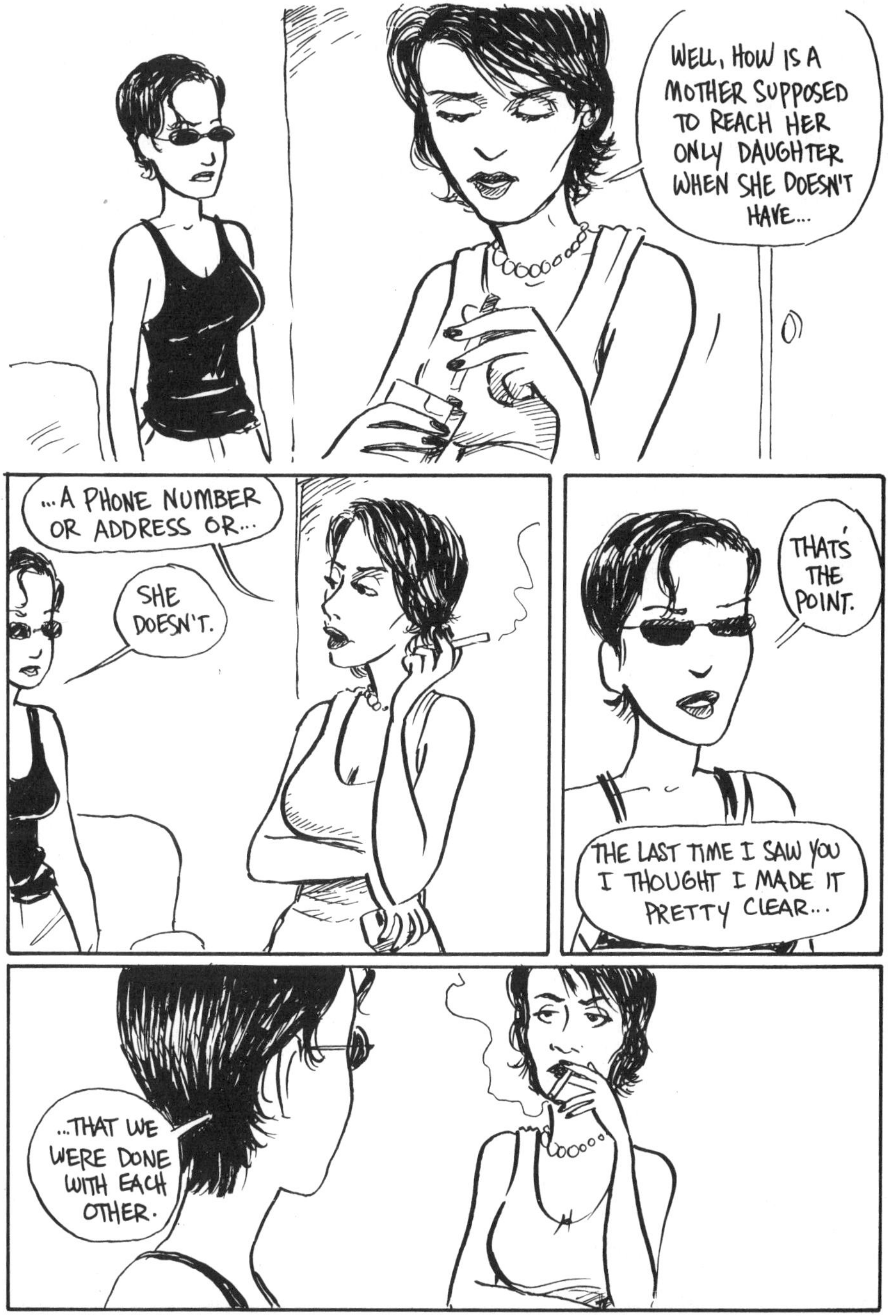
WELL, HOW IS A MOTHER SUPPOSED TO REACH HER ONLY DAUGHTER WHEN SHE DOESN'T HAVE...
...A PHONE NUMBER OR ADDRESS OR...
SHE DOESN'T.
THAT'S THE POINT.
THE LAST TIME I SAW YOU I THOUGHT I MADE IT PRETTY CLEAR...
...THAT WE WERE DONE WITH EACH OTHER.

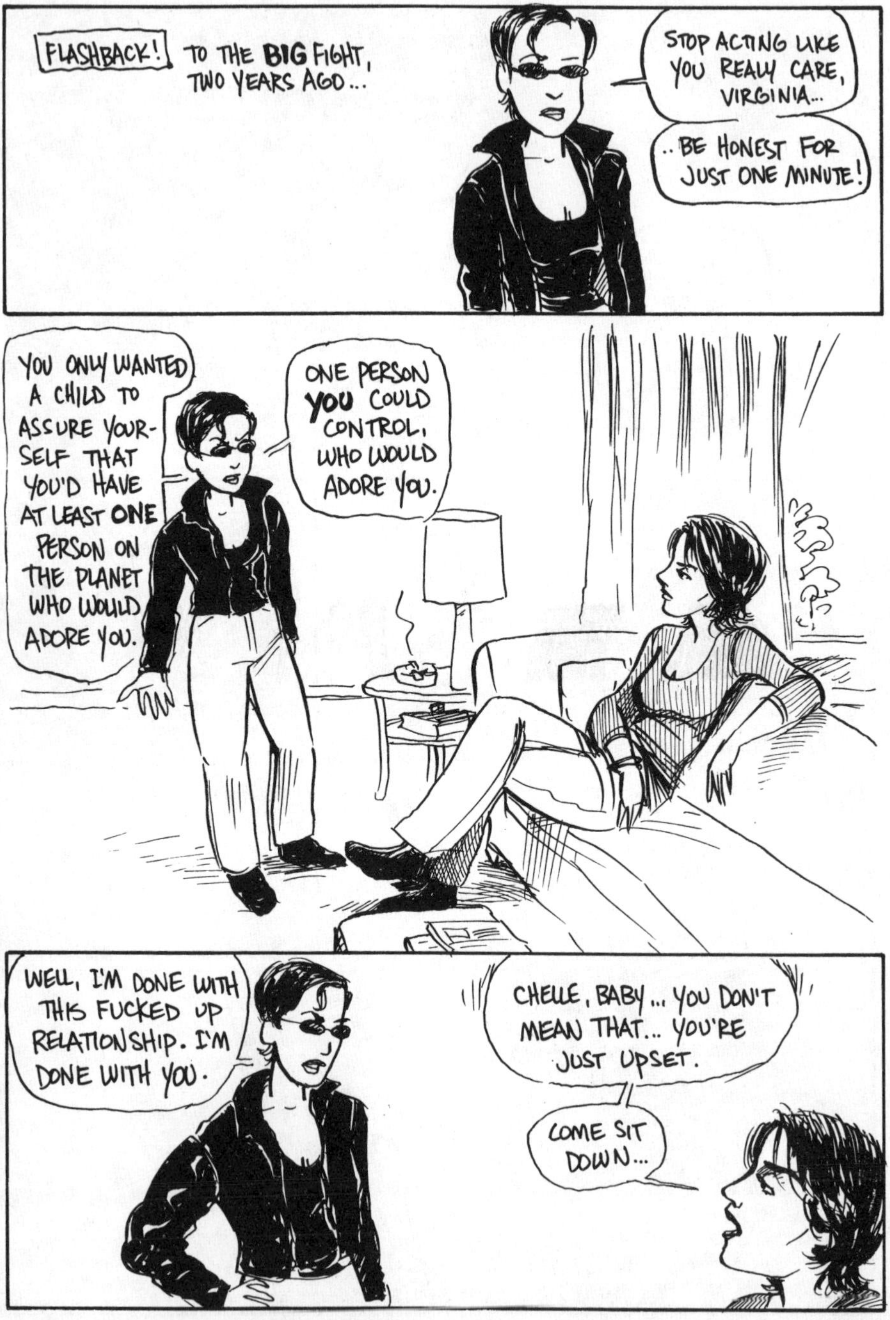
FLASHBACK!
TO THE BIG FIGHT, TWO YEARS AGO...
STOP ACTING LIKE YOU REALLY CARE, VIRGINIA...
..BE HONEST FOR JUST ONE MINUTE!
YOU ONLY WANTED A CHILD TO ASSURE YOURSELF THAT YOU'D HAVE AT LEAST ONE PERSON ON THE PLANET WHO WOULD ADORE YOU.
ONE PERSON YOU COULD CONTROL, WHO WOULD ADORE YOU.
WELL, I'M DONE WITH THIS FUCKED UP RELATIONSHIP. I'M DONE WITH YOU.
CHELLE, BABY... YOU DON'T MEAN THAT... YOU'RE JUST UPSET.
COME SIT DOWN...

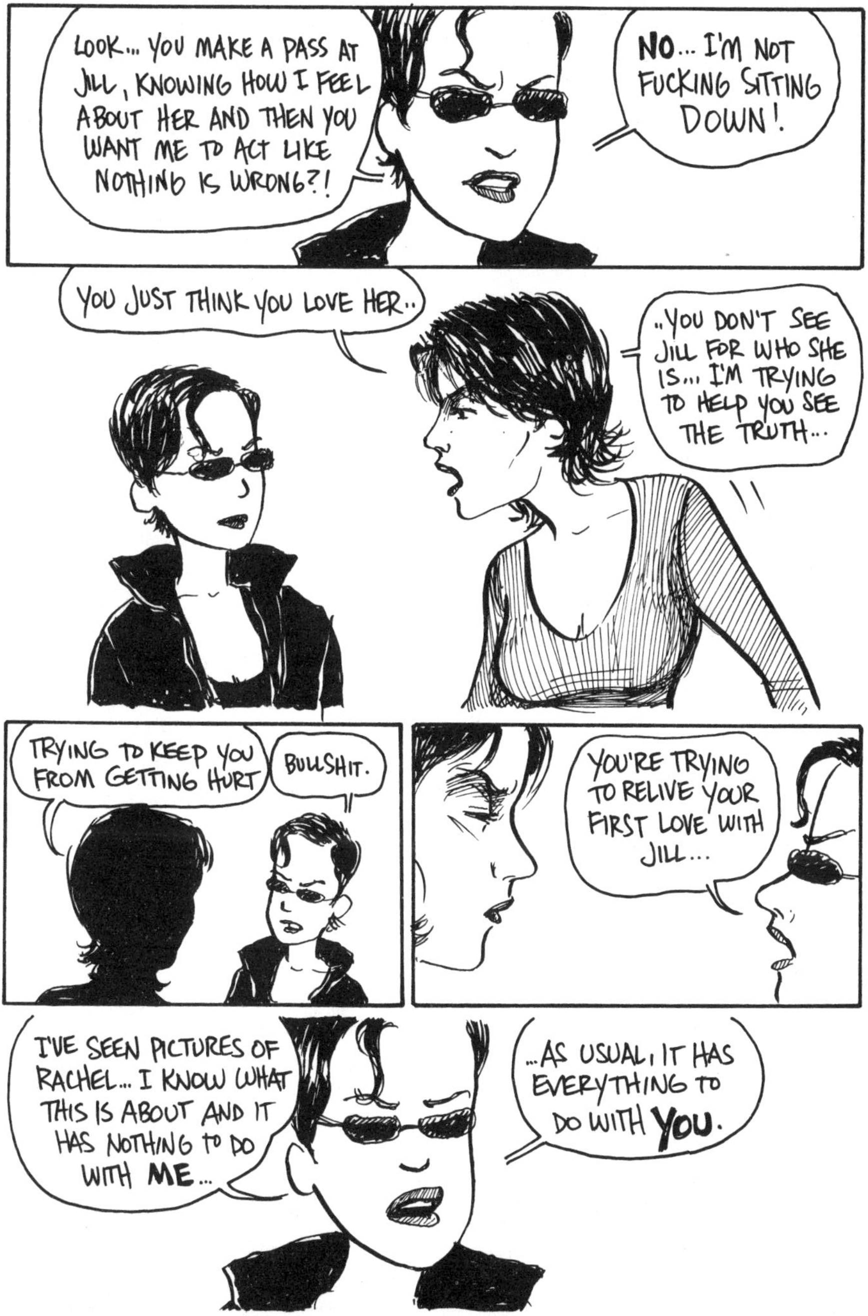
LOOK... YOU MAKE A PASS AT JILL, KNOWING HOW I FEEL ABOUT HER AND THEN YOU WANT ME TO ACT LIKE NOTHING IS WRONG?!
NO... I'M NOT FUCKING SITTING DOWN!
YOU JUST THINK YOU LOVE HER..
..YOU DON'T SEE JILL FOR WHO SHE IS... I'M TRYING TO HELP YOU SEE THE TRUTH...
TRYING TO KEEP YOU FROM GETTING HURT
BULLSHIT.
YOU'RE TRYING TO RELIVE YOUR FIRST LOVE WITH JILL...
I'VE SEEN PICTURES OF RACHEL... I KNOW WHAT THIS IS ABOUT AND IT HAS NOTHING TO DO WITH ME...
...AS USUAL, IT HAS EVERYTHING TO DO WITH YOU.

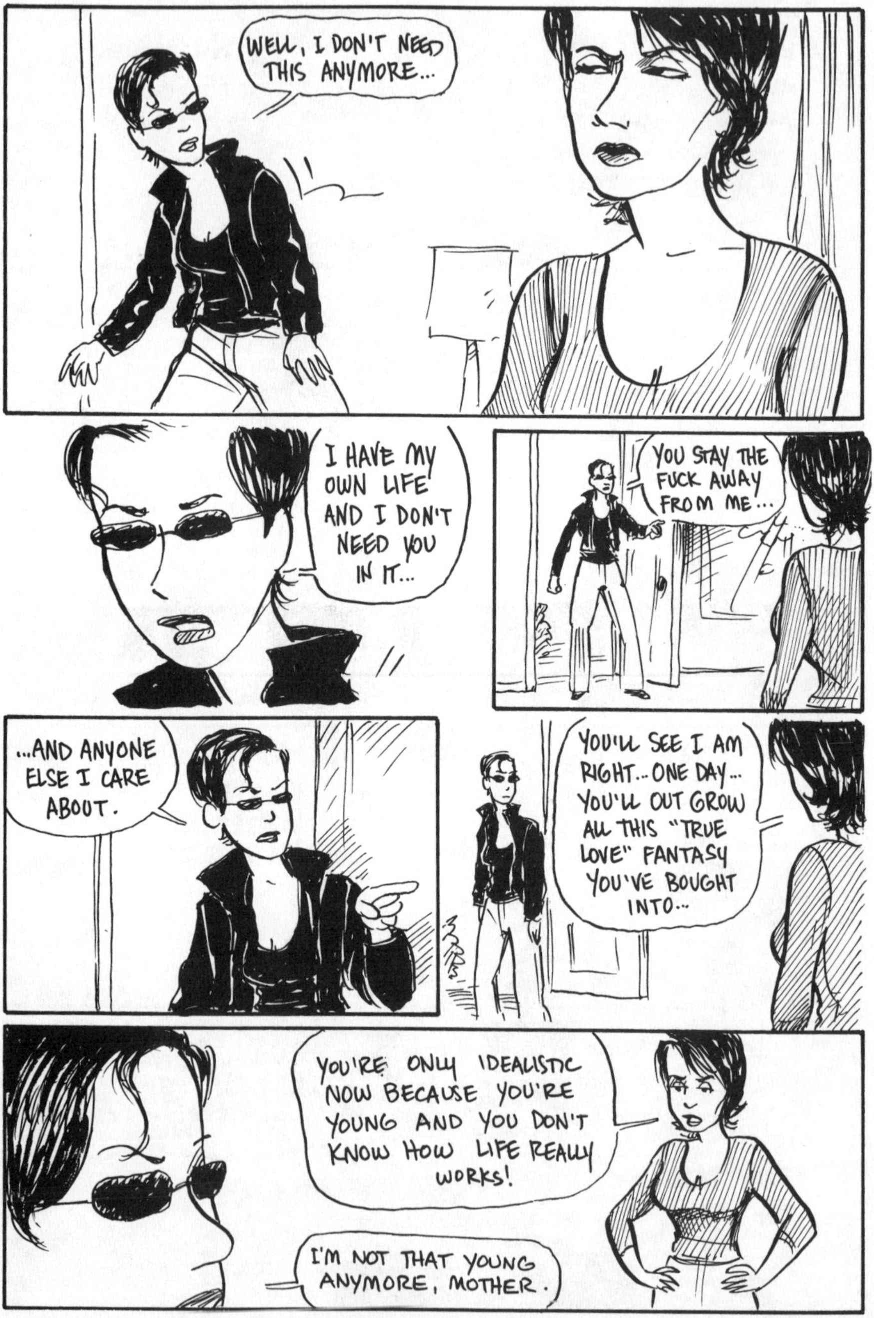

WELL, I DON'T NEED THIS ANYMORE...
I HAVE MY OWN LIFE AND I DON'T NEED YOU IN IT...
YOU STAY THE FUCK AWAY FROM ME...
...AND ANYONE ELSE I CARE ABOUT.
YOU'LL SEE I AM RIGHT... ONE DAY... YOU'LL OUT GROW ALL THIS "TRUE LOVE" FANTASY YOU'VE BOUGHT INTO...
YOU'RE ONLY IDEALISTIC NOW BECAUSE YOU'RE YOUNG AND YOU DON'T KNOW HOW LIFE REALLY WORKS!
I'M NOT THAT YOUNG ANYMORE, MOTHER.

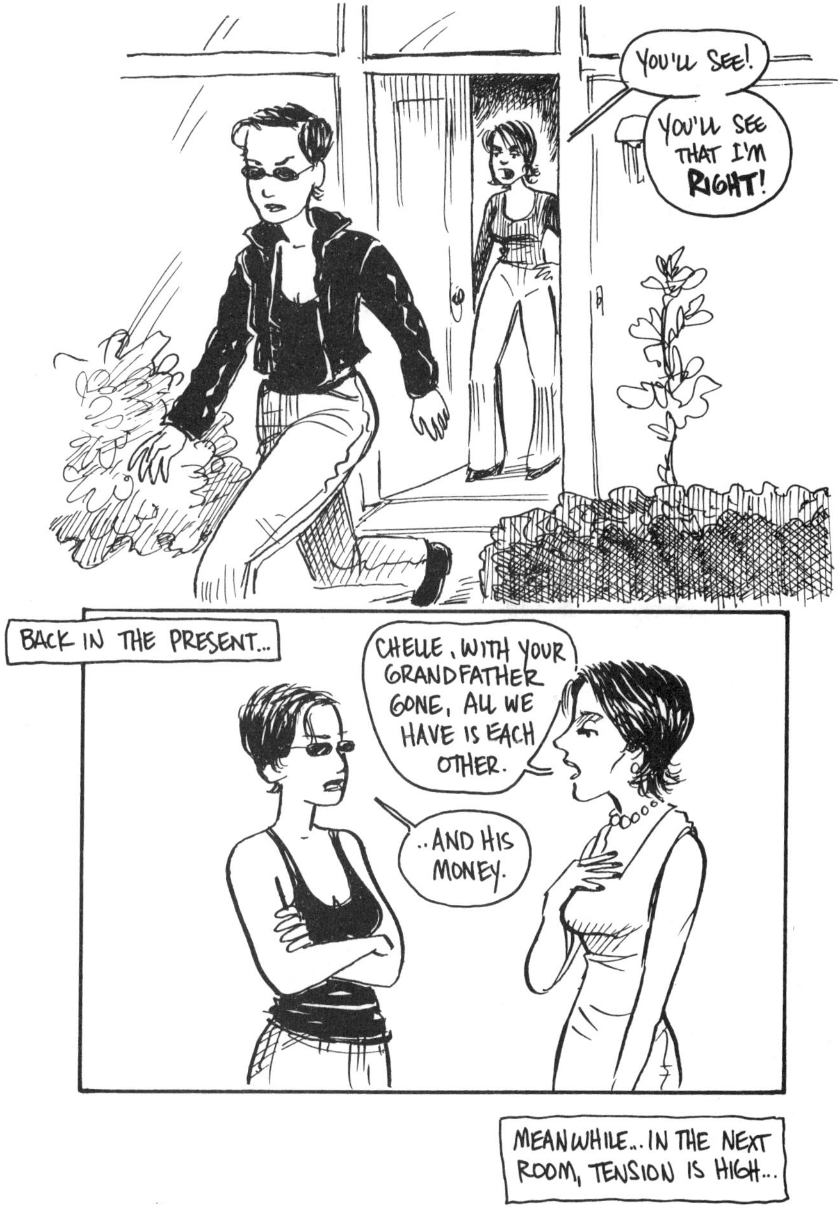
YOU'LL SEE!
YOU'LL SEE THAT I'M **RIGHT**!
BACK IN THE PRESENT...
CHELLE, WITH YOUR GRANDFATHER GONE, ALL WE HAVE IS EACH OTHER.
..AND HIS MONEY.
MEANWHILE.. IN THE NEXT ROOM, TENSION IS HIGH...

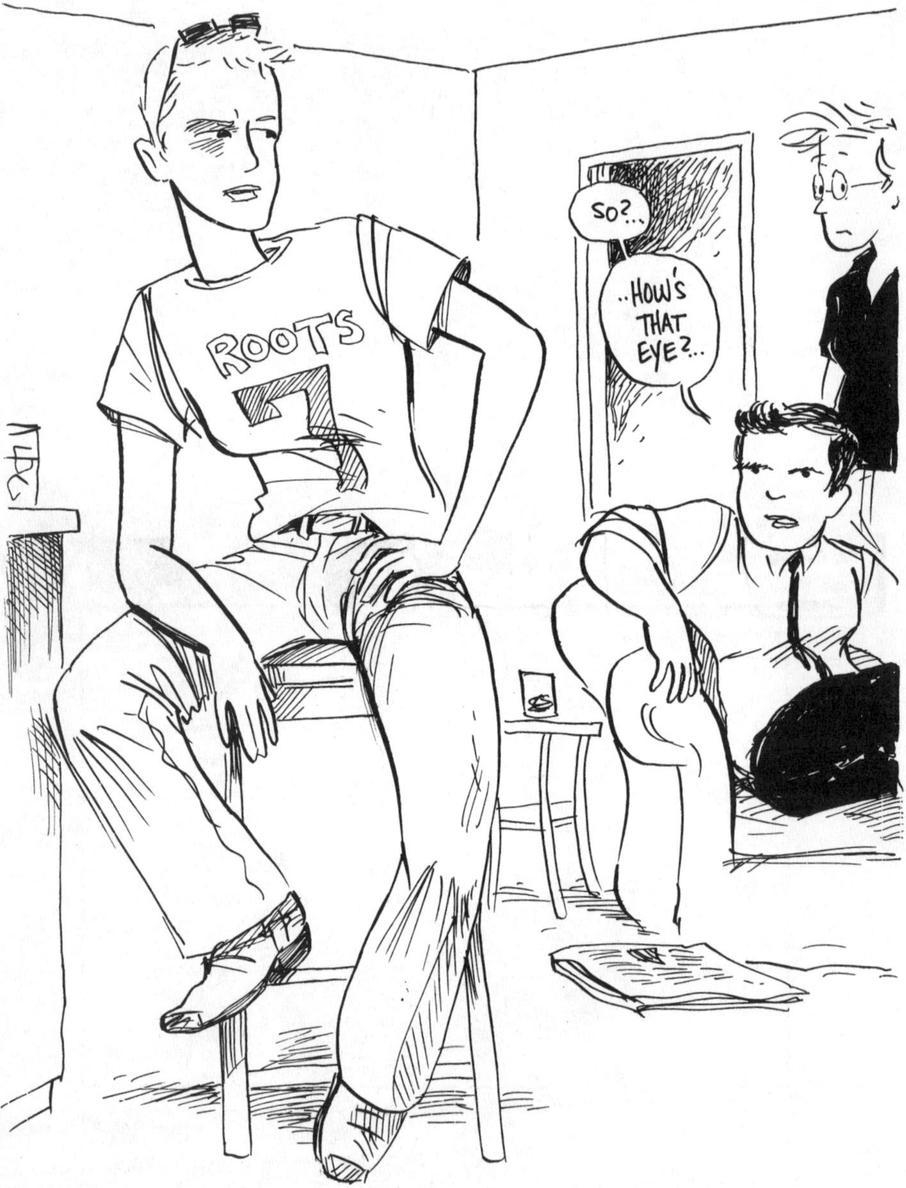
SO?...
..HOW'S THAT EYE?...
ROOTS

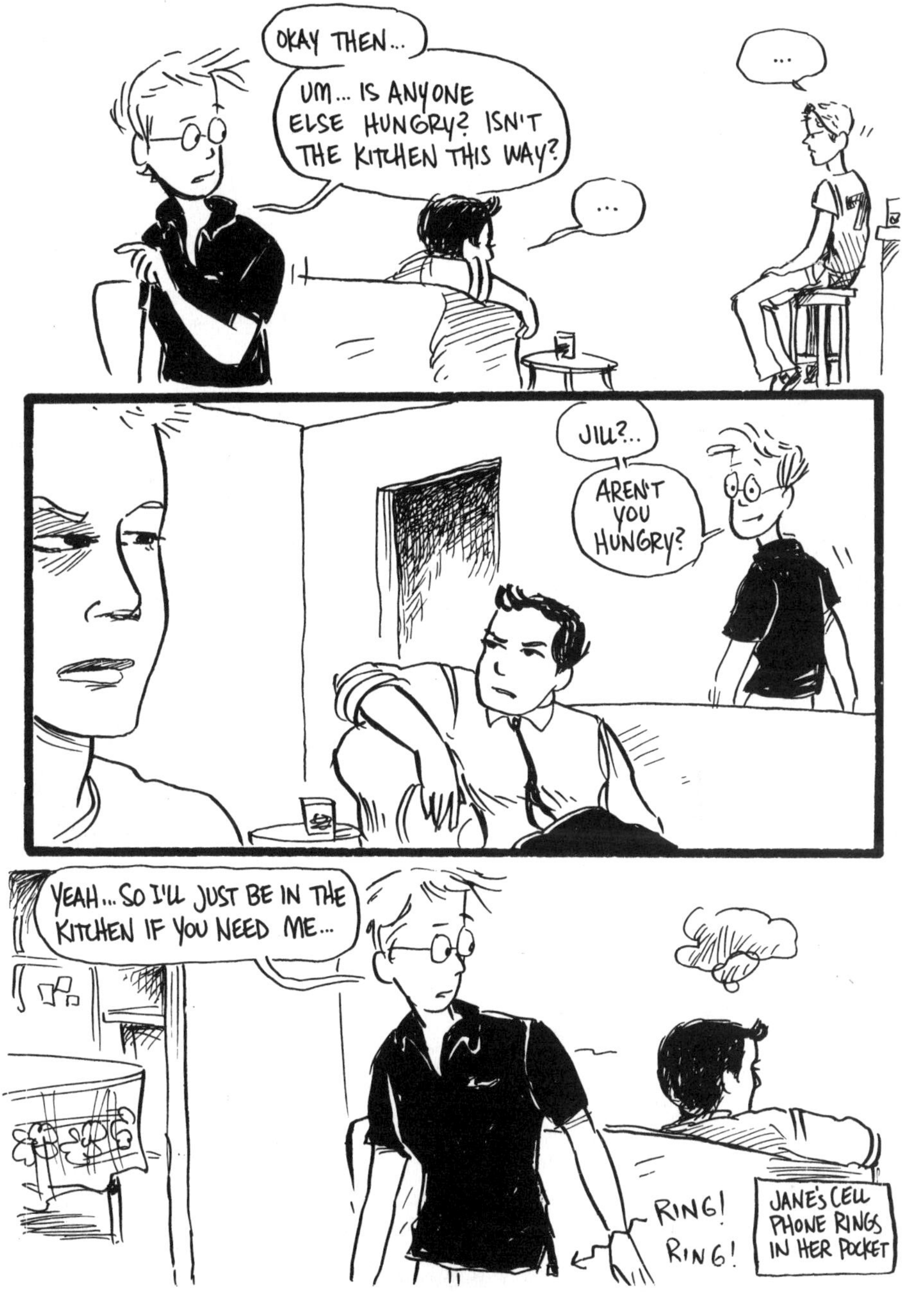
OKAY THEN...
UM... IS ANYONE ELSE HUNGRY? ISN'T THE KITCHEN THIS WAY?
...
...
JILL?...
AREN'T YOU HUNGRY?
YEAH... SO I'LL JUST BE IN THE KITCHEN IF YOU NEED ME...
RING! RING!
JANE'S CELL PHONE RINGS IN HER POCKET

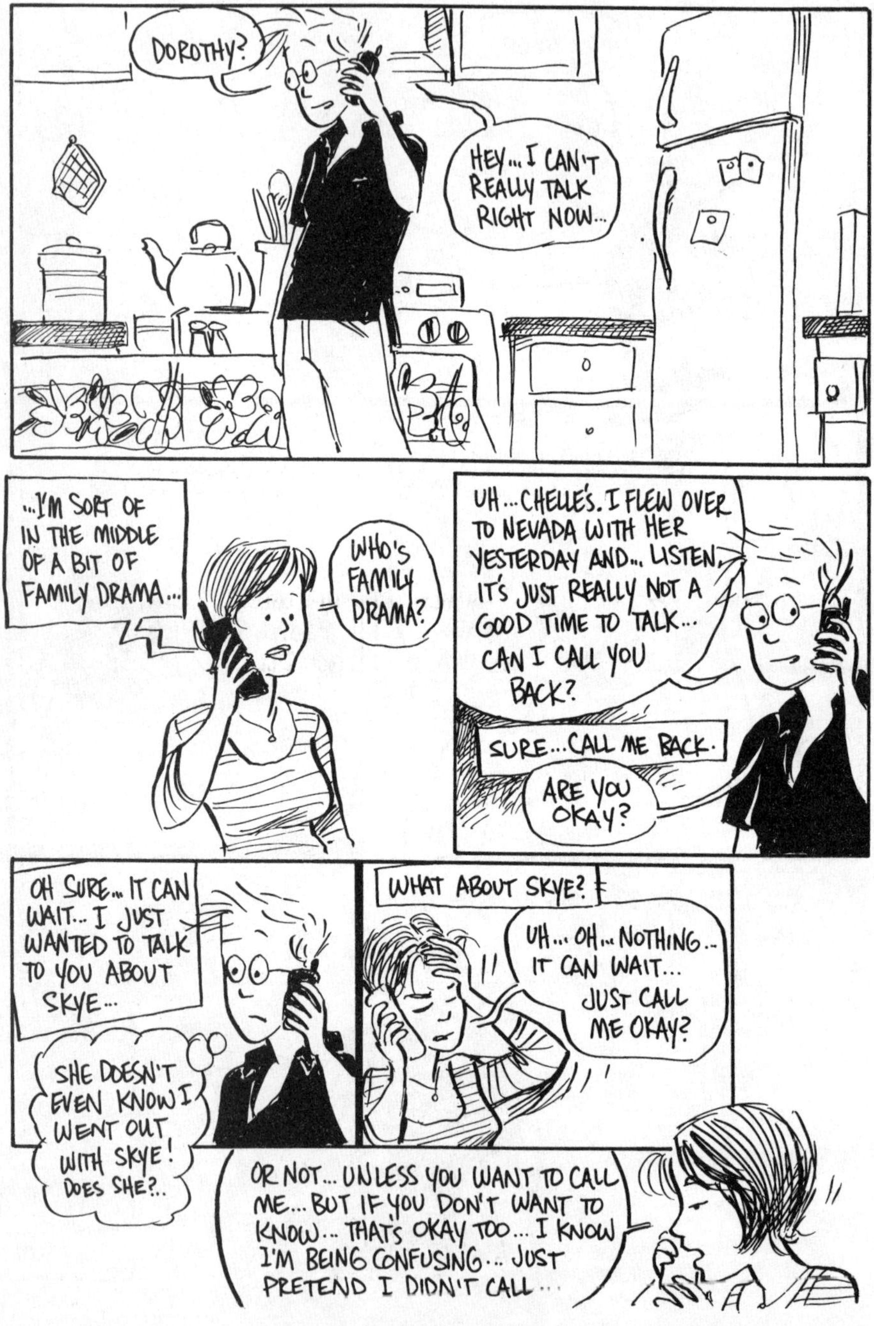
DOROTHY?
HEY... I CAN'T REALLY TALK RIGHT NOW...
...I'M SORT OF IN THE MIDDLE OF A BIT OF FAMILY DRAMA...
WHO'S FAMILY DRAMA?
UH... CHELLE'S. I FLEW OVER TO NEVADA WITH HER YESTERDAY AND... LISTEN, IT'S JUST REALLY NOT A GOOD TIME TO TALK... CAN I CALL YOU BACK?
SURE... CALL ME BACK.
ARE YOU OKAY?
OH SURE... IT CAN WAIT... I JUST WANTED TO TALK TO YOU ABOUT SKYE...
SHE DOESN'T EVEN KNOW I WENT OUT WITH SKYE! DOES SHE?..
WHAT ABOUT SKYE?
UH... OH... NOTHING... IT CAN WAIT... JUST CALL ME OKAY?
OR NOT... UNLESS YOU WANT TO CALL ME... BUT IF YOU DON'T WANT TO KNOW... THAT'S OKAY TOO... I KNOW I'M BEING CONFUSING... JUST PRETEND I DIDN'T CALL...

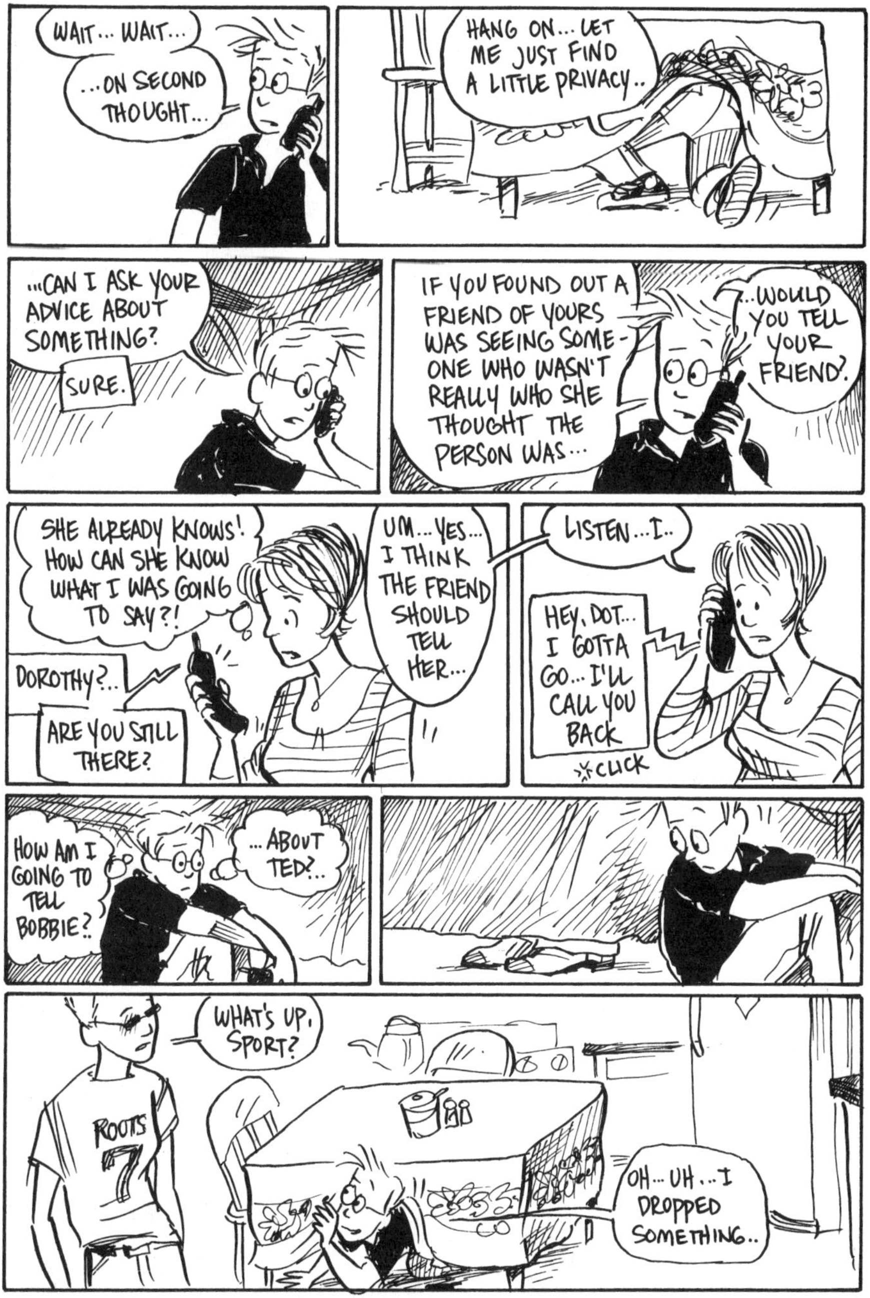
WAIT... WAIT...
...ON SECOND THOUGHT...
HANG ON... LET ME JUST FIND A LITTLE PRIVACY..
...CAN I ASK YOUR ADVICE ABOUT SOMETHING?
SURE.
IF YOU FOUND OUT A FRIEND OF YOURS WAS SEEING SOME-ONE WHO WASN'T REALLY WHO SHE THOUGHT THE PERSON WAS...
...WOULD YOU TELL YOUR FRIEND?
SHE ALREADY KNOWS! HOW CAN SHE KNOW WHAT I WAS GOING TO SAY?!
DOROTHY?..
ARE YOU STILL THERE?
UM... YES... I THINK THE FRIEND SHOULD TELL HER...
LISTEN...I..
HEY, DOT... I GOTTA GO... I'LL CALL YOU BACK
CLICK
HOW AM I GOING TO TELL BOBBIE?..
...ABOUT TED?...
WHAT'S UP, SPORT?
ROOTS 7
OH... UH... I DROPPED SOMETHING..

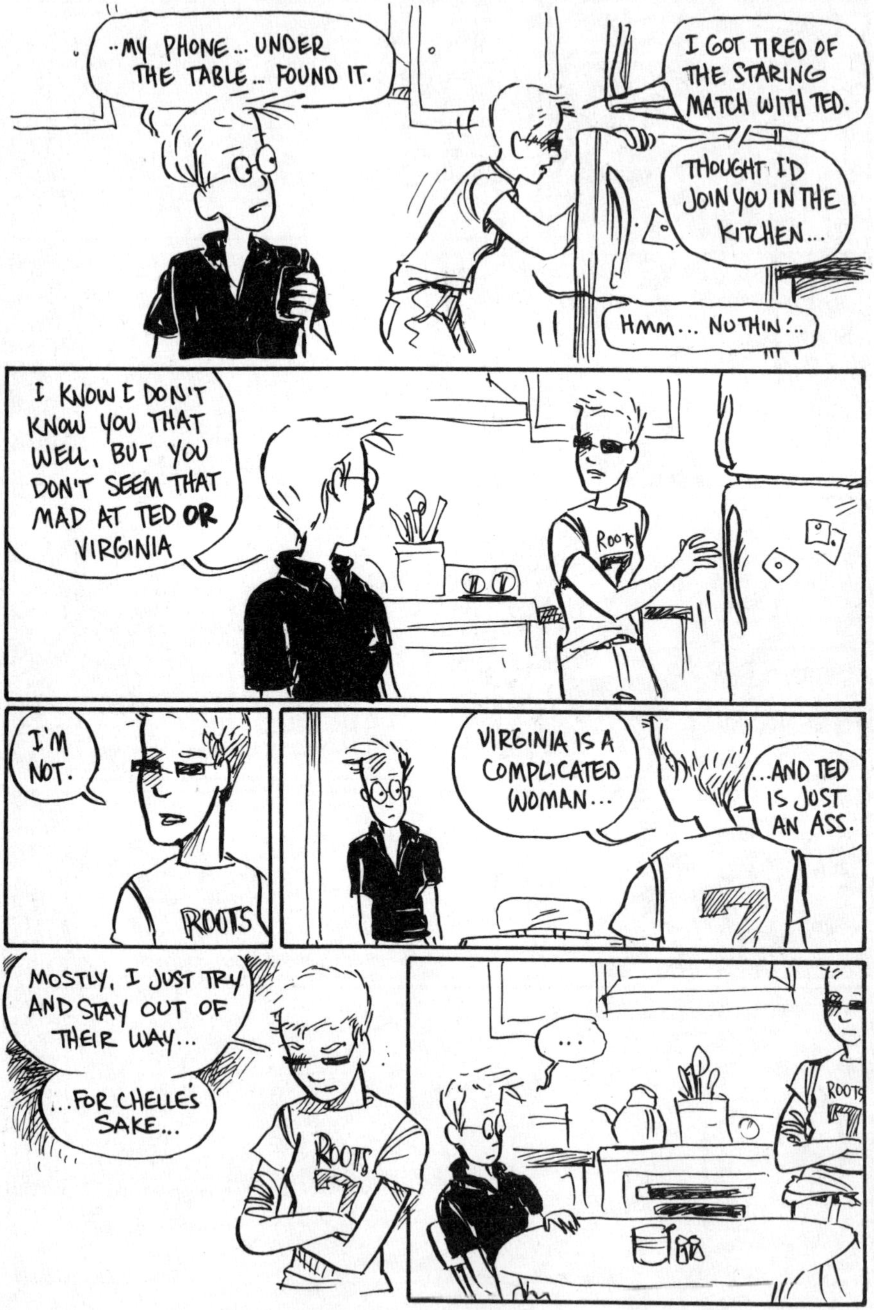
..MY PHONE... UNDER THE TABLE... FOUND IT.
I GOT TIRED OF THE STARING MATCH WITH TED.
THOUGHT I'D JOIN YOU IN THE KITCHEN...
HMM... NUTHIN'..
I KNOW I DON'T KNOW YOU THAT WELL, BUT YOU DON'T SEEM THAT MAD AT TED OR VIRGINIA
ROOTS
I'M NOT.
ROOTS
VIRGINIA IS A COMPLICATED WOMAN...
...AND TED IS JUST AN ASS.
MOSTLY, I JUST TRY AND STAY OUT OF THEIR WAY...
...FOR CHELLE'S SAKE...
ROOTS
...
ROOTS

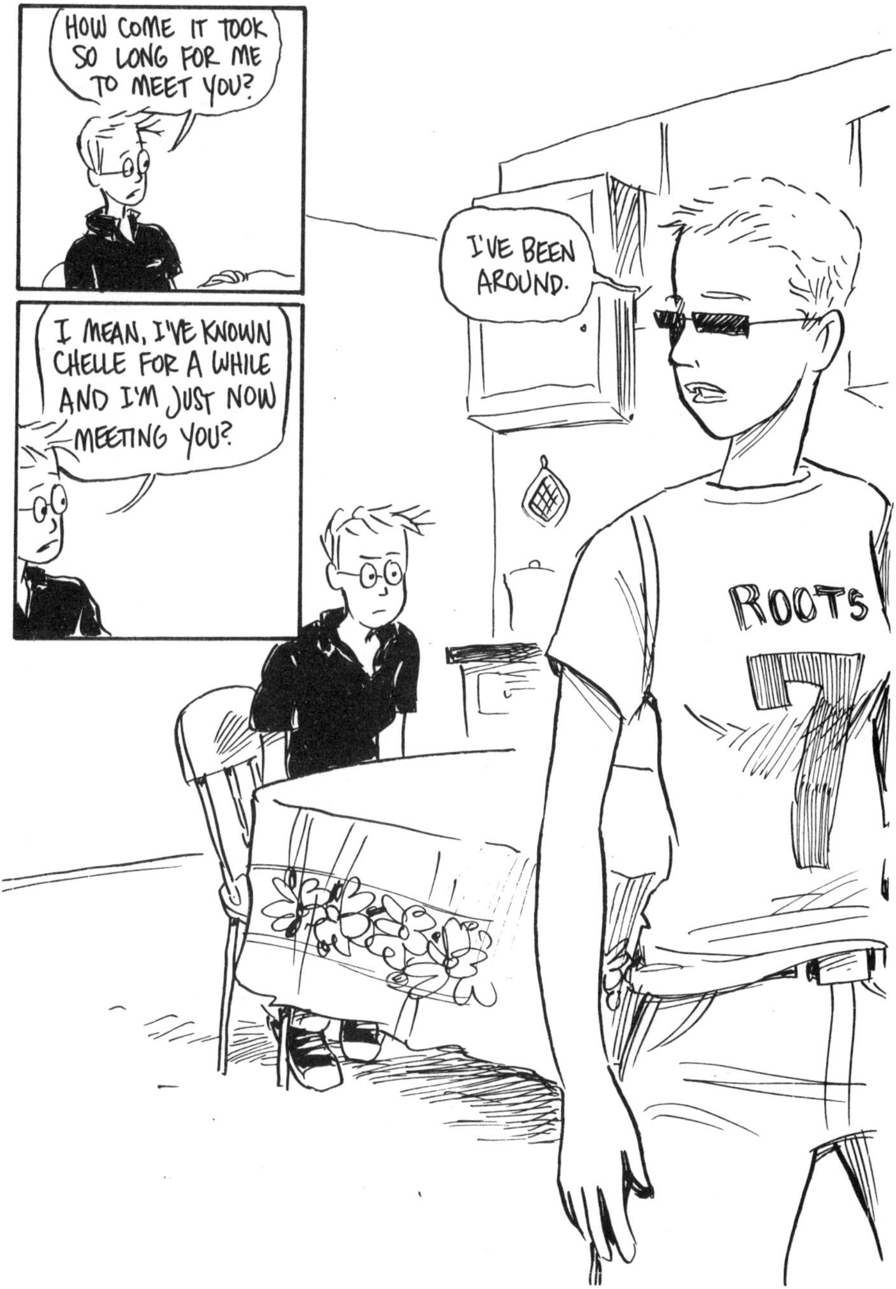
HOW COME IT TOOK SO LONG FOR ME TO MEET YOU?
I MEAN, I'VE KNOWN CHELLE FOR A WHILE AND I'M JUST NOW MEETING YOU?
I'VE BEEN AROUND.
ROOTS
7

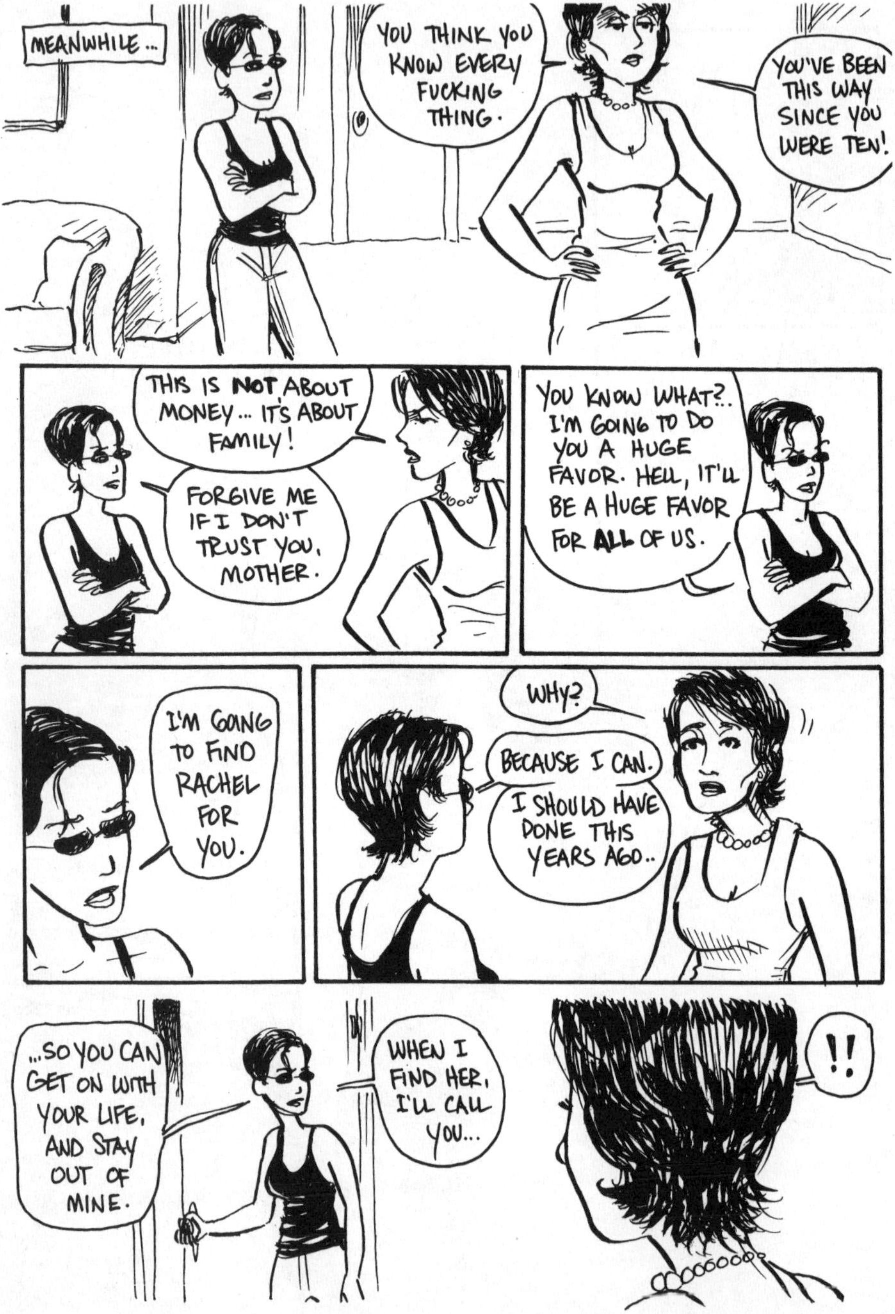
MEANWHILE...
YOU THINK YOU KNOW EVERY FUCKING THING.
YOU'VE BEEN THIS WAY SINCE YOU WERE TEN!
THIS IS NOT ABOUT MONEY... IT'S ABOUT FAMILY!
FORGIVE ME IF I DON'T TRUST YOU, MOTHER.
YOU KNOW WHAT?.. I'M GOING TO DO YOU A HUGE FAVOR. HELL, IT'LL BE A HUGE FAVOR FOR ALL OF US.
I'M GOING TO FIND RACHEL FOR YOU.
WHY?
BECAUSE I CAN.
I SHOULD HAVE DONE THIS YEARS AGO..
...SO YOU CAN GET ON WITH YOUR LIFE, AND STAY OUT OF MINE.
WHEN I FIND HER, I'LL CALL YOU...
!!

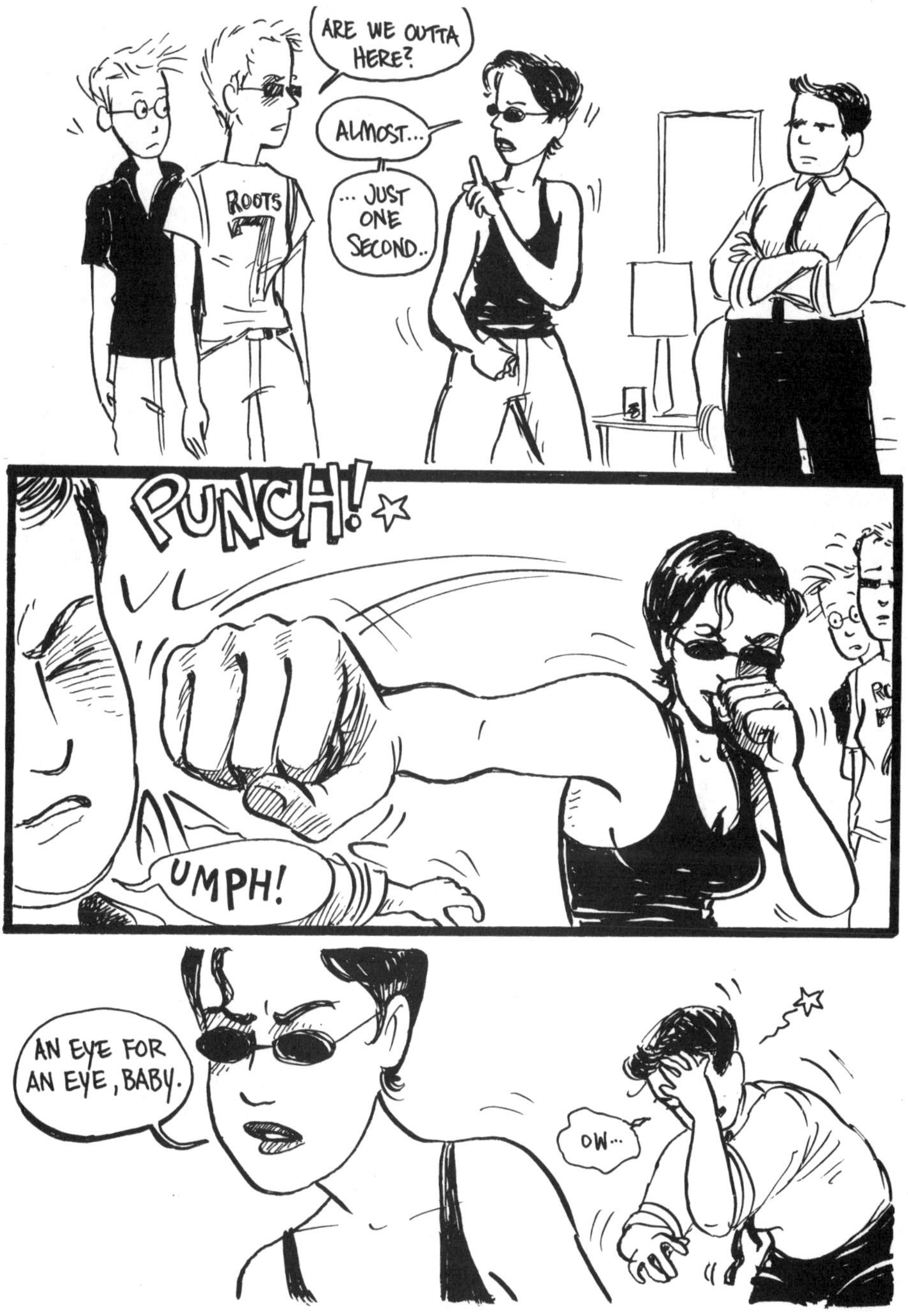
ARE WE OUTTA HERE?
ALMOST...
... JUST ONE SECOND..
PUNCH!
UMPH!
AN EYE FOR AN EYE, BABY.
OW...

48 hours later, back at Spud Point...

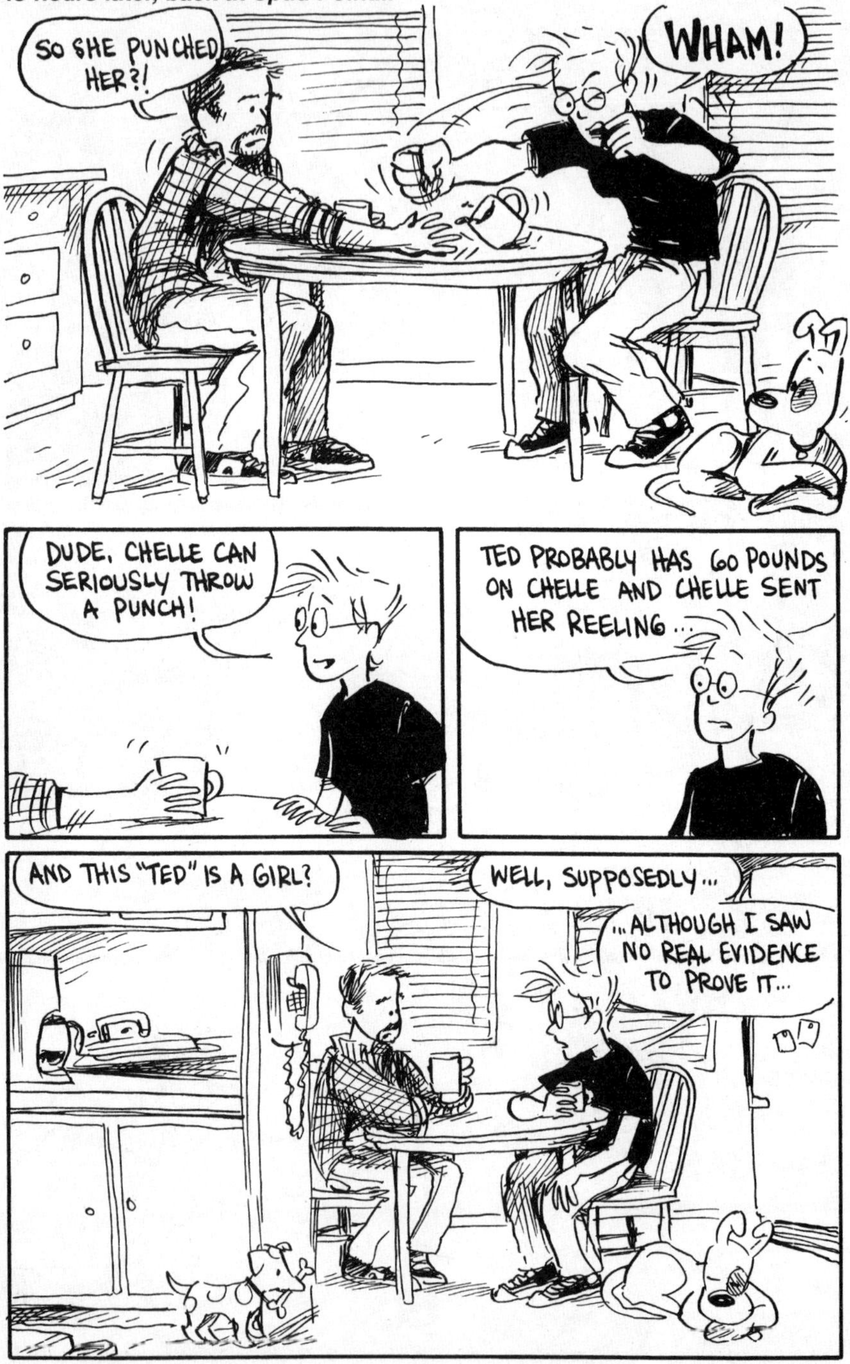
SO SHE PUNCHED HER?!
WHAM!
DUDE, CHELLE CAN SERIOUSLY THROW A PUNCH!
TED PROBABLY HAS 60 POUNDS ON CHELLE AND CHELLE SENT HER REELING...
AND THIS "TED" IS A GIRL?
WELL, SUPPOSEDLY...
...ALTHOUGH I SAW NO REAL EVIDENCE TO PROVE IT...

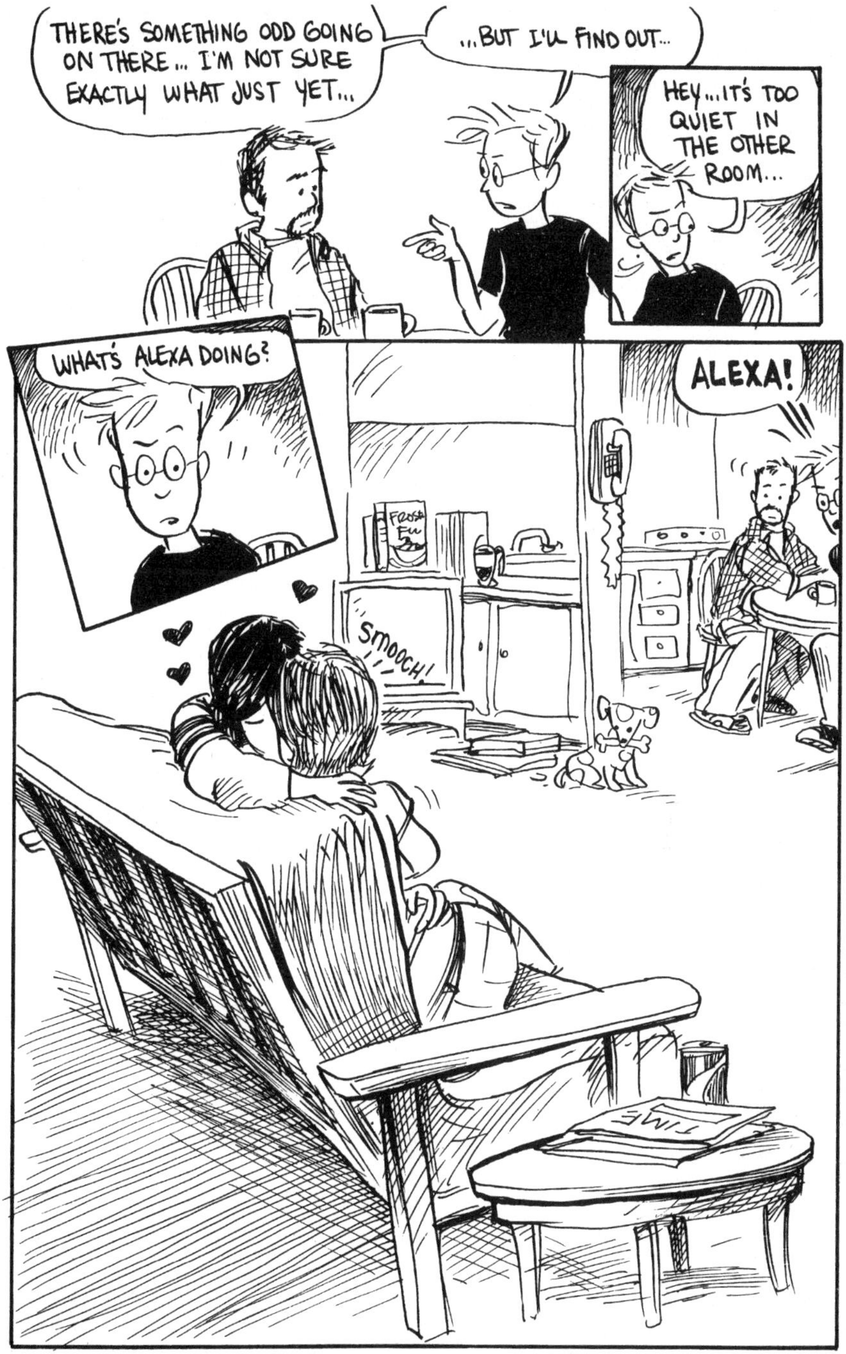
THERE'S SOMETHING ODD GOING ON THERE... I'M NOT SURE EXACTLY WHAT JUST YET...
...BUT I'LL FIND OUT...
HEY...IT'S TOO QUIET IN THE OTHER ROOM...
WHAT'S ALEXA DOING?
ALEXA!
SMOOCH!
TIME

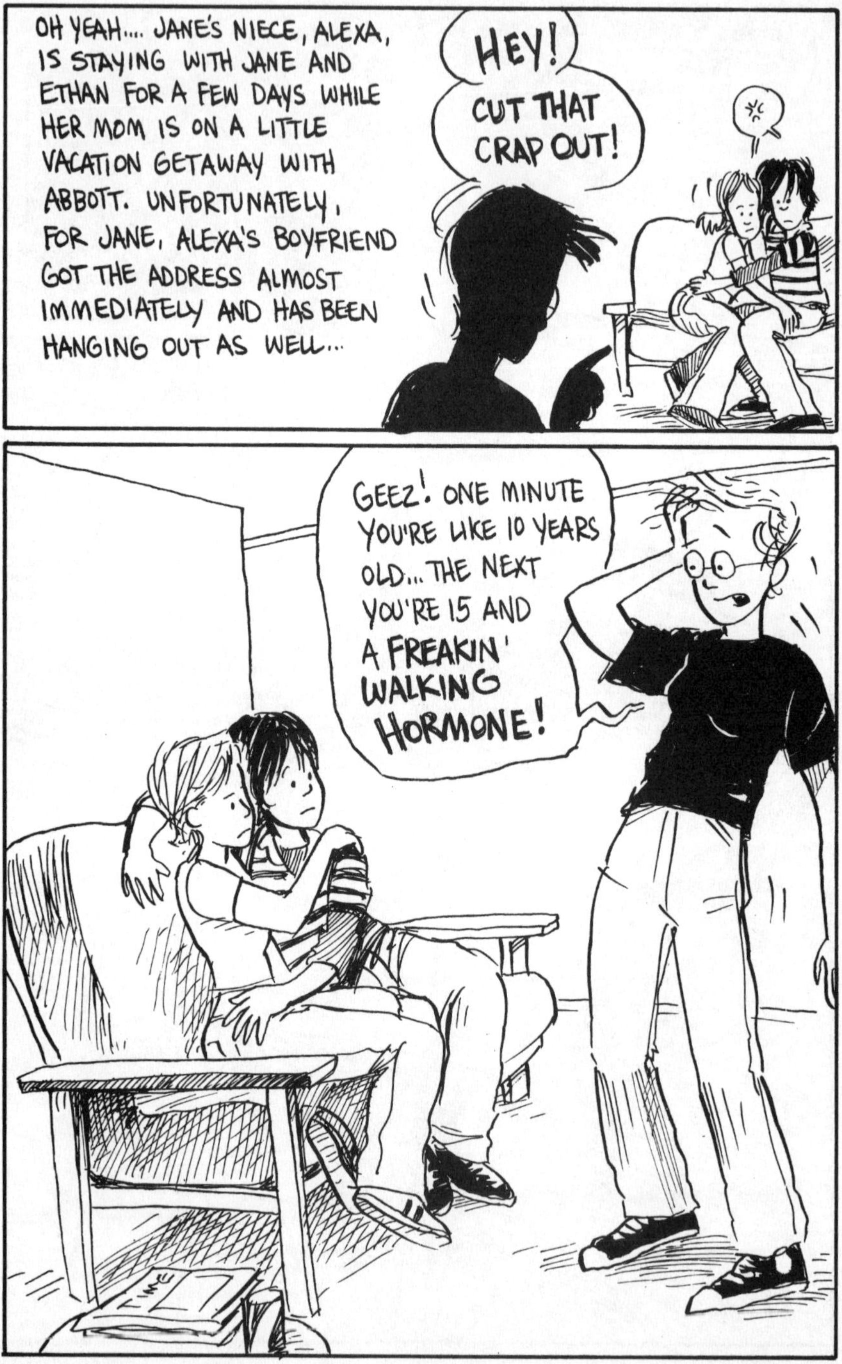
OH YEAH.... JANE'S NIECE, ALEXA, IS STAYING WITH JANE AND ETHAN FOR A FEW DAYS WHILE HER MOM IS ON A LITTLE VACATION GETAWAY WITH ABBOTT. UNFORTUNATELY, FOR JANE, ALEXA'S BOYFRIEND GOT THE ADDRESS ALMOST IMMEDIATELY AND HAS BEEN HANGING OUT AS WELL...
HEY!
CUT THAT CRAP OUT!
GEEZ! ONE MINUTE YOU'RE LIKE 10 YEARS OLD... THE NEXT YOU'RE 15 AND A FREAKIN' WALKING HORMONE!
TIME

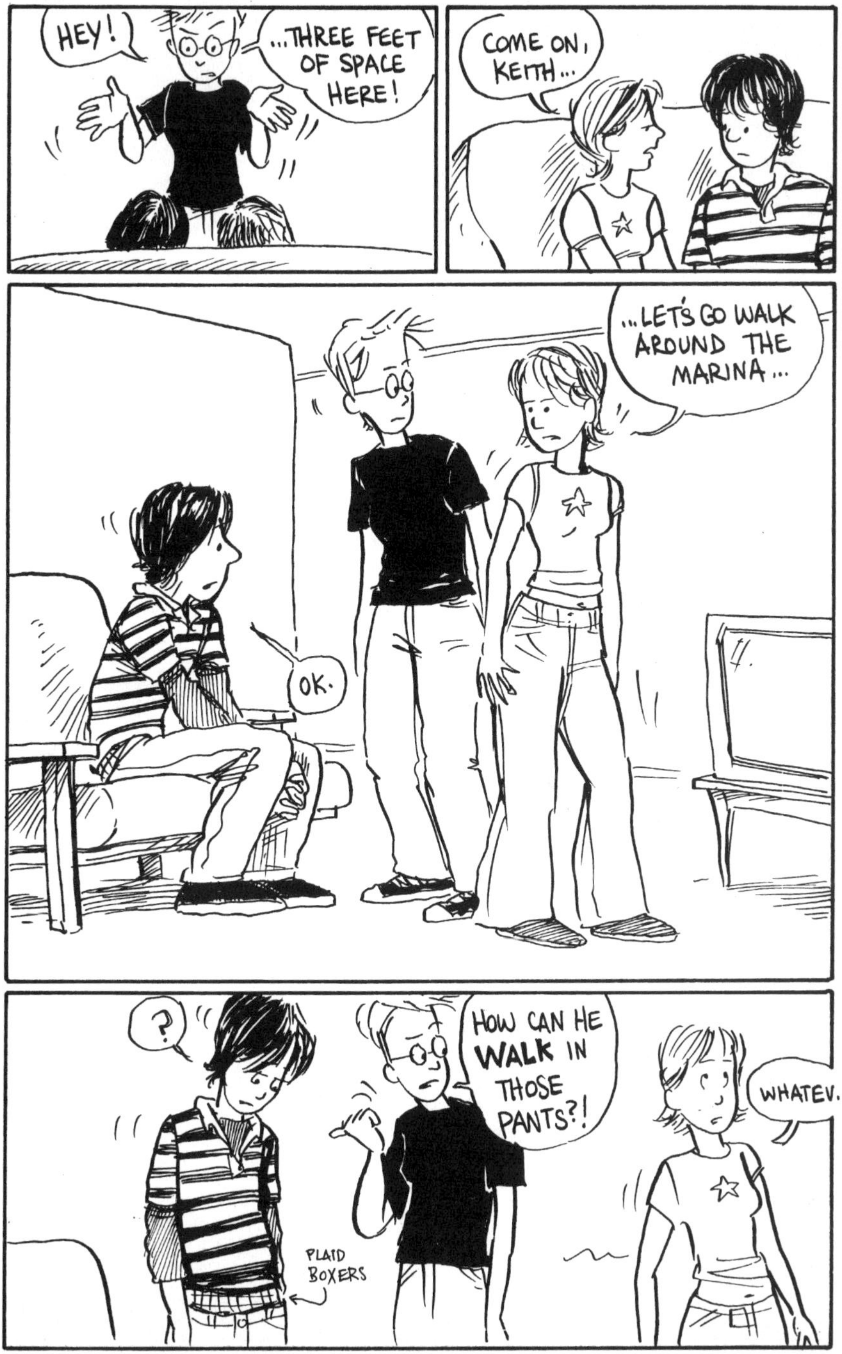
HEY!
...THREE FEET OF SPACE HERE!
COME ON, KEITH...
...LET'S GO WALK AROUND THE MARINA...
OK.
?
HOW CAN HE **WALK** IN THOSE PANTS?!
WHATEV.
PLAID BOXERS

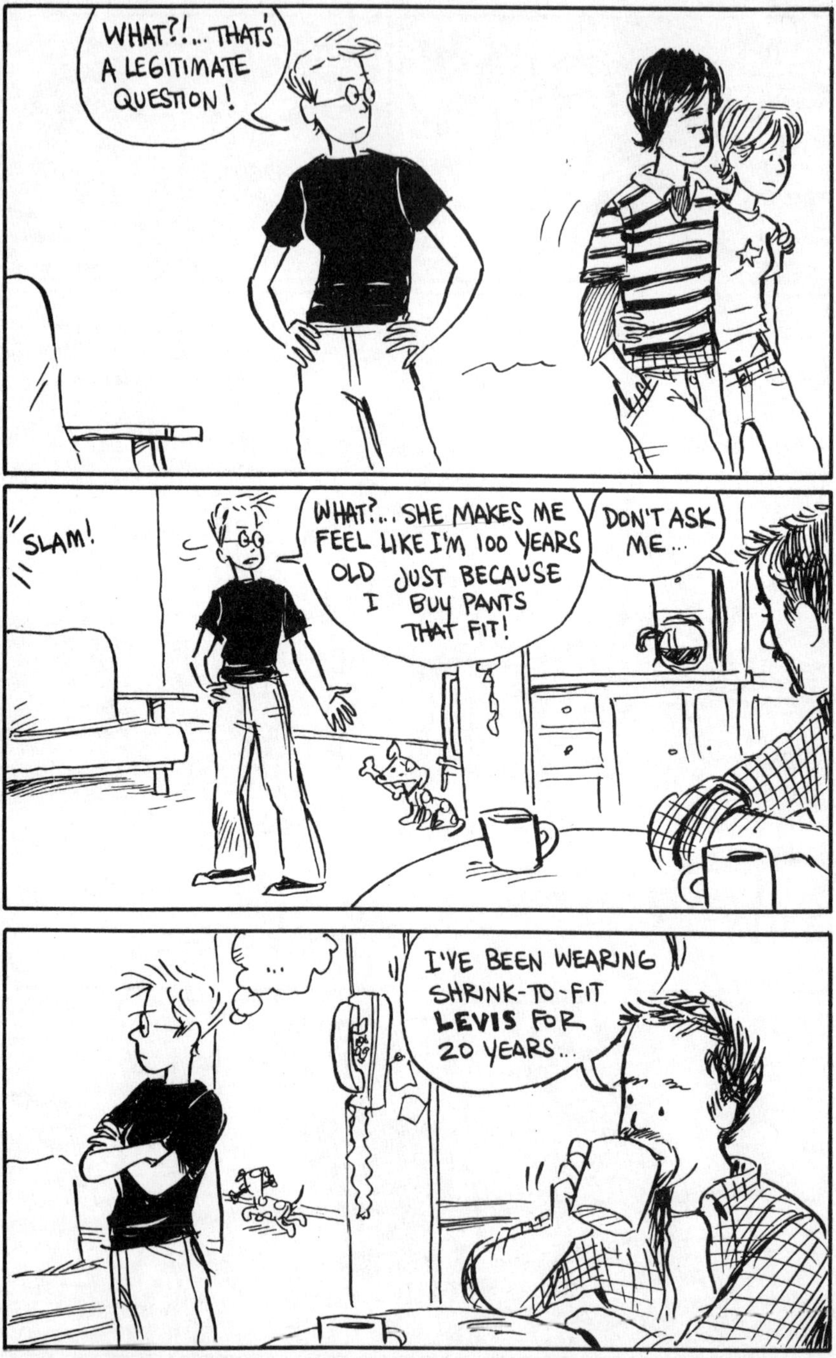
WHAT?!... THAT'S A LEGITIMATE QUESTION!
SLAM!
WHAT?... SHE MAKES ME FEEL LIKE I'M 100 YEARS OLD JUST BECAUSE I BUY PANTS THAT FIT!
DON'T ASK ME...
...
I'VE BEEN WEARING SHRINK-TO-FIT **LEVIS** FOR 20 YEARS...

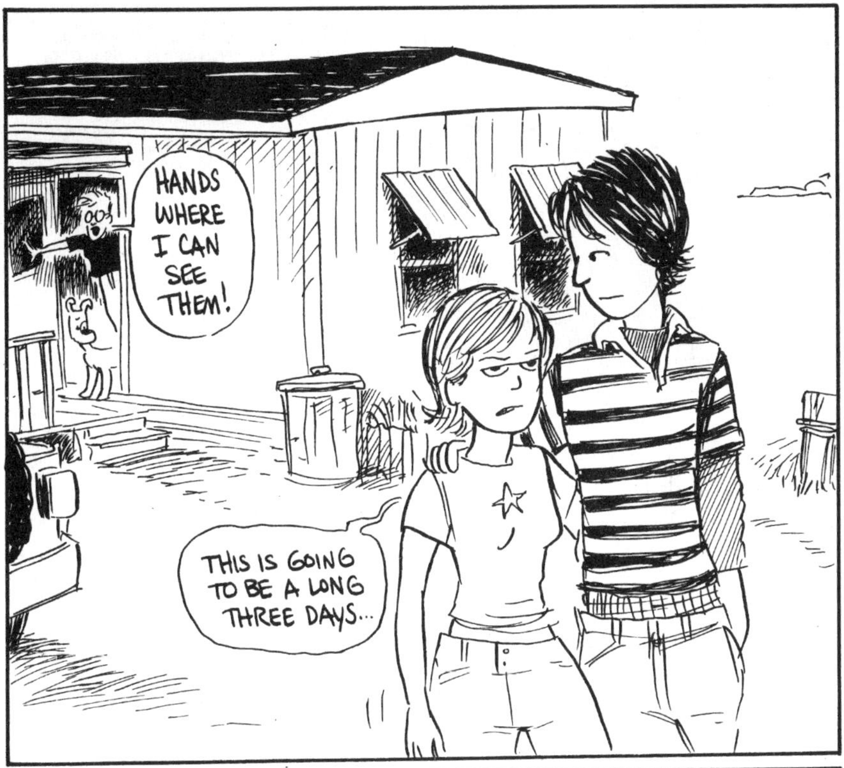
HANDS WHERE I CAN SEE THEM!
THIS IS GOING TO BE A LONG THREE DAYS...

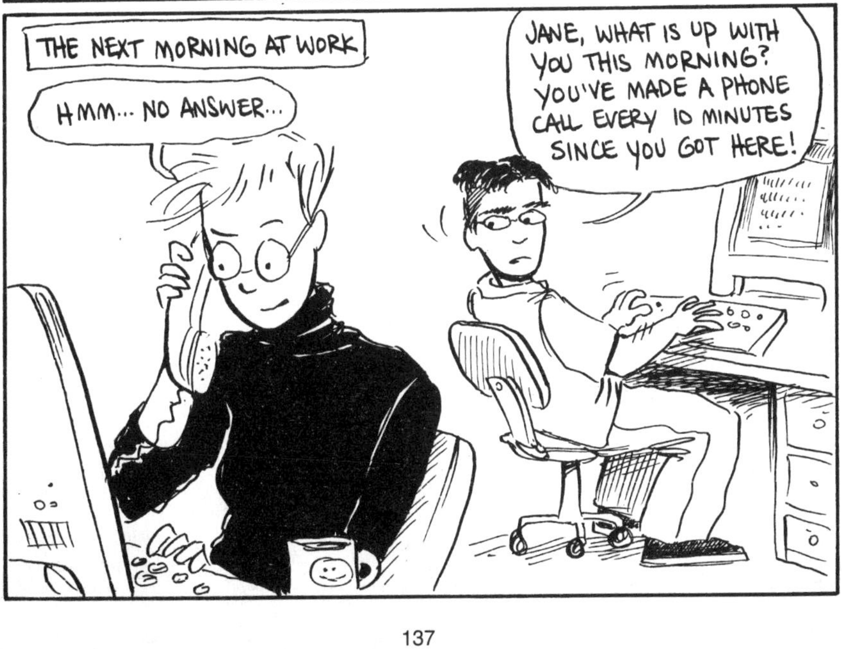
THE NEXT MORNING AT WORK
HMM... NO ANSWER...
JANE, WHAT IS UP WITH YOU THIS MORNING? YOU'VE MADE A PHONE CALL EVERY 10 MINUTES SINCE YOU GOT HERE!

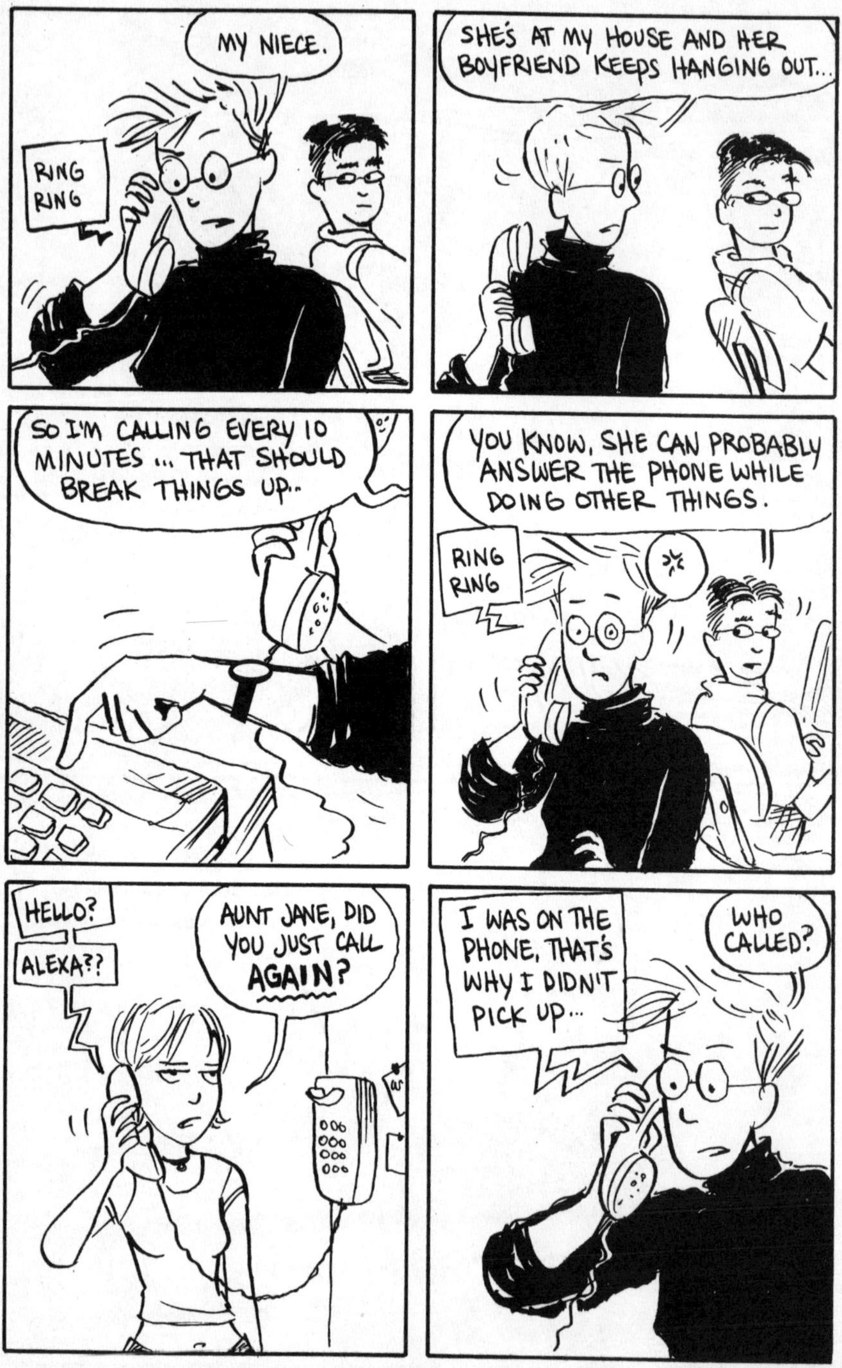
MY NIECE.
RING RING
SHE'S AT MY HOUSE AND HER BOYFRIEND KEEPS HANGING OUT...
SO I'M CALLING EVERY 10 MINUTES ... THAT SHOULD BREAK THINGS UP..
YOU KNOW, SHE CAN PROBABLY ANSWER THE PHONE WHILE DOING OTHER THINGS.
RING RING
HELLO?
ALEXA??
AUNT JANE, DID YOU JUST CALL AGAIN?
I WAS ON THE PHONE, THAT'S WHY I DIDN'T PICK UP...
WHO CALLED?

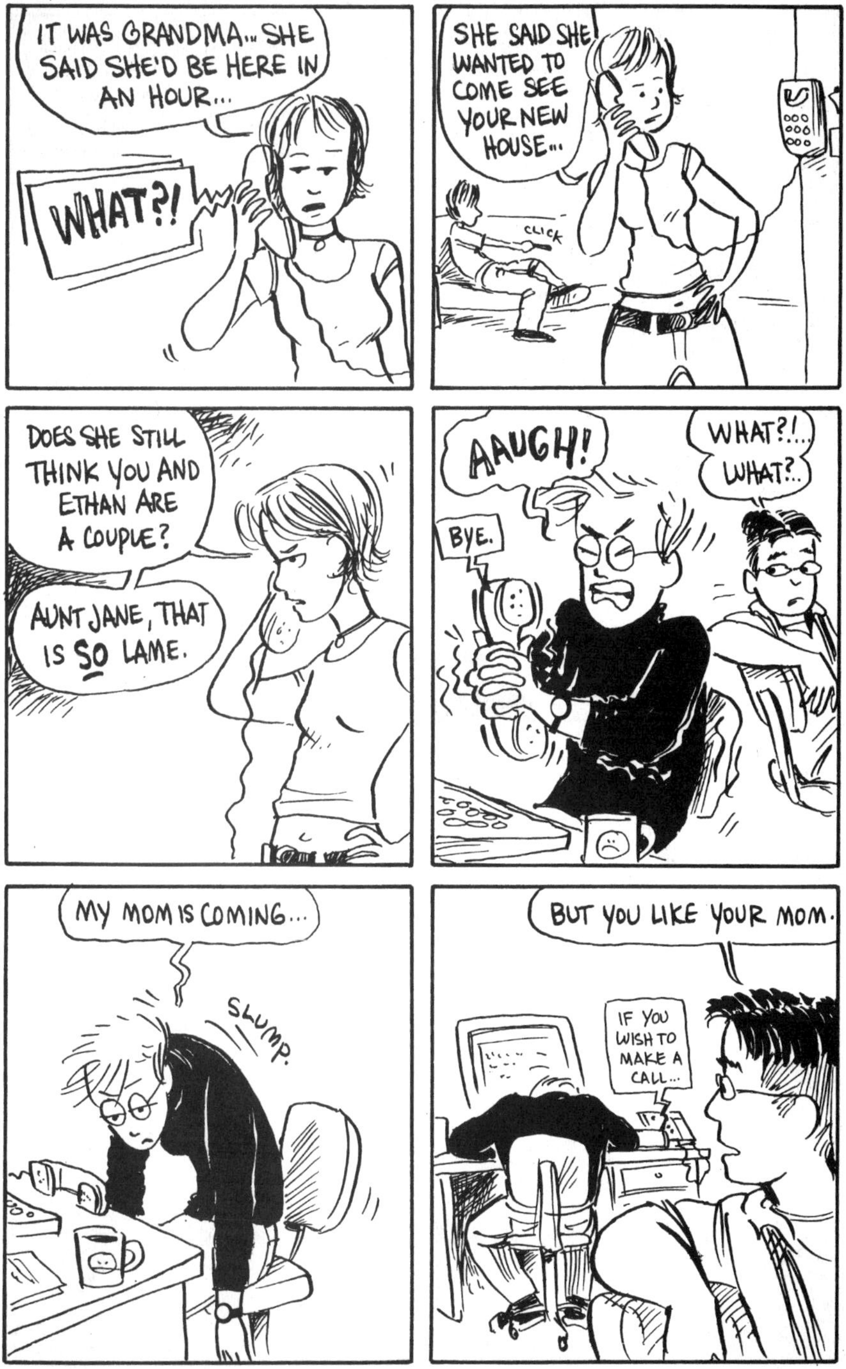
IT WAS GRANDMA... SHE SAID SHE'D BE HERE IN AN HOUR...
WHAT?!
SHE SAID SHE WANTED TO COME SEE YOUR NEW HOUSE...
CLICK
DOES SHE STILL THINK YOU AND ETHAN ARE A COUPLE?
AUNT JANE, THAT IS SO LAME.
AAUGH!
BYE.
WHAT?!... WHAT?..
MY MOM IS COMING...
SLUMP.
BUT YOU LIKE YOUR MOM.
IF YOU WISH TO MAKE A CALL...

YEAH, BUT REMEMBER?... SHE THINKS ETHAN AND I ARE A COUPLE. I'VE GOTTA FIND ETHAN **ASAP.**

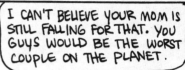

I CAN'T BELIEVE YOUR MOM IS STILL FALLING FOR THAT. YOU GUYS WOULD BE THE WORST COUPLE ON THE PLANET.

SHORTLY...

CAFE SQUEEZE

CAFE SQUEEZE

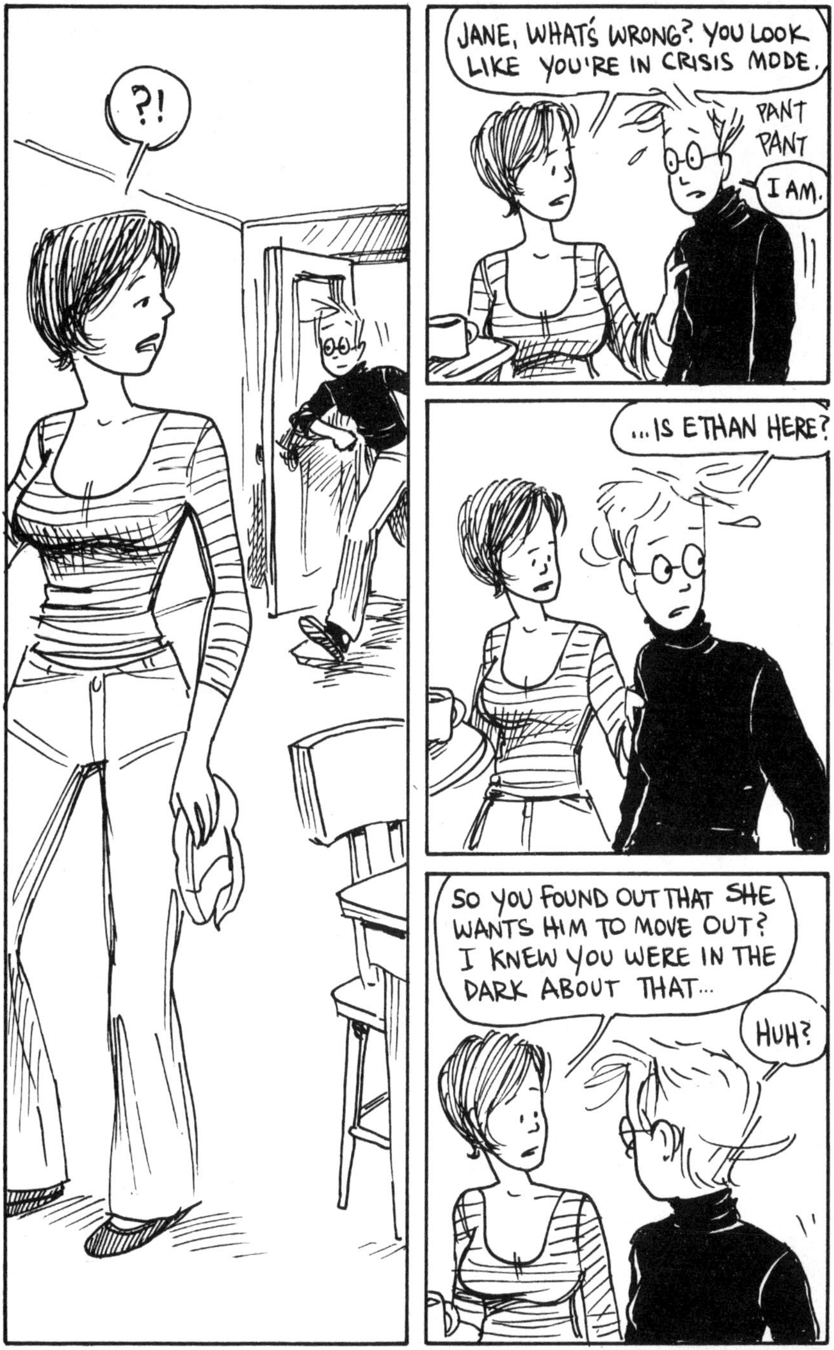
?!
JANE, WHAT'S WRONG? YOU LOOK LIKE YOU'RE IN CRISIS MODE.
PANT PANT
I AM.
...IS ETHAN HERE?
SO YOU FOUND OUT THAT SHE WANTS HIM TO MOVE OUT? I KNEW YOU WERE IN THE DARK ABOUT THAT...
HUH?

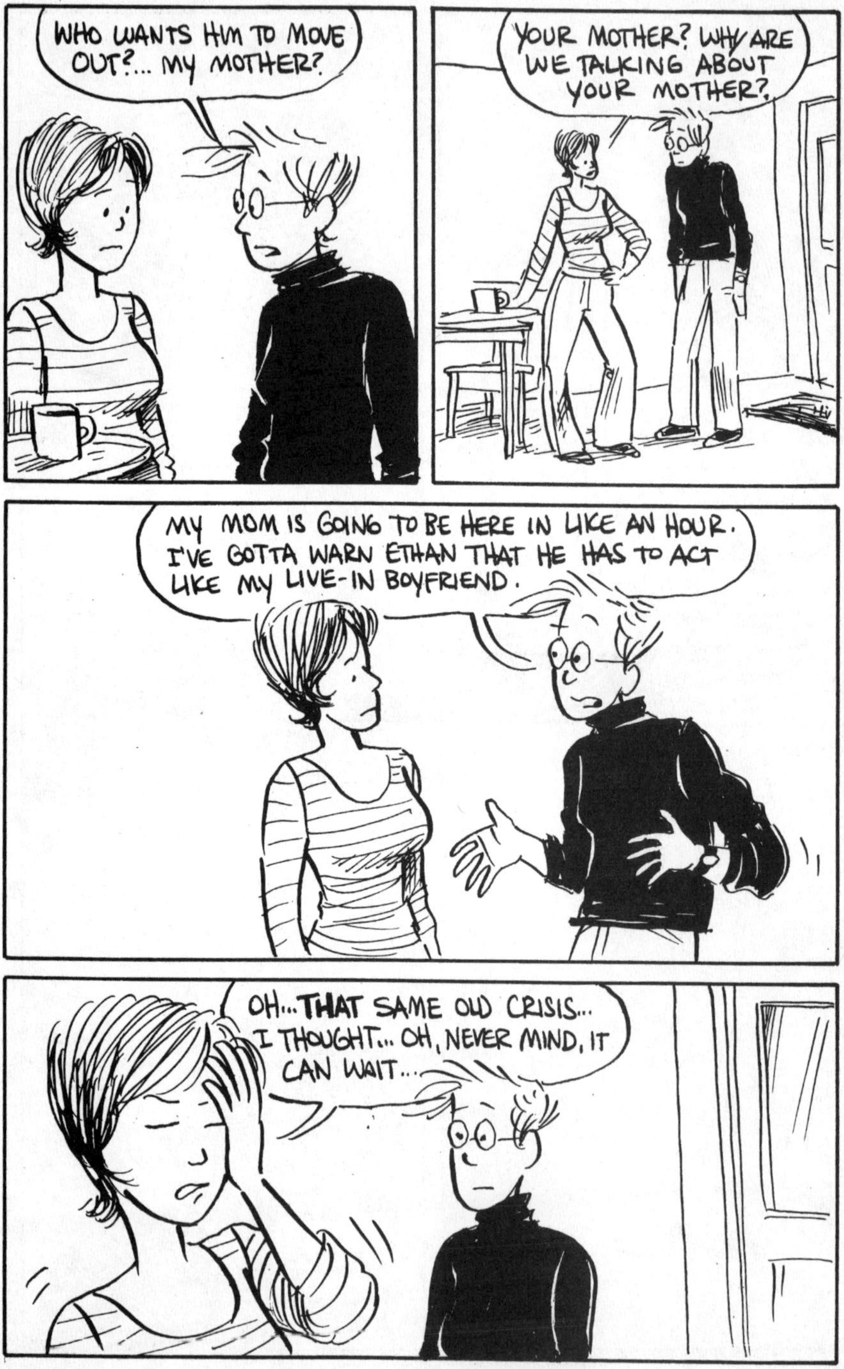
WHO WANTS HIM TO MOVE OUT?... MY MOTHER?
YOUR MOTHER? WHY ARE WE TALKING ABOUT YOUR MOTHER?
MY MOM IS GOING TO BE HERE IN LIKE AN HOUR. I'VE GOTTA WARN ETHAN THAT HE HAS TO ACT LIKE MY LIVE-IN BOYFRIEND.
OH... THAT SAME OLD CRISIS... I THOUGHT... OH, NEVER MIND, IT CAN WAIT...

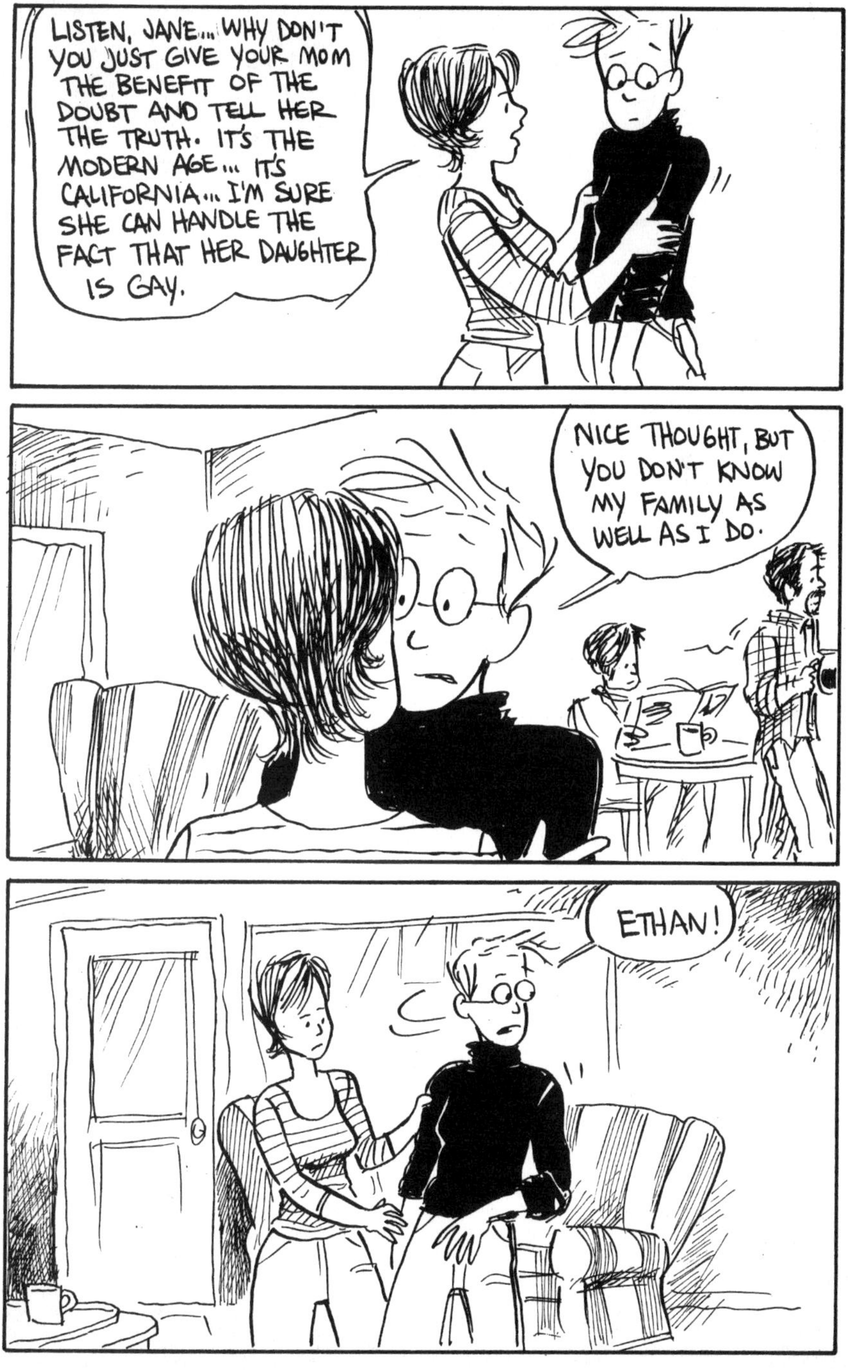
LISTEN, JANE... WHY DON'T YOU JUST GIVE YOUR MOM THE BENEFIT OF THE DOUBT AND TELL HER THE TRUTH. IT'S THE MODERN AGE... IT'S CALIFORNIA... I'M SURE SHE CAN HANDLE THE FACT THAT HER DAUGHTER IS GAY.
NICE THOUGHT, BUT YOU DON'T KNOW MY FAMILY AS WELL AS I DO.
ETHAN!

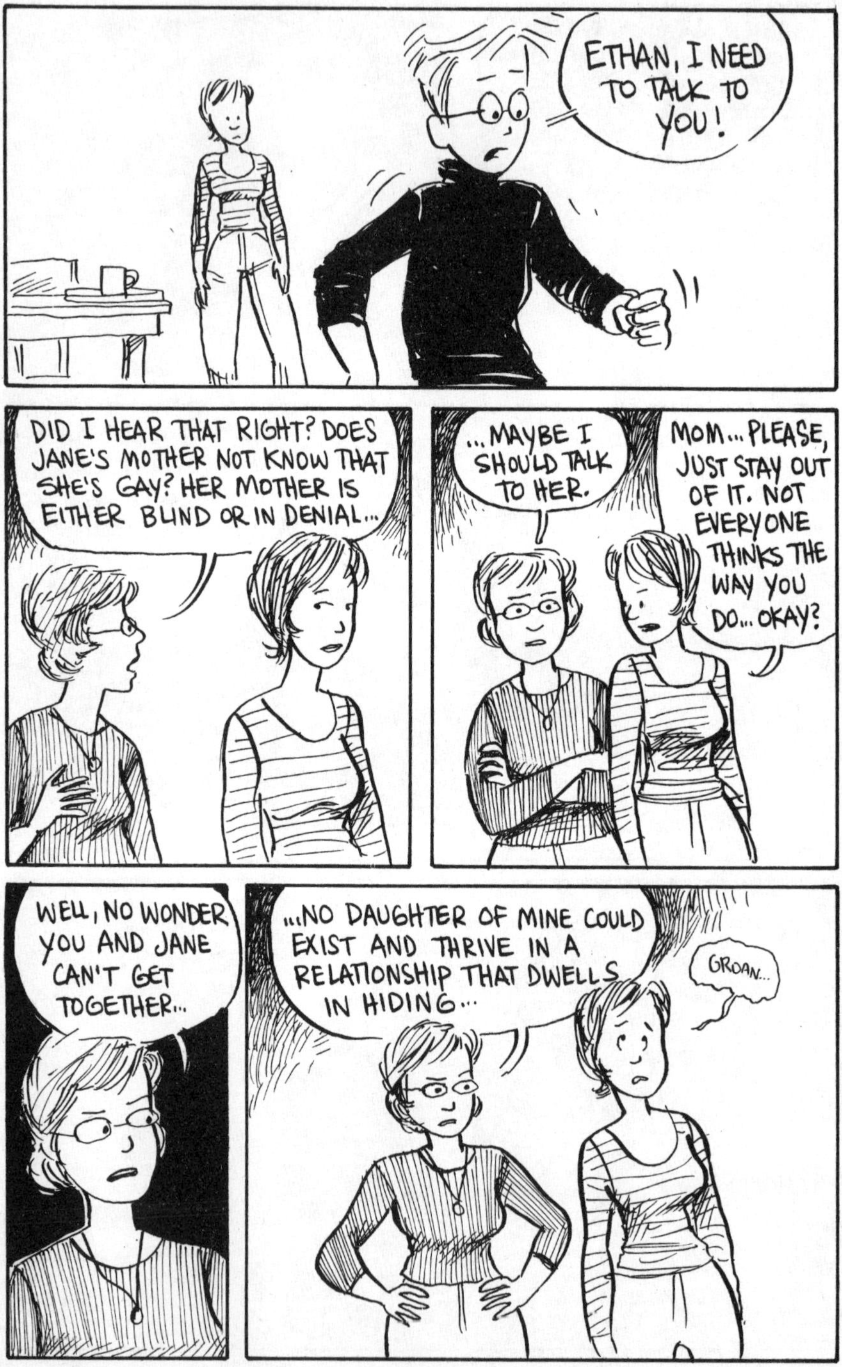
ETHAN, I NEED TO TALK TO YOU!
DID I HEAR THAT RIGHT? DOES JANE'S MOTHER NOT KNOW THAT SHE'S GAY? HER MOTHER IS EITHER BLIND OR IN DENIAL...
...MAYBE I SHOULD TALK TO HER.
MOM... PLEASE, JUST STAY OUT OF IT. NOT EVERYONE THINKS THE WAY YOU DO... OKAY?
WELL, NO WONDER YOU AND JANE CAN'T GET TOGETHER...
...NO DAUGHTER OF MINE COULD EXIST AND THRIVE IN A RELATIONSHIP THAT DWELLS IN HIDING...
GROAN...

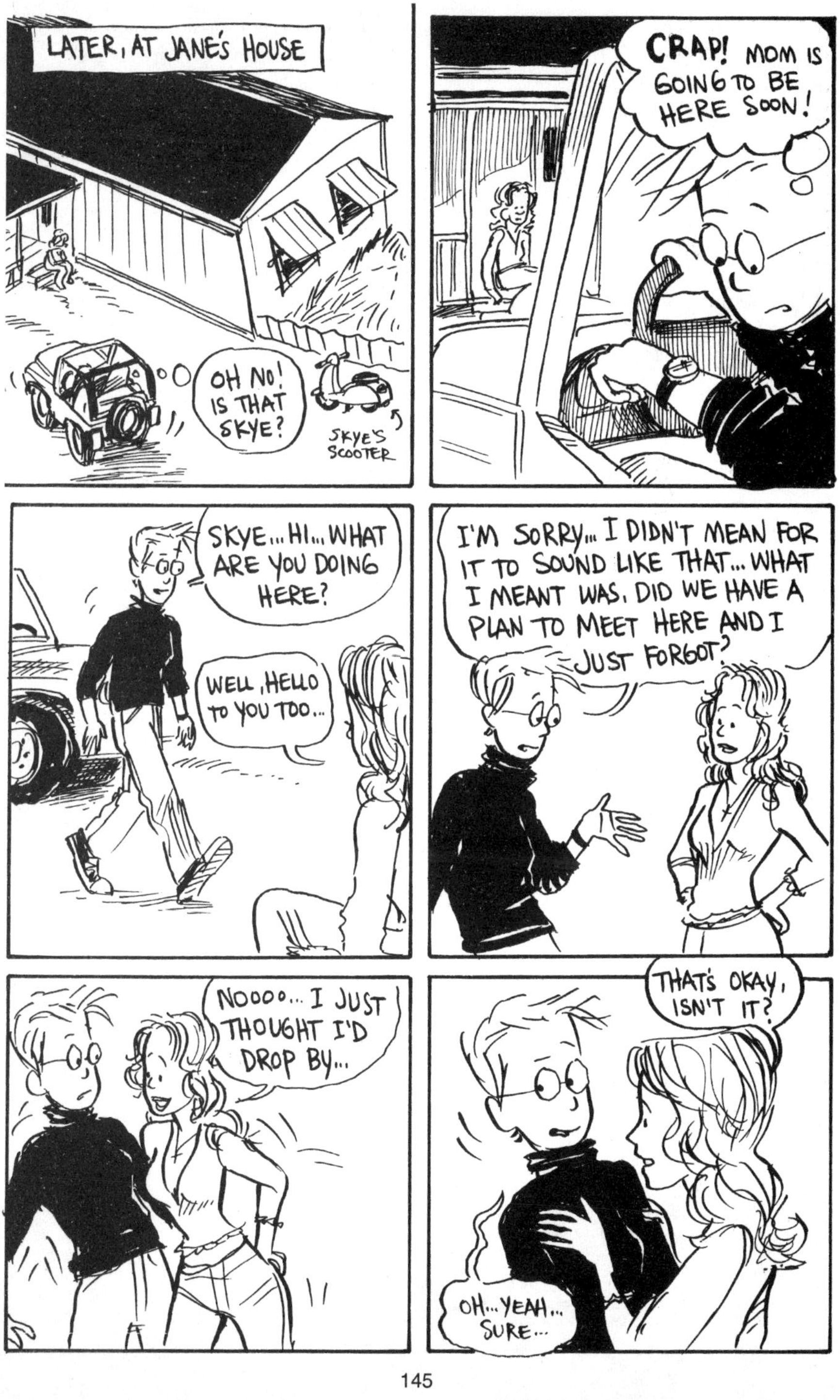
LATER, AT JANE'S HOUSE
OH NO! IS THAT SKYE?
SKYE'S SCOOTER
CRAP! MOM IS GOING TO BE HERE SOON!
SKYE... HI... WHAT ARE YOU DOING HERE?
WELL, HELLO TO YOU TOO...
I'M SORRY... I DIDN'T MEAN FOR IT TO SOUND LIKE THAT... WHAT I MEANT WAS, DID WE HAVE A PLAN TO MEET HERE AND I JUST FORGOT?
NOOOO... I JUST THOUGHT I'D DROP BY...
THAT'S OKAY, ISN'T IT?
OH... YEAH... SURE...

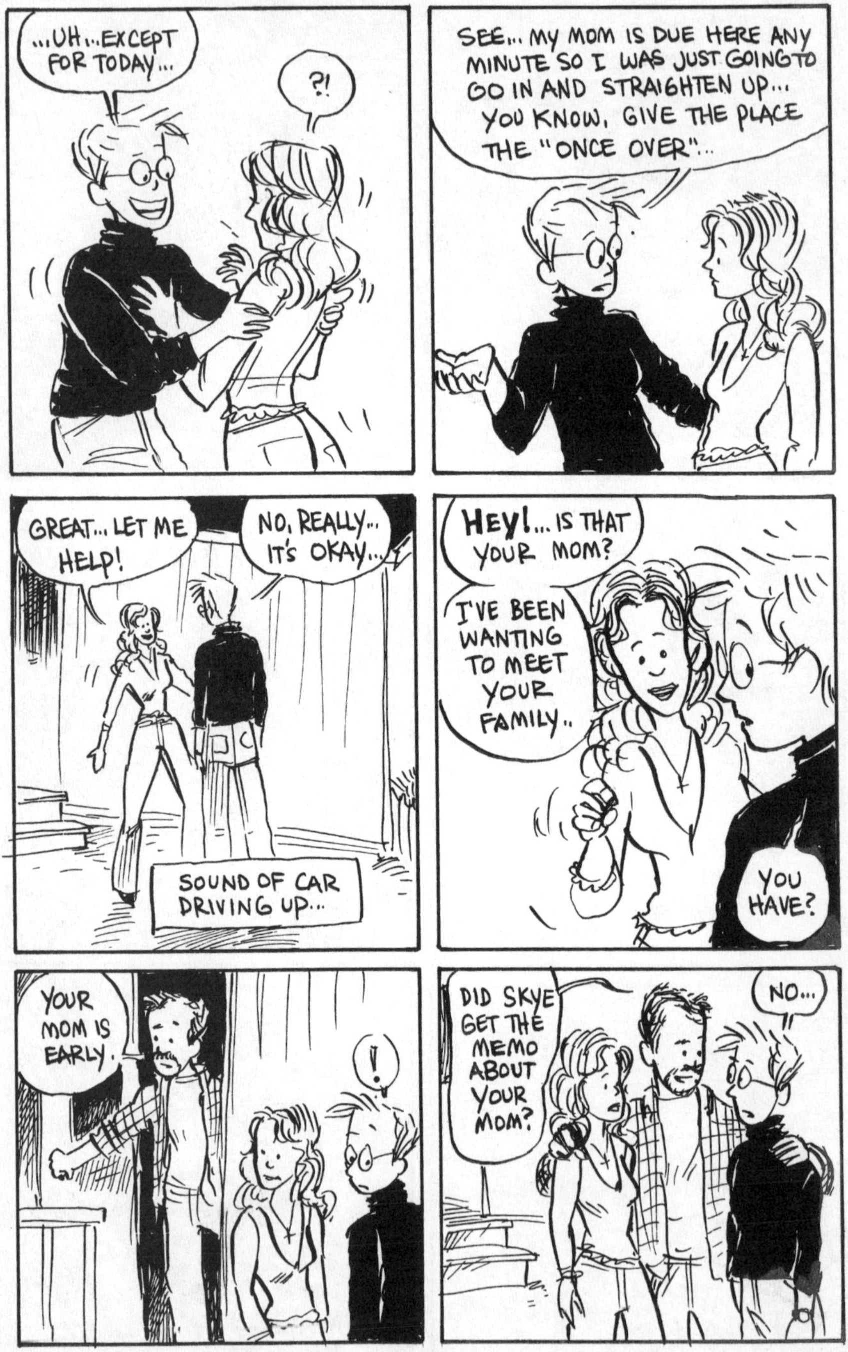
...UH...EXCEPT FOR TODAY...
?!
SEE... MY MOM IS DUE HERE ANY MINUTE SO I WAS JUST GOING TO GO IN AND STRAIGHTEN UP... YOU KNOW, GIVE THE PLACE THE "ONCE OVER"...
GREAT... LET ME HELP!
NO, REALLY... IT'S OKAY...
SOUND OF CAR DRIVING UP...
HEY!... IS THAT YOUR MOM?
I'VE BEEN WANTING TO MEET YOUR FAMILY..
YOU HAVE?
YOUR MOM IS EARLY.
!
DID SKYE GET THE MEMO ABOUT YOUR MOM?
NO...

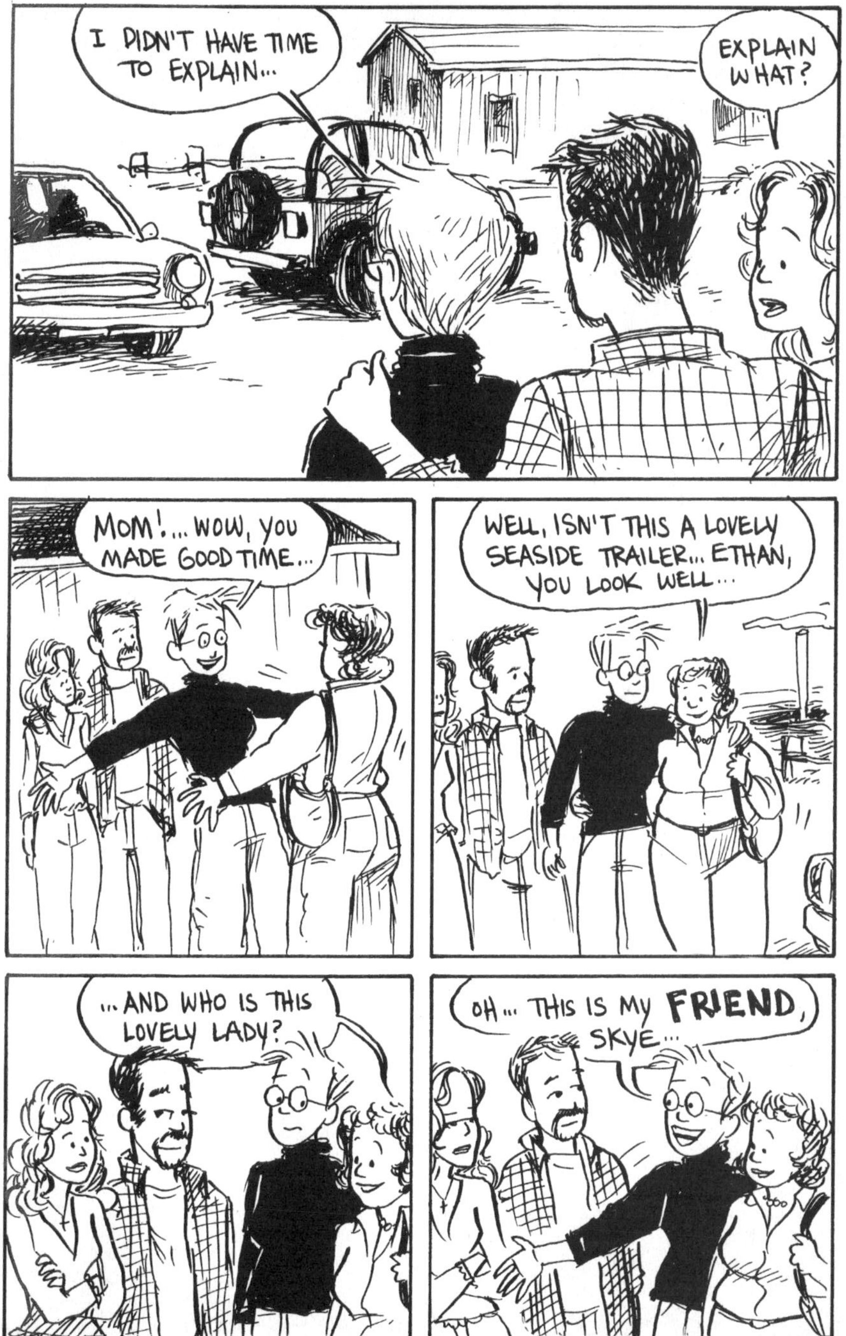
I DIDN'T HAVE TIME TO EXPLAIN...
EXPLAIN WHAT?
MOM!... WOW, YOU MADE GOOD TIME...
WELL, ISN'T THIS A LOVELY SEASIDE TRAILER... ETHAN, YOU LOOK WELL...
...AND WHO IS THIS LOVELY LADY?
OH... THIS IS MY **FRIEND**, SKYE...

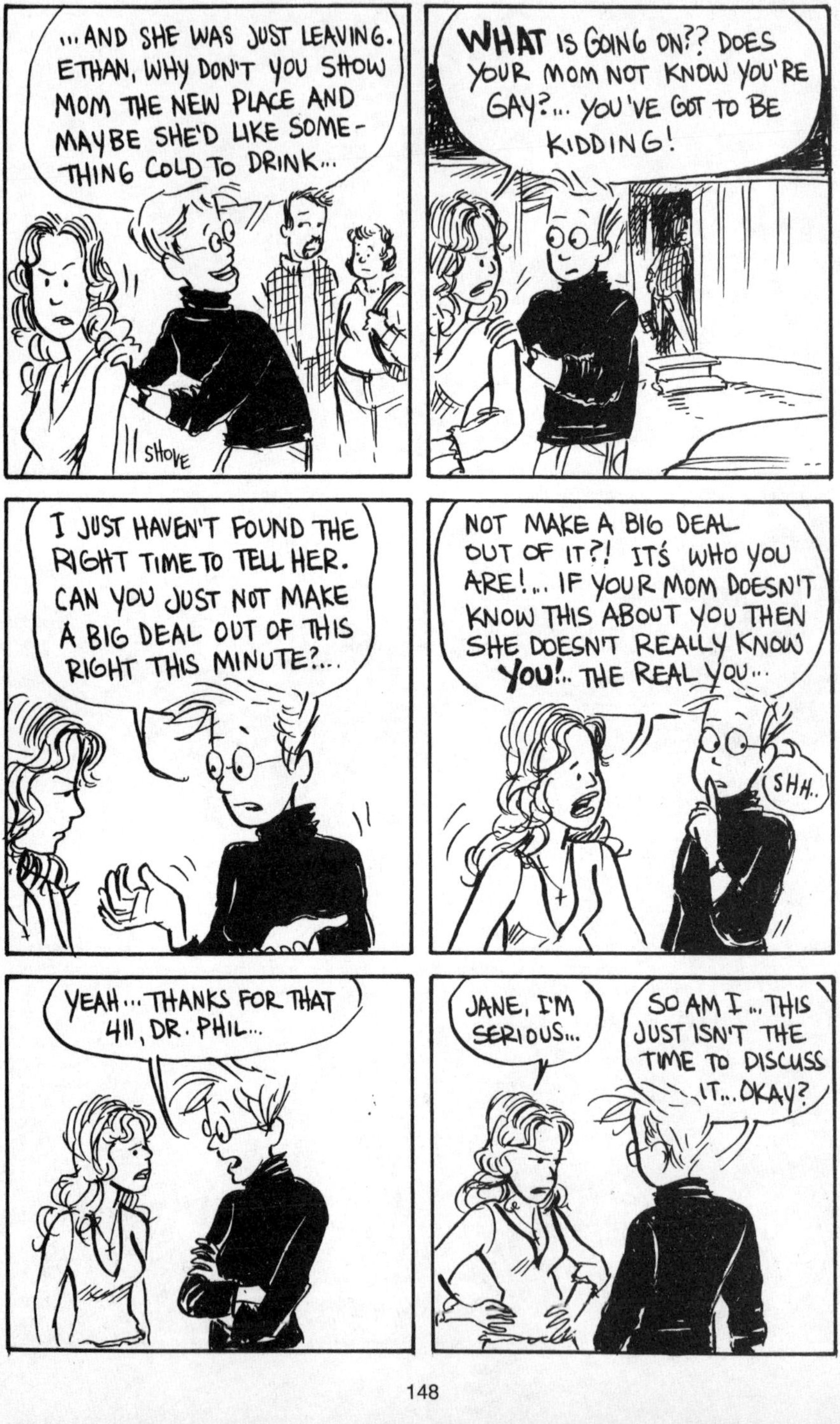
...AND SHE WAS JUST LEAVING. ETHAN, WHY DON'T YOU SHOW MOM THE NEW PLACE AND MAYBE SHE'D LIKE SOME-THING COLD TO DRINK...
SHOVE
WHAT IS GOING ON?? DOES YOUR MOM NOT KNOW YOU'RE GAY?... YOU'VE GOT TO BE KIDDING!
I JUST HAVEN'T FOUND THE RIGHT TIME TO TELL HER. CAN YOU JUST NOT MAKE A BIG DEAL OUT OF THIS RIGHT THIS MINUTE?...
NOT MAKE A BIG DEAL OUT OF IT?! IT'S WHO YOU ARE!... IF YOUR MOM DOESN'T KNOW THIS ABOUT YOU THEN SHE DOESN'T REALLY KNOW YOU!.. THE REAL YOU...
SHH..
YEAH... THANKS FOR THAT 411, DR. PHIL...
JANE, I'M SERIOUS...
SO AM I... THIS JUST ISN'T THE TIME TO DISCUSS IT... OKAY?

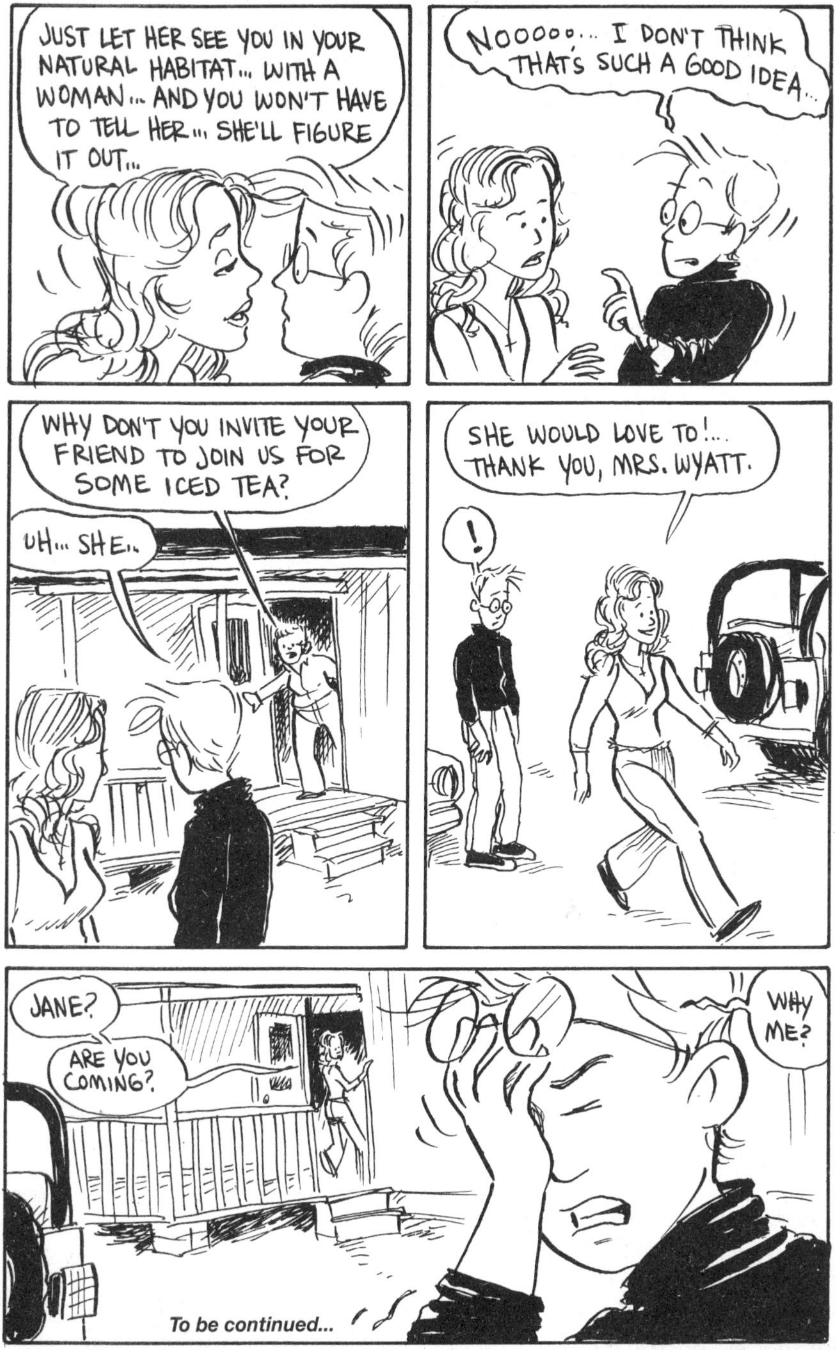
JUST LET HER SEE YOU IN YOUR NATURAL HABITAT... WITH A WOMAN... AND YOU WON'T HAVE TO TELL HER... SHE'LL FIGURE IT OUT...
NOOOOO... I DON'T THINK THAT'S SUCH A GOOD IDEA...
WHY DON'T YOU INVITE YOUR FRIEND TO JOIN US FOR SOME ICED TEA?
UH... SHE...
!
SHE WOULD LOVE TO!... THANK YOU, MRS. WYATT.
JANE?
ARE YOU COMING?
WHY ME?
To be continued...

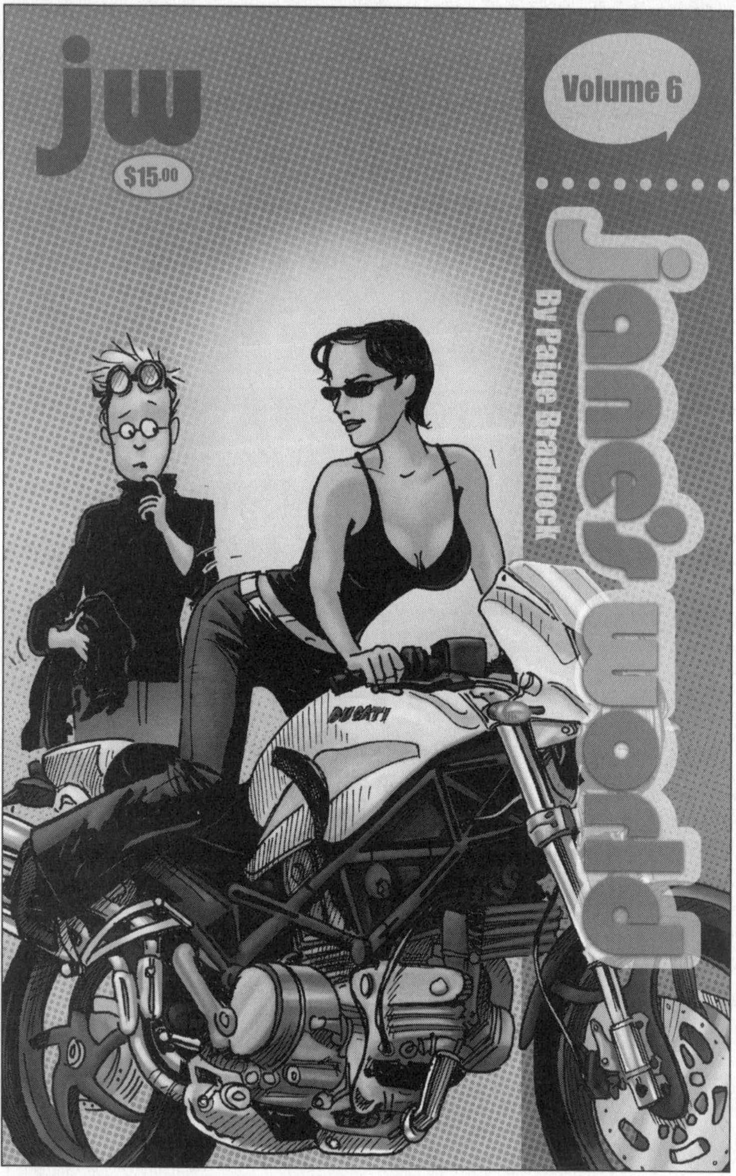
jw
$15.00
Volume 6
Jane's World
By Paige Braddock
DUCATI

Coming in September 2006:
Jane's World Vol. 6
ISBN 0-9766707-7-1

"I didn't set out to do a gay comic, but given the current political and religious climate in this country, I feel it is important as a gay person, and a Christian, to create stories with humor and honesty. My hope is that the characters in these stories help those outside our community gain understanding, and help those who might be isolated within our community feel a little less alone."

-- Paige Braddock